POSTHUMANIST VULNERABILITY

THEORY IN THE NEW HUMANITIES

Series editor: Rosi Braidotti

Theory is back! The vitality of critical thinking in the world today is palpable, as is a spirit of insurgency that sustains it. Theoretical practice has exploded with renewed energy in media, society, the arts and the corporate world. New generations of critical "studies" areas have grown alongside the classical radical epistemologies of the 1970s: gender, feminist, queer, race, postcolonial and subaltern studies, cultural studies, film, television and media studies. This series aims to present cartographic accounts of emerging critical theories and to reflect the vitality and inspirational force of on-going theoretical debates.

Editorial board
Stacy Alaimo (University of Texas at Arlington, USA)
Simone Bignall (Flinders University, Australia)
Judith Butler (University of Berkeley, USA)
Christine Daigle (Brock University, Canada)
Rick Dolphijn (Utrecht University, The Netherlands)
Matthew Fuller (Goldsmiths, University of London, UK)
Engin Isin (Queen Mary University of London, UK, and University of London Institute in Paris, France)
Patricia MacCormack (Anglia Ruskin University, UK)
Achille Mbembe (University Witwatersrand, South Africa)
Henrietta Moore (University College London, UK)

Other titles in the series:
Posthuman Glossary, edited by Rosi Braidotti and Maria Hlavajova
Conflicting Humanities, edited by Rosi Braidotti and Paul Gilroy
General Ecology, edited by Erich Hörl with James Burton
Philosophical Posthumanism, Francesca Ferrando
The Philosophy of Matter, Rick Dolphijn
Vibrant Death, Nina Lykke
Visceral Prostheses, Margrit Shildrick
From Deleuze and Guattari to Posthumanism, ed. Christine Daigle and Terrance H. McDonald
Materialist Phenomenology, Manuel DeLanda
More Posthuman Glossary, edited by Edited by Rosi Braidotti, Emily Jones and Goda Klumbytė

POSTHUMANIST VULNERABILITY

An Affirmative Ethics

Christine Daigle

BLOOMSBURY ACADEMIC
LONDON • NEW YORK • OXFORD • NEW DELHI • SYDNEY

BLOOMSBURY ACADEMIC
Bloomsbury Publishing Plc
50 Bedford Square, London, WC1B 3DP, UK
1385 Broadway, New York, NY 10018, USA
29 Earlsfort Terrace, Dublin 2, Ireland

BLOOMSBURY, BLOOMSBURY ACADEMIC and the Diana logo are trademarks of Bloomsbury Publishing Plc

First published in Great Britain 2023

Copyright © Christine Daigle, 2023

Christine Daigle has asserted her right under the Copyright, Designs and Patents Act, 1988, to be identified as Author of this work.

For legal purposes the Acknowledgments on p. viii constitute an extension of this copyright page.

Cover image: Polyps of orange sun coral (Tubastrea faulkneri),
Felidhu Atoll, Maldives
(© RGB Ventures / SuperStock / Alamy Stock Photo)

All rights reserved. No part of this publication may be reproduced or transmitted in any form or by any means, electronic or mechanical, including photocopying, recording, or any information storage or retrieval system, without prior permission in writing from the publishers.

Bloomsbury Publishing Plc does not have any control over, or responsibility for, any third-party websites referred to or in this book. All internet addresses given in this book were correct at the time of going to press. The author and publisher regret any inconvenience caused if addresses have changed or sites have ceased to exist, but can accept no responsibility for any such changes.

A catalogue record for this book is available from the British Library.

A catalog record for this book is available from the Library of Congress.

ISBN: HB: 978-1-3503-0287-7
PB: 978-1-3503-0288-4
ePDF: 978-1-3503-0289-1
eBook: 978-1-3503-0290-7

Series: Theory in the New Humanities

Typeset by Deanta Global Publishing Services, Chennai, India

To find out more about our authors and books visit www.bloomsbury.com and sign up for our newsletters.

CONTENTS

List of Figures vii
Acknowledgments viii

Meandering 1: In Lieu of a Preface 1

Introduction: By Way of Getting Started 3

Meandering 2: Land Acknowledgment 9

Chapter 1 The Transjective: A Posthumanist Material Feminist Ontology 15

Meandering 3: Charlie and Me 35

Chapter 2 Our Polyp-Being 39

Meandering 4: Feeling/Being Out of Place 55

Chapter 3 Affective Fabric and Collective Agency 61

Meandering 5: Inoculation 77

Chapter 4 Of Selves and Agents 83

Meandering 6: Inosculation 99

Meandering 7: 4:00 a.m. by the Train Tracks 103

Chapter 5 Vulnerability 105

Meandering 8: World in Turmoil 121

Chapter 6 Manifold Toxicity 127

Meandering 9: Cohabitating 143

Chapter 7 Ethical Thriving 151

Notes 165
References 196
Index 204

FIGURES

3.1-3.4	Charlie making its way in 37
4.1	Self-constitution? 55
4.2	A messy assemblage 56
5.1	No selfie for me, busy as I was handling my fear and trying to not completely collapse out of sheer anxiety 80
5.2	Blood pressure's best friend 82
6.1	Ash and Birch embrace 100
6.2	Ash and Birch embrace 101
6.3	Dead tree very much alive 102
9.1	Kits up the crabapple tree 144
9.2	Kits by the water bowl 145
9.3	Kits playing on the railing 147
9.4	Curious kit 148
9.5&9.6	Doves nesting in the vine 149

ACKNOWLEDGMENTS

This book is the outcome of many years of learning, reading the inspiring work of colleagues and friends, engaging in wonderful conversations, individual and collective questionings, puzzlements, and ruminations. I want to express my deepest thanks for these various encounters and entanglements generated by such incredible individuals. Rosi Braidotti's unwavering support and essential work fuel my thinking, and I cannot thank her enough. Ada Jaarsma, Antonio Calcagno, Simone Bignall, Xin Liu, Ilaria Santoemma, Astrida Neimanis, Olga Cielemęcka, Patricia MacCormack, Tuija Pulkkinen, Erika Ruonakoski, Rick Dolphijn, Danielle Sands, and Matthew Hayler have been invaluable interlocutors. I am convinced I am forgetting many and I apologize for that.

Marie-Andrée Robitaille's exciting work on circus art opened new ways of thinking for me, and I am grateful for her generosity in commenting on a chapter in this book. The PostPhenomenology group at Helsinki run by Erika Ruonakoski has provided great opportunities for me to present drafts of my work. The feedback received in these meetings was invaluable and for this I thank Martta Heikkilä, Irina Poleshchuk, Janne Vanhanen, Jaakko Vuori, Joonas Martikainen, Olli-Pekka Paananen, and, of course, Erika herself again.

I was able to engage with this group during my tenure as Core Fellow and Research Director at the Helsinki Collegium for Advanced Studies (HCAS). The fellowship at HCAS provided me with the perfect working and intellectual environment to start the writing of this book. A large portion of the manuscript was written there. I am thankful for the friendship and support provided by Tuomas Forsberg (Director), Hanne Appelqvist (Deputy Director), Kaisa Kaakinen (Research Coordinator), and other fellows such as Jaana Simola and Maijastina Kahlos, with whom many lunches were shared in the Common Room as well as Pedro Oliveira and Ayesha Hameed with whom I crossed paths as our fellowships overlapped all too briefly but with whom great conversations were had. I am happy to count you all as my friends. Such a brilliant and inspiring group! Not to mention all the other Cool Kids from HCAS. You know who you are!

A lot of the preparation for the book was done at my house working in my summer office, aka back deck, which is where I completed it after my fellowship. The many yard critters and bugs, wild nonhuman animals and pets with whom I shared portions of my life, including Oscar, Charlie, Rowdy Kit, and a new addition from the summer 2022, Killer the red squirrel, have all contributed to shape my thinking and my being as has this character home with all its quirks and its funky yard.

I am also very thankful for Christinia Landry's skepticism toward my project, which forced me to think harder but also for her unwavering friendship and support. I am truly lucky to have her as a friend.

Thanks are also due to a number of very talented PhD students from the PhD in Interdisciplinary Humanities at Brock who worked as research assistants for me over the years, accomplishing numerous tasks that supported my project. Andrew McEwan, Terrance McDonald, Mitch Goldsmith, Camila Mugan, and Julie Gemuend have done great work. And my special thanks go to Brett Robinson who patiently and expertly edited my writing, challenging me to think harder on some of the issues I was tackling. I also wish to thank Cristina Santos for her help with one of the meanderings.

Dr. Hany Hanna gave me timely advice as he was giving me my allergy shot. I mentioned being a little stuck in my writing at the beginning of May 2022 and he said: "It has to come from the heart." When I thanked him a week later because it really got me unstuck—I wrote what he said down on a post-it that I stuck on my computer, next to the keyboard and trackpad—he said it had been a message from heaven. Thanks to him for uttering or conveying the message, whether it was from heaven or not.

Liza Thompson and Lucy Russell at Bloomsbury have been wonderful to work with. Many thanks to them and all the other staff at Bloomsbury for making this book happen. Thanks to the anonymous reviewers who offered excellent constructive criticism that allowed me to improve the book. The work of reviewers is often unacknowledged or underappreciated and yet their work is key to pushing authors to do their best work. Thank you for engaging with my work before it was ready to go to print and contributing to making it ready.

I have developed some of the arguments in this book over the years and earlier versions of these have been published in the following essays and articles: "Trans-subjectivity/Trans-objectivity," *Feminist Phenomenology Futures*. Helen Fielding and Dorothea Olkowski (eds), Bloomington: Indiana University Press, 2017, 183–99; "Can Existentialism be a Posthumanism?: Beauvoir as Precursor to Material Feminism," *Philosophy Today*, volume 64, no. 3, Summer 2020, 763–80; "Deleuzean Traces: The Self of the Polyp," *From Deleuze and Guattari to Posthumanism*. Christine Daigle and Terrance McDonald (Eds). London, Bloomsbury, 2022, 41–62; "Moving beyond Humanism in a Constructive Manner: The Case for Posthumanist Material Feminism," *Rivista Per la Filosofia. Filosofia e insegnamento*, special issue on "Postumano," coedited by Anna Maria Pezzella and Antonio Calcagno, XXXVIII/113, Fall 2021, 81–95; coauthored with Olga Cielemęcka, "Posthuman Sustainability: An Anti-anthropocentric Ethos for Our Anthropocenic Future," *Theory, Culture & Society*, volume 36, Nos. 7–8, 2019, 67–87; "The (Post)human and the (Post)pandemic: Rediscovering Our Selves," In *The Posthuman Pandemic*. Tihomir Topuzovski and Saul Newman (eds). London: Bloomsbury, 2022, 27–42.

Finally, I want to thank Brock University's Humanities Research Institute and Research Services for the support provided through various internal grants. I also want to acknowledge that this book draws on research supported by the Social Sciences and Humanities Research Council of Canada.

MEANDERING 1
IN LIEU OF A PREFACE

If the claims of this book are convincing, its somewhat unconventional form may be partly responsible. The academic book has its raison d'être, but the many requirements of its format act as constraints on one's thinking. This book will be academic, but it will also venture into more experimental and personal territory. I felt that a combination of interconnected theoretical essays and interludes (in which specific personal experiences, fuzzy thoughts, or encounters are discussed but not theorized upon) would provide me and the reader with spaces and moments to ponder, breathe in, and literally incorporate the many entanglements that we are and of which this book is now a part. Engaging with a book is an affective experience that contributes to shape who/what one is, whether one writes or reads it. It matters how, when, where, with whom, and why one puts thoughts on paper. It matters how, when, where, with whom, and why one encounters the thoughts conveyed on paper.

Of course, while this may be unconventional, it is not radically new. Feminist thinkers have advocated in favor of and practiced writing that makes room for something other than the traditionally championed disembodied mind speaking the truth to its readers. The recognition that the human is much more than a rational being and that, in fact, its rationality is of the embodied and embedded kind—always and ever-entangled with myriad beings and affects—requires that our explorations be of a tentative rather than a definitive kind. Indeed, the definitive is never quite so in a world of swarming, dynamic interrelations and intra-action. Therefore, it would be very presumptuous to attempt to offer a definitive account of anything. Further, there is value in meandering alongside theorizing. The motion of thinking and feeling, the affective fabric generated by the assemblage we call "book" and which you are engaging with now, advances one's thinking and relating, for author and reader alike. Not that I hold onto some kind of naïve notion of progress toward better thinking that my book—or any other book for that matter—would help initiate. This is not what I understand by "advance." But a lack of movement, standing firm in one's thinking and being, would constitute a refusal of dynamic becoming that would amount to a denial of one's existence as the beings we are. The encounter with the ideas that follow—my own as I was developing them and the reader's as they make their way through them—generates movement of one kind or another.

Who/what is doing the writing? I am an assemblage of encounters with the thoughts of others through conversations, listening to talks and reading books and essays. Even the thoughts of that other that I was and that I encounter in notebooks enter the assemblage, not as memories of thoughts formed and articulated by me but as those ideas had by an other, the past "me." Gathering thoughts—those of others and of past me as another other—as one does when preparing to write is to be overwhelmed by these thoughts and one's thoughts as they emerge in the new set of relations generated by this preparatory work. And then the act of writing itself is a way to let these thoughts merge, confront one another, bounce off each other, modulate, and morph into that assemblage that the book is becoming. Its becoming does not end when one is done writing it, when a copyeditor has diligently helped improve its prose, and when it is off to press. It continues to become, in multiple ways, through its encounter with readers as their own assemblage enters in relation with it. A book is never done and yet here it is.

INTRODUCTION
BY WAY OF GETTING STARTED

The human is a strange creature that seems to resist any attempt at fully theorizing itself or its experiences. It often feels like something falls through the cracks and is not entirely captured by one's conceptualization or even remains entirely opaque. The philosophies I worked with until encountering posthumanism and material feminism certainly had their ambiguous or blind spots. Existentialism and phenomenology offer great insights on human beings as embodied and intersubjective beings. A sprinkle of structuralism and poststructuralism comes in handy to understand the ways in which humans are part of systems of meaning and power that inflect their experiences as individuals. Nietzsche's understanding of the human as a subjective multiplicity embodied in a body—Nietzsche calls it a great reason (a *große Vernunft*)—serves to explain that reason, a fetish of centuries of Western philosophizing, is a rather limited tool at the hand of the somatic—a tool we use to make sense of the world—but is still merely a tool that is directed by the passions and drives at work in the body. A few decades later, Sartre focused his attention on the operations of consciousness with a concern for the relations between the individual and others. "Hell is other people!" is Garcin's "Eureka!" moment in Sartre's *No Exit*, a play first staged in 1944. While this damning sentence was taken as a final pronouncement, it was instead pointing to the problem at the heart of ethical thinking: How do we exist with others and how do we do so ethically? Beauvoir's unprecedented attention to the body in the phenomenological analyses of *The Second Sex* revived the notion that it matters what body one is. Although she does not go as far as material feminists do nowadays, she sowed the seeds of many of their reflections. What I am describing here is the philosophical pathway that took me to posthumanist theory and material feminism. The philosophers I had concentrated my work on each talked about the body, theorized the body, and acknowledged the importance of embodiment for consciousness—the fact that consciousness only exists *as* embodied and situated—and yet the materiality of this body was not fully explored.[1] Likewise, while they all acknowledge human situatedness—the human as being-in-the-world as Heidegger would have it—they do not explore the materiality of this worldly embeddedness—what it means existentially and fundamentally for a human to exist in material surroundings constituted by concrete and bricks or by wood and fields, surroundings permeated by pollution or extreme weather conditions, and surroundings that amount to a small town or a megalopolis. Sure, Sartre talks about a boulder on his path while out hiking. The boulder is material and presents a formidable obstacle as it blocks the path and transforms the hiker's project of carrying on down the path. The boulder, however, is considered as obstacle or tool only in the human project, an instrument in the decision-making of the one who encounters it. Its material stubbornness is closed upon itself.

What I want to do here is think this materiality through, with the help of posthumanist theory and material feminism. This, however, should not be taken as a rejection of the insights gained by the philosophies I have been working with thus far. The insights are many and helpful in understanding the subjective and intersubjective aspects of our lives, and I will appeal to them throughout the book. However, they are not as helpful to understand our materiality and the various material entanglements that constitute us and that are also of influence on the subjective and intersubjective. What I am seeking, therefore, is a supplement or a complement that may indeed end up transforming some of these insights, but these transformations will not amount to an outright rejection. While some may think that these approaches are mutually exclusive, I contend they are not.[2]

Mostly, I am seeking to develop a proposal for an ethics that will allow us to render our ontological vulnerability generative. It seems obvious to me that the ethical norms and principles we have lived by have failed us. This failure is due partly to the fact that too many people in positions of power only pretend to hold to these norms and principles but in fact don't care. Their decision-making is thereby infused by other values and pursuits. But the failure is also due to the fact that these norms and principles are erected on a flawed onto-epistemology. Therefore, the first task is to step back and revisit our ontology and, thereafter, reconceptualize the human, the nonhuman, the notion of agency, responsibility, and ethical thriving. Those are, in a nutshell, the motions I will go through in this book. While the world is such a garbage fire with the multiple crises we face, this pursuit may seem trivial. I contend that, on the contrary, it is the most pressing and most fundamental pursuit we may undertake. In Chapters 2 and 6, I mention and very briefly discuss the sixth mass extinction event, one of the many crises we are confronted with. It is thanks to the fact that this mass extinction event—including our own demise as a species—is a slow process that we can afford to pause, reflect, and take stock, not to stop the extinction—it is always already unfolding—but to think a better future, the future of the being that is emerging: a posthumanist human. While the process of extinction is slow, it is urgent that we tackle the problems facing us if there is to be an "us" at all in the future.

I think it is important to deal with some potential distractions here. The first one is the term "posthumanism" itself and its adjectival form "posthumanist," which is found in a prominent position in the title of my book along with another distraction: "vulnerability"—I discuss it later. The term "posthumanism" has an interesting history that comprises many mishandlings and misunderstandings. A philosophical position that claims to be posthumanist often runs the risk of being readily dismissed as some kind of transhumanist pursuit of human enhancement, what amounts to a hyperhumanism, or some misguided critique of humanism. Posthumanism is a philosophical stance that wants to move beyond humanism, literally an after humanism. It is a position that rejects the central tenets of humanism and wants to reconceptualize things, look at the world through new lenses, and offer alternatives to the human exceptionalism and anthropocentrism so dear to humanism along with its love affair with rationalism. When anyone embracing this philosophical stance explains that they would rather focus on a non-anthropocentric perspective that emphasizes our entanglements with the more-than-human and reconceive the human in those terms, it is not atypical to be offered the objection: "But, not all humanism!" And to be fair, not all humanism embraces human exceptionalism in the same way—not all is necessarily oppressive and exploitative of nonhumans—and some concepts put forward by humanism may be worth rescuing, although that may only be possible once they are revisited through a posthumanist material feminist lens. I think, however, that this is merely a distraction. Those who object "not all humanism!" often accuse posthumanist thinkers of targeting a strawman. But what if this strawman actually is that set of beliefs, values, and principles that folks put to work in their lives? If humanism has been misinterpreted and people have geared their existence along the lines of this misinterpretation, then it is justified to criticize and reject it if we consider it to be detrimental, which I do.

Furthermore, it is sometimes the case that posthumanism is perceived as a dangerous nihilistic enterprise by those who hold dear to humanism.[3] But even when it is correctly portrayed and its criticism of the humanist tradition well understood, the response often is that humanism does not always match the object of criticism as described by posthumanists. The suggestion is that humanism need not be anthropocentric and also that it is not necessarily exclusive. Humanism would be an "expansive and unfinished project."[4] My question in response to this is: How is humanism not necessarily anthropocentric when the term itself indicates its focus on the human? The Renaissance type of humanism, and its return to the ancients, was a means to focus on the human in this life. It is anthropocentric *and* androcentric even when its ontological and normative foundations are not exclusive: its *mise en oeuvre* is exclusive and oppressive. This means it can agree with certain notions like entanglement but still, in practice, advocate for non-entanglement or, rather, champion acts and values that amount to ignoring entanglement. Is posthumanism an anti-humanism then? It is a mode of thinking that seeks to go beyond it. Is it anti-human? It is only against a certain conceptualization of the human. The humanist human is an obsolete and dangerous misconception of the kind of being we are.

In any case, I am not offering an extensive theorization of posthumanism and what it might be even if I embrace this theoretical orientation, agree with many of its theorists, and think alongside them as will be obvious through my citation practices here. The label encompasses many different philosophical positions,[5] and a few theorists whose projects match the aims or fundamental positions of posthumanist theory resist the label.[6] Is posthumanism a philosophy? A theory? A mode of theorizing? A theoretical lens through which we apprehend and think ourselves and the world? A curation of our selves, the others we meet, and the world we are embedded in?[7]

"Vulnerability" and "trauma" are two other potential distractions. In recent years, the literature on vulnerability has exploded. No doubt Judith Butler's explorations of precariousness and grievability have played a role in this increased interest. I invoke Butler's important analyses in my chapter on vulnerability as well as in the last chapter. There is, however, simply too much to give a full account of and I am not so much interested in providing an account of the various theories, something like a literature review, but instead of elaborating a view on vulner—ability that stems from a posthumanist material feminist ontology. The same holds for trauma. Trauma theory is a whole field and rich with insightful approaches defining trauma and its operations. While traumatic experiences are invoked in my discussion of the concept of transjective vulner—ability, I do not provide a review of various theories on trauma. I am interested in traumatic experiences insofar as they provide a magnifying lens to unearth the ways in which experiences of any kind leave the traces they do in our transjective beings. While my reflections on traumatic experiences such as rape and war as well as exposure to violent images were the trigger for the current project—because the theories I was working with were failing to fully explain them—my focus is not on trauma itself but on transjectivity, ontological vulner—ability, and what an ethical project might be for a transjective being.

Posthumanism is often met with much anxiety. But what makes me even more anxious is our failure to acknowledge the materiality of our entanglements and how materiality and subjectivity are radically intertwined. That is why the overall emphasis in this book will be placed on these insights and why I won't delve into the insights of existential phenomenology, structuralism, or poststructuralism concerning subjectivity and intersubjectivity. I consider those as more or less settled and agree with much of what Nietzsche, Sartre, and Beauvoir had to say about these topics (and I have already written on these issues somewhat extensively). But with that said, and despite all the emphasis I want to place on the materiality of matter, it remains that this is a book written for human readers (are there any others?). Therefore, while the notion of transjectivity I elaborate in Chapter 1 applies to all living beings—human and nonhuman—it is still mostly about transjective human beings that I write. It is interesting to push our thinking and speculate on what it may be like to exist as a nonhuman transjective being, as is the project of Chapter 2. All transjective beings are affective beings, as per Chapter 3, and they only exist as part of collective assemblages, collective agencies, as per Chapter 4. All transjective beings are vulner—able as affect—able, as per Chapter 5, and they exist as embedded and therefore permeated by various toxicities, as per Chapter 6. But the ethical concern that emerges is one that is more strictly human, at least as far as we know. It is as transjective, affective, vulner—able, collective, embedded, and toxic agents and assemblages that we ask ourselves the question of how to live in the best way and what conditions we can contribute to create to allow for our individual and collective flourishing, as discussed in Chapter 7. The foundational theory of this book applies for all beings, but the ethical implications discussed are relevant for the specific being that the human is. So, while my book offers an ontological perspective on all being as relational, transjective, and vulner—able, it is to human transjective beings that I appeal. Because in the end, this book is a call for us to rediscover ourselves, embrace humility, and seek to thrive while pursuing thriving for all. This is what fuels the affirmation alive in this book.

MEANDERING 2
LAND ACKNOWLEDGMENT

Land acknowledgments have become widespread in recent years in Australia, Canada, and New Zealand. They are becoming more common in the United States as well. Some have lamented that their ubiquity—at the beginning of events or meetings, in syllabi, in email signatures, and so on—may actually have the opposite effect than what is intended, namely to draw attention to the colonial history of oppression and suppression of Indigenous peoples and the relation of settlers to these peoples, to this history, and to the land. Indeed, when performed mechanically, in order to tick a box on a political correctness checklist, land acknowledgments not only fail to serve their intended purpose, but they may even be detrimental to decolonization.[1]

What is a land acknowledgment? At a minimum, it should recognize the Indigenous territories one occupies, the Indigenous peoples who lived and continue to live on it, the treaties governing the land, and one's intention in acknowledging the land. This is important in terms of bringing to light the history of the land, reflecting on it, and relating to it individually and collectively. I think land acknowledgments, when performed appropriately, can reveal the manifold entanglements of which we are. My university's official statement for events and which I have adopted to include on the first page of my syllabi goes as follows:

> We acknowledge the land on which we gather is the traditional territory of the Haudenosaunee and Anishinaabe peoples, many of whom continue to live and work here today. This territory is covered

by the Upper Canada Treaties and is within the land protected by the Dish with One Spoon Wampum agreement. Today this gathering place is home to many First Nations, Metis, and Inuit peoples and acknowledging reminds us that our great standard of living is directly related to the resources and friendship of Indigenous people.

Brock University is located in St. Catharines in Southwestern Ontario, between Lake Ontario and Lake Erie. The institution's namesake is Sir Isaac Brock, who commanded the British troops in the 1812 war against the Americans. He allied himself with Shawnee chief Tecumseh who also was seeking to stop American expansion. Tecumseh's support and troops were instrumental in Brock's victory at Fort Detroit in August 1812. And yet, this is majorly underplayed as he is acknowledged only through the name of a university center, while the whole institution is named after the General with a bronze statue of him in front of the main building and, as of recently, his name on the road leading to the campus entrance—ongoing colonialism at work in the twenty-first century.

The land acknowledgment is a good tool to start a process of decolonizing. It makes settlers reflect on the history behind our presence and how the people and the land and their interactions have shaped current beings and actions. But it needs to be rightly done. With my students, I spend almost an hour unpacking the statement that opens my syllabus at the beginning of each course. Students are, just like I was when discussions about decolonization and reconciliation started, genuinely curious. Unlike Indigenous students in the classroom, non-Indigenous students often know little about colonial history and what knowledge they might have is frequently tainted by a settler perspective. It is important for all students—Indigenous and settlers alike—that we collectively acknowledge and discuss how the spaces we use exist as a result of a long history of land appropriation. The story of the collaboration and friendship between Brock and Tecumseh romanticizes what were in fact oppressive relations. The Dish with One Spoon Wampum agreement is one between different Indigenous peoples—the Anishinaabe, Mississauga, and Haudenosaunee—to share and protect the land, the dish out of which one eats. Settlers invited themselves to this dish and imposed their presence, disrupting the land and dispossessing the peoples. They mapped the land, partitioned it, and sold it. I "own" a piece of that land which is therefore both mine—I bought the house sitting on the lot delimited by a fence—and not mine—it was never my ancestors' to take. My workplace is located in the city next to mine and those cities' boundaries do not reflect the Indigenous mapping of the land. They are colonial superimpositions. Slowly making our way through the land acknowledgment and learning about each element—the land, the peoples, the treaties and agreements, the past and the future—is a learning experience through which we can better understand our location and how the political process of colonization has superimposed various socio-cultural constructs on the land we inhabit.

To truthfully acknowledge colonial history is crucial to reconciliation and decolonization. It allows for settlers' expressions of thankfulness to Indigenous peoples for accepting their presence and entering agreements that pointed to collaborative futures. But it is also for expressions of shame and regret at our colonial ancestors' behavior. The "new" world was only new and up for grabs to colonizers. It "belonged" to Aboriginal people. It was the peoples. Accepting that one is a settler can be a difficult process. The knee-jerk reaction to first being referred to as a settler is to think: "My ancestors may have been settlers, but I have merely inherited the world they made for me. I did not take part in colonization myself. I am not to be blamed for past and present inequities and discrimination." Once one gets over this reaction and really thinks about one's own being as radically entangled, one needs to also consider oneself as temporally entangled with both one's past and one's future. Quite simply, neither settlers nor Indigenous people can cut themselves off from their past. For settlers, it means learning about their ancestors' actions and taking responsibility for them. For Indigenous people, it means recognizing and keeping alive the history of what was done to their ancestors and being responsible for them in the present, by advocating for restoring dignity to their ancestors, for example.[2] We are also responsible for the futures we make together, settlers and Indigenous people being collaboratively responsible for how we understand and enact our relationship and entanglement. Land acknowledgments, when properly done as a reflective process on one's own location and ensuing responsibility/response-ability, can prompt an ethical decolonizing response that aims at the elimination of discrimination and inequities. Indigenous peoples continue to this day to be among the least privileged citizens. I could list many examples but will give just one which in itself brings shame on all Canadian settlers of which I am one: the fact that there are still many Indigenous communities without access to clean drinking water. Access to water and sanitation is a human right. Indigenous peoples without access continue to be treated as less than human. Insofar as this state of affairs continues to be accepted by settlers today—actively or passively by ignoring it—they behave like their colonial ancestors who took the land for themselves and continue to deny Indigenous peoples' rights to the land.

We are constituted by the matter surrounding us, including the land and all beings inhabiting it. Acknowledging that the spaces, buildings, and land we use and occupy have a much broader history that is often not noticed by settlers, taking into account how settlers are entangled with Indigenous peoples and their history of dispossession is essential if Canadians are to better understand themselves as well as understanding what their ethical duties to one another are, at least in part. Land acknowledgments when performed meaningfully rather than mechanically can lead to this outcome. But are they falling short? If we are going to fully think through our relation to the land, its occupants—past, present, and future—and our relation to them, ought we not to further expand these statements?

The thought came to me when I received an email from Mitch Goldsmith, one of our PhD students and a long-time animal rights activist and queer theorist. His email signature contains the following land acknowledgment:

> Brock University is located on the traditional territory of Anishinaabe and Haudenosaunee peoples. This land is also comprised of much ecological diversity and many other-than-human persons including birds, mammals, reptiles, amphibians, fish, insects, rivers, lakes, and rock formations. We acknowledge this land and history as we work toward environmental justice, decolonization, and the renewal of Indigenous sovereignty.[3]

This expanded acknowledgment reflects a sensibility common in Indigenous worldviews by capturing the fact that the land is not merely a construct "for humans." The other-than-human persons inhabiting it are in relation with the land, with each other, and with humans. As transjective beings, humans and other-than-humans are entangled in this web of relations and affect I have been discussing. To acknowledge only a section of this complex ecosystem is to obscure the role some nonhuman beings play, devalue them, and thereby dismiss any ethical duty we may have toward them. The land on which I live and work makes me just as it is a foundation for Anishinaabe and Haudenosaunee peoples, for the settlers who took it and toiled it. It makes and grounds (literally) Charlie, rowdy kit, and the doves nesting by my wall. It is the coyotes I heard howl and yap in the middle of the night the other day. It grounds that vine that tore down the fence, the land of the stones at the foundation of my house, the land of the wild garlic growing in the backyard and of the milkweed hosting monarchs in the front yard's flower bed. This land shapes these monarchs on their migratory way. All these statements also capture different temporal scales which crisscross: the land that was used in the past by Indigenous peoples and then taken by settlers, the land that continues to belong to Indigenous peoples, but which was seized by settlers, is the land on which I live and must reckon with the past, and prepare a future by letting milkweed grow, letting bugs and critters be and wild plants do their thing. Each being unfolds its life at its own temporal scale and relates to all other beings and temporalities. Enmeshment is deep and manifold. We can say and ought to say "Mitakuye-Oyasin," the Lakota phrase for "all my relations," indicating that one is part of a whole and related to all beings. An Indigenous friend and colleague remarked pointedly to me that settlers speak too much. When we recite a land acknowledgment, we speak but we ought to listen. And we also ought to reflect on the meaning of "all my relations" or "this land has this history of which I am the inheritor." We need to ask what it means for us and how we, as settlers, have wrongly conceived of ourselves as special and entitled. Understanding oneself as settler is not a means to cut oneself off from this web of relations, to the contrary. When done meaningfully and expanded to include all beings forming the land, a land acknowledgment is a lesson in humility. It is a lesson in ethical dwelling and relating in one's land.

As you are reading this book, you are located on a land. Who dwells in it with you? What are the many different intertwined histories that now constitute you and your location on this land? How are you shaping its future? What traces will you leave through your relations to other dwellers and the land itself and to its past? How are you building the future?

1 THE TRANSJECTIVE

A POSTHUMANIST MATERIAL FEMINIST ONTOLOGY

The target of posthumanist theory is the humanist subject that thinks of itself as exceptional and radically separated from all other beings. The humanist subject is a mind in a body that goes about the world in a position of superiority, whether it is as user and depleter of resources or as carer and steward. One sees oneself as superior and in charge in both scenarios. In this view of the humanist subject, it is the capacity to think and use one's reason, even—or particularly—against one's bodily urges and needs that makes it exceptional. A mechanistic and instrumentalist conception of the body, which went along with the understanding on the part of some hardcore rationalists that animals are merely machines, served to separate the human mind from everything around it. Further, some humans suffered a dehumanizing fate, as their sex, sexual orientation, gender expression, race, ability, or combination thereof did not match that of the superior white, hetero, cisgender, and able-bodied male. Regimes of patriarchy and colonialism contribute to perpetuate these self-serving views that lay at their foundation.

Before posthumanism emerged and set its sight on this target of critique, feminist and postcolonial theory started to dismantle these views as did disability studies, critical animal studies, and queer theory. Posthumanism is indeed the heir of the efforts waged by key predecessors from these fields. One may want to say that it takes the critique one or many more steps further by proposing a new ontology. This ontology repositions and reconceptualizes the human without doing away with it. This entails placing the human back in the web of relations between humans, nonhumans, and various assemblages—communities, ecosystems, the Earth system, and the human itself as an assemblage—and no longer making it the center of attention.[1] Post-anthropocentrism is key to the posthumanist stance and that of material feminism in particular.

Material feminists have adopted this anti-humanist post-anthropocentric perspective and moved on to an examination of the very materiality of bodies. From Haraway (1991) to Barad (2007), to Frost (2016), Bennett (2010), Alaimo (2010), and others, attention shifted from the body as lived—embodied consciousness—to the atoms, cells, and organs that we literally are and the material relations we are (in) even while we like to think of ourselves and act as if we were disembodied minds.

Material Feminist Perspectives

One of the first feminists to take into consideration the materiality of beings is Simone de Beauvoir who, in *The Second Sex*, devoted a whole chapter to "the givens of biology."[2] She is mostly interested in biological processes of reproduction and whether and how they constitute the sexes and their roles for the species. To explore this, she also examines how these processes unfold for other species. She notes that the role of the sexes diverges greatly according to whether they are highly differentiated or not, with males being almost useless in some instances of lesser differentiation and females being more subjected to the reproductive service to the species in cases of higher differentiation. At the end of the spectrum for the latter, human females are the most subjected to reproductive service with longer pregnancies and care for infants. But, as Beauvoir claims opening Book II of her study, "one is not born, but rather becomes a woman" (2011: 283). It is the cultural, religious, and social constructions of that reproductive service that makes it oppressive for women.

If I am making this brief incursion into the foundation of Beauvoir's overall argument in *The Second Sex* it is because I see the roots of a material feminism there. Importantly, by investigating the biological processes of reproduction across species and by discussing sexual differentiation as universal, Beauvoir is implicitly holding to the view that these processes are the same. The mechanics may differ, but reproduction and the perpetuation of the species cut across all species. If this is true of reproductive processes, it is also true of other biological processes. This serves to dismantle human exceptionalism. Further, she insists that the real problem lays with the social construction of biological facts rather than with the facts themselves, saying: "In truth these facts cannot be denied: but they do not carry their meaning in themselves" (Beauvoir 2011: 46). What matters is how they are constructed and experienced by individual humans. In the following chapter, "The Psychoanalytic Point of View," she also points out that "it is not the body-object described by scientists that exists concretely but the body lived by the subject" (Beauvoir 2011: 49). As a phenomenologist and an existentialist, Beauvoir's focus ends up being placed on this lived experience. But that also means having a sound understanding of the situation in which a subject exists. Since consciousness is defined as situated and constituted through its intentional relation to that situation—which includes one's body as well as geographical, social, political, religious, and other settings—it is essential to understand it. It also helps dismantle the regimes of oppression that rest upon a misunderstanding—deliberate or not—of the facts of the situation. In this case, being born female may lead one to become woman if one's becoming is shaped by the patriarchal regime. This, however, is not a necessary outcome if other modes of thinking are embraced. This constitutes a charge against the humanist subject, which is a patriarchal subject.[3]

I am not claiming that Beauvoir was a material feminist avant la lettre. She was not. However, there is no question that her attention to biology opened the way for feminists after her. Just like the distinction she makes between sex and gender—a distinction she does not name as such—the one she makes between the biological body and the social body—again, a distinction not labeled as such but operative throughout *The Second Sex*—has launched or nourished essential feminist inquiries. The new attention to the body as more than something that is experienced is key. Granted, her approach remains grounded in humanist thinking but its rejection of dichotomic structures of thought that drive oppressive regimes such as patriarchy is foundational.[4] If Beauvoir's position is one that ends up championing a humanist feminism,[5] its introduction of a "new brand of materialism of the embodied and embedded kind" which allows for "new and more accurate analyses of power" is a fundamental step forward according to Rosi Braidotti (2013: 22). This attention to the body and biological processes was unprecedented and prepared the ground for subsequent feminist thinkers who investigated the materiality of our existence and relations.

Another foundational figure is Donna J. Haraway who, with her *Cyborg Manifesto* and its concluding provocative statement, "I would rather be a cyborg than a goddess" (2016a: 68),[6] dismantles the human/

animal and the human-animal/machine distinctions and thus also does away with the notion of "woman." The cyborg as hybrid is what we need in a post-gender world and, one might want to add, in a posthumanist world, even while Haraway herself rejects the label.[7] Her trajectory, from *A Cyborg Manifesto* to *Staying with the Trouble* via a study of companion species and technoscience, is an exploration of the multiple assemblages and co-constitutions that form the beings we are. She emphasizes the natureculture and humanimal continuums and defines the cyborg as "a kind of disassembled and reassembled, postmodern collective and personal self" (Haraway 2016a: 33). This, as we will see, resonates with what I wish to capture in the notion of transjective being. Haraway's recent discussion of holobionts and humans as humus (2016b: 32; 58–60) decidedly grounds being in materiality and biological processes while also capturing the world-making activities we engage in. She explains that "[o]ntologically heterogeneous partners become who and what they are in relational material-semiotic worlding. Natures, cultures, subjects, and objects do not pre-exist their intertwined worldings" (Haraway 2016b: 13). This means that no being makes itself. Sympoiesis is the name of the game, and holobionts are sympoietic assemblages, "knots of diverse intra-active relatings in dynamic complex systems" (Haraway 2016b: 60). The holobiont as sympoietic is a becoming-with an expandable set of players. Not only is this set expandable but also dynamic itself as some co-constitutive beings engage in and disengage from co-constitution. What Haraway is describing—and calling us to embrace by "staying with the trouble"—is a dynamic unfolding assemblage of beings materially and subjectively (semiotically) constituted. This assemblage cannot be pulled apart, and any attempt to make sense of it via the binaries inherited from the humanist tradition is bound to fail.[8] The feminist project launching this whole trajectory finds its best solution: an anti-identitarian post-gender cyborg holobiont cannot be reduced to either "woman" or "man."[9]

Material feminism emerges from this fertile ground and further inquires into the intricacies of matter and its functioning. One might say that after years of theorizing the outer world via the lens of physics or biochemistry,[10] scholars like Karen Barad and Samantha Frost make the distinction of inner/outer world finally collapse by taking scientific insights seriously and applying them to our understanding of human beings as fundamentally material.[11] By demonstrating that physical and biochemical phenomena are universal—they occur in beings of every kind—they establish firmly the notion that humans are not to be separated from nature and do not partake in any kind of exceptionality, consciousness notwithstanding. We are beings constituted by physical and biochemical processes which also always make us interconnected to other beings and the world. There are a number of salient ideas in their analyses, but I will focus on three specific and interrelated ones: interconnectivity, the dynamism of matter, and the reconceptualization of agency that they necessitate.

As mentioned, posthumanist material feminism criticizes and rejects the notion of an independent and autonomous human subject that is separate from and superior to other beings. Philosophers have long recognized the notion of intersubjectivity, a form of interconnectivity, but in most cases, it is to be found only between human subjects and has not been grounded in any kind of material entanglement among them aside from the encounter between embodied *consciousnesses* in shared spaces. Interconnectivity among humans has been construed in terms of conscious engagement from subject to subject, and interconnectivity between humans and other beings—such as nonhuman animals, plants, and objects—has been construed in terms of a relation of stewardship or domination: the human was placed in the world and has for a mission to look after it but is also entitled to consume from it as it pleases given its position of superiority.[12] There is an interconnection but it is one ridden by dependence and exploitation whereby the human depends on the creatures it exploits. These understandings of interconnectivity also posit discrete entities interacting with one another. But, if we take the quantum plunge and if we also investigate biochemical processes, this will lead to an undermining of "the metaphysics of individualism," as Barad would put it (2007: 23).

Indeed, the interconnectivity we uncover at these levels is multiple and occurs among particles so small that any notion of "individual" as we have traditionally posited it is evacuated. There is no inside or outside of an individual, even an individual cell or atom, since relations and interconnections unfold within and through them. It is not a case of not having found yet the smallest individual entity since, as Barad shows, the entanglement of which every particle is a part constitutes phenomena just as much as particles do. It is phenomena that are ontologically primitive and not individual bodies or entities. They say that "*phenomena are the ontological inseparability/entanglement of intra-acting 'agencies.'* That is, phenomena are ontologically primitive relations—relations without pre-existing relata*" (Barad 2007: 139). Objects do not precede their relations but rather emerge through these relations, the relations between entities and "measuring agencies." This is what Barad refers to as intra-activity. Phenomena are produced "through complex agential intra-actions of multiple material-discursive practices or apparatuses of bodily production" (Barad 2007: 140). A key aspect of Barad's agential realism proposal is that agency is not an attribute, it is "the ongoing reconfigurings of the world. The universe is agential intra-activity in its becoming" (Barad 2007: 141) and humans "are intra-actively (re)constituted as part of the world's becoming" (Barad 2007: 206). Quantum physics and its examination of particle behavior allow for this dismantling of individualism and the humanist notion of agency. Agency is distributed across being and when we think we are able to isolate one agent or the course of action they initiated, we are—deliberately or not—ignoring the manifold of intra-acting agencies at work. Coole (2005) uses the term "agentic capacity" to refer to this notion of distributed agency. This moves us further away from any subject/object dichotomy of the metaphysics of individualism according to which an identifiable, individual, and delimited subject can be pinpointed as an agent. To say that all matter and material beings have agentic capacity allows for capturing the way in which we are done and undone by our material entanglements and serves to further undermine the fantasy of human mastery and exception.[13] As Samantha Frost puts it, "there are many more agents afoot in the world than human exceptionalism has allowed" (2016: 10). Both a forest fire and a microbe have agentic capacity and often times the extent of their agency far surpasses that of the human.[14] Frost claims that we need a new theory of the human and proposes to conceive of ourselves as biocultural creatures by looking into biochemical operations and the atomic relations of energy that ground them. I want to take a close look at this.

Frost demonstrates that biological processes have intentless direction. This, she says, allows us to "account for the precision and directedness of biological activity without that activity being reducible to anything at all" (Frost 2016: 28). Indeed, once one looks into the atomic field, one discovers the strict mechanics governing energy relations between particles. Frost's strategy is to track this through the atom, molecules, various types of chemical bondings, the operations of permeable membranes, and the role proteins and oxygen play, showing that these processes are distributed throughout all matter, including the matter composing us. It serves to escape the indeterminacy and unpredictability of the quantum field, and it allows for the establishment of some stability through the rules and intentless direction of biological processes. Frost resists the charge of biological determinism—the *überbiological* as she refers to it—by showing that our corporeal history, our temporal unfolding, and the levels of stability we may attain within change—what she calls our "itness"—allow us to exercise some intentional direction amid the intentless direction at work in our material foundation. As she puts it, the organism is permeated by its habitat and relies on the traffic of atoms and cells through its numerous membranes for its persistence, for life to unfold, but it also "composes and recomposes itself continuously in response to and through engagement with its habitat" (Frost 2016: 145). In this context, to speak of an inside and an outside is completely meaningless. There is no such distinction. She recuperates agency through whichever moments of consolidation an agent may achieve upon the intentless processes from which it arises. This amounts to a minimal locus of agency that is barely individuated. Since it rests upon a manifold of processes, it can be said to be collective, to be an assemblage, even in its tenuous individuated form.[15] Barad posits that "[t]here is no discrete 'I' that precedes its actions . . . even in our becoming there is no 'I' separate from the intra-active becoming of the world" (2007: 394).[16] Likewise, there is no "I" separate from its biochemical unfolding.

Frost's points about the permeability of membranes and how life depends on the traffic through those membranes are crucial. No traffic, no life. No intermingling with one's habitat, no life. Entanglement is fundamental to life processes when one bases one's analysis on the atom and up, focusing on biochemical reactions, like Frost does. This coheres with my view of the transjective being and gives it a biochemical foundation. It is transjective and not merely transobjective because Frost recognizes culture and agency as not entirely material but as grounded in matter. The transjective being is transobjective, that is, materially entangled in the dynamic relationality that biochemical processes delineate. There are different approaches to material entanglement among material feminists and bringing together these threads provides us with a solid—no pun intended—albeit dynamic understanding of matter and its agentic capacity. Some theorists, like Jane Bennett, return to Spinoza as well as Deleuze and Guattari's Spinoza-inspired notion of assemblage to discuss matter and its operations. Bennett posits that all matter is lively and that agency is distributed among the material. For her, "all bodies are kin in the sense of [being] inextricably enmeshed in a dense network of relations" (Bennett 2010: 13). She grounds her view in Spinoza's notion of the affective body and speaks of an "effervescence of agency" (Bennett 2010: 29) that is distributed within and across individuals in the assemblage. This leads to a displacement of the subject, a deflation of the notion of agent, and a rediscovery of what we always were: beings engaged in a dance with other beings, human and nonhuman, and an "interfolding network of humanity and nonhumanity" (Bennett 2010: 31). The human "individual"—or more properly, the dividual—is itself an assemblage that operates within what she refers to as congregational assemblages. Entanglement is multilayered and runs within and through the layers. Stacy Alaimo's transcorporeal being partakes in this since, as she says, "the human is always the very stuff of the messy, contingent, emergent mix of the material world" (2010: 11). Our bodies have permeable boundaries—the skin, mucous surfaces, orifices—making us porous beings speared by the materiality surrounding us at the same time we seep into that materiality. The human being as material is "subject to the agencies of the compromised, entangled world" (Alaimo 2016: 158). As such, it "opens up a mobile space that acknowledges the often unpredictable and unwanted actions of human bodies, nonhuman creatures, ecological systems, chemical agents, and other actors" (Alaimo 2010: 2). From this, she concludes that we are toxic bodies with exceedingly leaky borders and as such, we are posthumanist. Indeed, the humanist subject is a solid, autarkic entity that does not leak or is not permeated by other beings. But transcorporeality tells a different tale about the beings we are.[17]

While material feminists turn their gaze to matter in an effort to make matter *matter* again,[18] this does not entail a rejection of other modes of existence such as the subjective and the intersubjective. Barad, Frost, Alaimo, and Bennett all emphasize what matter does and how it does it, but the entanglements they unearth are also entanglements with the subjective, with the cultural, with the discursive. For example, Alaimo explicitly acknowledges that her notion of transcorporeality is indebted to Judith Butler's idea of the subject as also immersed in networks of discursive systems while adapting it to materiality. Any discursive constitution of a subject is always going to unfold as entangled in materiality.[19] From a Spinozist perspective, which is animating the views of many material feminists and certainly Bennett's take on vibrant matter, we can say that bodies are driven by the desire to persist (*conatus*), which is inflected by the traces left by the bodies with which we are interconnected. Disentangling these is impossible.[20] For human bodies—

and for any body for that matter—material entanglement is multiple: it is the entanglements of quantum particles, atoms, cells, and bodies of flesh, but it is also the intermingling of the multiplicity of bodies we occupy, as Arthur Kroker puts it, the intermingling of the "imaginary, sexualized, disciplined, gendered, laboring, technologically augmented bodies" (2012: 2).[21] This is what the concept of transjectivity aims to capture, namely materiality itself in its dynamism and vibrancy but also materiality as existed and interpreted, materiality as subjectivized and subjectivity as materialized. Before I turn to transjectivity and an attempt at a definition, I want to consider one potential consequence of deflating and distributing agency, which is a key outcome of the emphasis on materiality, interconnectivity, and dynamism of matter, as offered by material feminists.

A Flat Ontology?

Does emphasizing agentic capacity while deflating the traditional understanding of agency amount to a flattening of ontology? Is a posthumanist material feminist ontology flat? In his Actor-Network Theory (ANT), Bruno Latour did posit that the world is populated by various *actants* and that these are all on the same plane while being vastly different. All entities act, whatever they are. Their presence in the world is a fact as is their action: they are; they are as *actants*. Given that, to introduce any hierarchy among beings is a mistake. While all entities may play different roles, transforming or transmitting meaning, all have the potential to play both roles. So, when theorists approach being and create categories of beings such as "the social," they are introducing what amounts to an arbitrary category which does not match the reality of entities out there. The theorist is in fact creating a narrative that introduces meaning in an ontological realm where there are no hierarchies and all entities exist with the same acting potential.[22] In this context, one may say that an ontology that speaks of classes of objects, categories, and hierarchies is nothing but a fiction.[23] Inspired by Latour's ANT, object-oriented ontology (OOO) and speculative realism (SR) have effected a return to ontology and objects.[24] The speculative character of OOO is at its peak in the inquiries Ian Bogost presents in his *Alien Phenomenology* (2012), where he discusses things and their experiences, such as the experience a house may have of having humans inside it. Such speculations are useful in terms of distancing ourselves from a human point of view and attempting to decenter it. However, and despite all these efforts, it remains that it is humans thinking those objects. This point allows me to make a more general one about OOO and SR, but also posthumanist material feminism—all manifestations of a post-anthropocentrism: no matter what efforts we make to think objects or materiality, to decenter our perspective and deflate the central position humanism has granted the human, this thinking is done by a human being. The human perspective cannot be dismissed. What matters, however, is that we better understand what the human is and how its perspective is articulated, how it is construed subjectively and materially. Post-anthropocentrism is not a posthuman position. It is a posthumanist position that dismisses humanist constructions of the human. The concept of transjectivity I propose, and to which I come shortly, still allows for a human perspective on things but one that understands how it unfolds in the midst of its entanglements—indeed its unfolding is the coalescence of these in a precarious assemblage—rather than a humanist objective, detached, god's eye point of view.

SR and OOO charge phenomenology with correlationism, whereby being is always thought in relation to the human. According to them, this anthropocentric position obscures objects as they are and renders ontology impossible. This is a problem and SR and OOO aim to think objects as they are in themselves, doing away with a human perspective altogether or at least with its centrality. In order to break the correlationist circle, Levi Bryant proposes a realist ontology, an ontology in which "humans are no longer monarchs of being but are instead *among* beings, *entangled* in beings, and *implicated* in other beings" (emphasis in original) (2011: 40).[25] As Graham Harman puts it, "We ourselves are things-in-themselves while inhabiting this very world, and so too are tables, hyenas, and coffee cups" (2016: 33). With all of its interest in objects, however, OOO is not a materialist position, according to Harman. He sees materialism, and especially the new kind, as overmining objects, as treating objects as "needlessly deep" (Harman 2016: 10). In this sense, materialism would be introducing hierarchies in an ontology that he wants to deal with as flat.

Bryant argues that one consequence of flat ontology as developed by OOO is that *the* world does not exist because "there is no super-object that gathers all other objects together in a single, harmonious unity" (2011: 246). It seems, then, that we are taken back to existential-phenomenological notions that distinguish between the realm of being—in which one simply is—and the world—in which one exists. Sartre famously concludes the introduction of *Being and Nothingness* titled "The Pursuit of Being" by saying, "Being is. Being is in-itself. Being is what it is" (1992: lxvi). The rest of the volume is devoted to an analysis of consciousness—the nothingness referred to in the book's title—and its relating to being which makes the world and consciousness emerge. The intentional consciousness of existential phenomenology constitutes the world via its encounter with being—a being it does not reach since at the very moment of encounter it gives it meaning. The layer of meaning introduces distance rather than proximity. At the same time, consciousness constitutes itself by becoming "full of world." The constitutive process at work is bidirectional. Just like Parmenides who is taken to be the first Western philosopher to inquire about the question of being, Sartre claims there is a very limited number of things we can say of being (granted Parmenides's list was more extensive, including characteristics such as spherical and limited).

There are separate questions here: What can we say about being as it is and what can we say about being and how we relate to it? Nietzsche who, I have argued, practices a wild kind of phenomenology,[26] goes further than those who posit a realm of being that is and dismisses it as insignificant and worthy of laughter. Indeed, if it is out of our reach and we cannot say anything about it as it is in itself, why bother with it? What matters is the world in which we exist and which is a fiction of our making, a fiction we created but forgot we did. Nietzsche claims that we are the colorists of the world: we make sense of things, order them, explain them, and load them with meaning, but these are merely convenient narratives that allow us to function and not any kind of true and accurate statements about the nature of being. So, what is ontology really about?

Ontology. *Ontos logos*: the science or discourse on being and their relations. Could it be that when we ask the question "What is being?" we can offer it an answer that posits a flat ontology but that when we ask the question "What are the relations among beings?," then all flatness disappears? I think this is the key to why so many theorists react quite adversely to the claim that ontology is flat. They are focused on relations among beings in which there is no flatness. But the claim that all there is are actants, individuals, or objects seems quite matter-of-factly and, frankly, true. One can then talk about the relations among those beings in terms that move away from flatness. Relations are not the same and it is when we look at the relations among beings that we see that these introduce the hierarchies and power relations that flat ontology denies. Or is this the case? To lump together beings as different as atoms, humans, spiders, rocks, corporations, and climate as beings with the same potential to act and affect and to refuse to classify them and introduce different kinds of beings according to some characteristic or other is in fact to also answer the question "What are the relations among beings?" by positing that, to that question too, we must answer with the notion of flatness. Indeed, if we adopt a Spinozist stance whereby all bodies stand to be affected and to affect, and if we zoom in on the notion of affect itself then we may understand all relations in terms of affecting, whether that affecting is of a small or great magnitude. Beings *qua* Spinozist bodies are and they are as affecting each other. Ontology is flat through and through whether one focuses on what being is or what relations exist among beings. Affective relations are flat in that it is affect circulating.

I make no claim to be an ontologist and most certainly have made statements about Latour, OOO, Spinoza, or Parmenides that could be debated. If I offer this potentially flawed account and want to raise the question of the possible flatness of ontology it is because it matters to a material feminist stance. We want to say that all beings share the same material constitution which we can understand once we take the quantum plunge with Barad or inquire into the biochemical processes constituting us with Frost or further understand beings as ephemerous and always changing dynamic assemblages of relations. To be able to claim that all beings are materially constituted in the same way and therefore that there is an ontological flatness among them is essential to combatting the various hierarchical and oppressive regimes that we have faced and continue to face. In pandemic time, a widespread claim has been that "we are all in this together."[27] This claim is both true and false. From a strict ontological point of view, in virtue of the fact that we exist, we are indeed all in this together. However, the relations that govern humans in the current world clearly posit some humans as more vulnerable than others. The circumstances faced by a large portion of humans are such that they are not equipped in the same way as others to face the threat posed by the virus. We are all in this together but not *in the same way*.

Going back to Nietzsche and Barad, an interesting pairing if there ever was one or any thinker of power relations such as Foucault, Beauvoir, or Fanon, we need to recognize that the relations that exist among beings often prevent us from even seeing or acknowledging the existence of some beings or relations. Some relations are construed in a hierarchical and oppressive way and deprive some beings and relations of existence or dismiss them as inferior or irrelevant.[28] Because the act of reading the real is structural, because we introduce categories, meanings, and quite literally read ourselves into the real, ontology is never and cannot be flat.[29] What purpose does a flat ontology serve? Could it be that positing a flat ontology is a strategy that ends up hiding or erasing hierarchies and, by the same token, denies the operations of power that are in fact at work? Is this why OOO is mostly put forward by white men? Is the flat ontology of OOO and like-minded theories the last hiccup of white male privilege?

Flat ontology serves to reject anthropocentrism and that is useful. It is anti-correlationist, but is that its fatal flaw? The inability to see that being is what we make it? It rejects under- (Plato, Kant) and overmining (Foucault, Butler, feminism presumably). So, a posthumanist material feminist ontology wants to reject anthropocentrism, but what about the rest? Another question that arises is whether flat ontology is the equivalent of zoe-egalitarianism as posited by Rosi Braidotti. What is zoe-egalitarianism? It is a position that embraces and values all life and rejects any form of exceptionalism. But it is not a position that ignores differences and the various relations among beings that are not equal. To say that all life ought to be embraced and valued is not to say that all life is the same. One can hold on to a notion of zoe-egalitarianism whereby there is equity of value—all life is valuable—and at the same time dismiss the notion of flat ontology—not all beings or instances of life are the same and their relating to one another generates inequities of which we must become mindful.

Can the notion of a weak ontology rescue us from this debate? In his *Sustaining Affirmation*, Stephen K. White offers a useful distinction between strong and weak ontologies. He argues that ontological commitments are entangled with questions pertaining to history and identity (White 2000: 4). He identifies an "ontological turn," initiated by the critiques put forward by Foucault, Derrida, and Lyotard and permeating other fields. One should add to that list of critiques that launched the ontological turn the work of feminists and postcolonial thinkers since they, too, brought forward the "deep reconceptualizations of human being in relation to its world" that White has in mind. These present the human being "as in some way 'stickier' than in prevailing modern conceptualizations" (White 2000: 5). The "stickiness" hinted to here, which is the main focus of the posthumanist material feminist stance I embrace, has to do with regrounding the human in materiality: the materiality of its own body and that of the world in which it is intertwined. While the impact of such reconceptualizations is extensive, the ontological proposals themselves are "weak." They consider the foundationalism of strong ontologies as contestable and believe that their claim to be able to tell us how the world and human nature truly are is dubious. At the same time, proponents of weak ontologies consider it essential or unavoidable to offer some claims about the nature of the human and the world in order to provide ourselves with some grounds to elaborate ethical and political thinking. In a later text, White further explains that weak ontology is not merely critique and must move beyond it. Susan Hekman, for example, offers what she calls a "social ontology of the subject" that adds to the discursive approaches of Foucault, Derrida, and others that posit language as constituting reality by also adopting a materialist stance. For Hekman, identity is both material and social.[30] White insists: it is crucial that nonfoundationalist ontologists make their ontological commitments explicit and robust and offer "a foundation that is universal yet contestable" (2005: 20). This is what posthumanist material feminists should aim to do and what I am attempting here.

I would claim that the proposal to conceive of beings as transjective is universal and contestable. How so? Positing being as dynamic and in flux, as constantly shifting and entering different kinds of assemblages, is making a universal claim about the non-fixity of being. It is a fluctuating foundation which makes any claim about the "true, permanent, and fixed" nature of any being contestable. This is what a posthumanist material feminist ontology offers us and, I argue, this provides us with a better understanding of what we are and how we exist as fluid and dynamic. To offer any kind of fixed notion of the nature of beings and the world is to force dynamic being into a straitjacket. Taking seriously scientific understandings of matter leads us to dismiss any notion of static being. Foundationalist ontologies that have proposed definitions of being that are universal and valid at all times and the moral ideals grounded on those as fixed goals to be attained by individuals have not only proposed inaccurate views but offered what amounted to alienating moral philosophies with demands impossible to fulfill.[31]

Transjectivity

My proposal is to understand the human, and all other beings, in terms of "transjectivity." "Transjectivity" is a compound term that I coin to capture the idea that beings are transsubjectively and transobjectively constituted. No being exists in isolation as an individual but one may have the phenomenological and subjective experience of being a self with one body. This subjectivity, however, is always already constituted by its intersubjective relations, its situation, and its location, as phenomenologists and feminists—such as Edmund Husserl, Maurice Merleau-Ponty, Jean-Paul Sartre, Simone de Beauvoir, Sarah Ahmed, and others[32]—have taught us. My relation to the other is crucial to my self-constitution and *vice versa*. We mutually constitute ourselves, be it positively or negatively, or even in a relatively neutral fashion as we simply cross paths or share a space without interacting, as one does waiting for a train at the station for example. Structuralists and poststructuralists—such as Michel Foucault, Judith Butler, Gilles Deleuze, and Félix Guattari—for their part, have drawn our attention to the various ways in which we are constituted by such things as language, socio-cultural institutions, and social imaginaries that dictate how we insert ourselves in the collective as individuals, but also how we become as individuals—that are never to be separated from the collective, one might want to add. However, while phenomenologists, feminists, structuralists, and poststructuralists have been attentive to our embodiment and situation and how it shapes our transsubjective beings, the attention to material constitution did not consider matter in itself. Even Butler, whose key theory rests upon the notion that bodies matter, fails to consider the materiality of bodies itself and its radical entanglements with all materiality and instead focuses on how human bodies are shaped and produced discursively and culturally.[33] As essential as the phenomenological, structuralist, and poststructuralist approaches to the human may be, they remain concerned with the transsubjective only. Attention is paid to the materiality of bodies only insofar as it inflects the subjective constitution of individuals. However, it is also essential to pay equal attention to the materiality of matter, to its innerworkings. This does not mean rejecting the insights of these approaches. With Astrida Neimanis, I agree that we can engage in "posthuman feminist phenomenology," one that acknowledges that "our experience as bodies is not only at the subjectivized human level" (2017: 24). This is what "transjectivity" captures: in addition to its transsubjective constitution, a being is also transobjectively, that is transmaterially,[34] constituted. Further, these modes of constitution cannot be isolated: they are always intertwined. This is why I opt for the prefix "trans" instead of "inter." Meaning "across," "beyond," or "in a different state," the prefix "trans" better conveys that there is "movement across different sites" (Alaimo 2010: 2).[35] The transjective being, human and nonhuman, is a being constituted by its dynamic subjective and material entanglements, one that emerges on the basis of this dynamic flux.[36]

Examining Merleau-Ponty's phenomenological account of intersubjectivity and embodiment, Vivian Sobchack criticizes his understanding of the process of objectification that occurs in the intersubjective encounter as a diminution of subjectivity. Instead, she proposes that experiencing oneself as object amounts to a "*sensual* and *sensible* expansion—and an enhanced awareness of what it is *to be material*" (Sobchak 2004: 290). She proposes the concept of interobjectivity to encompass the "complementary co-constitutive experience we have of ourselves and others as material objects" (Sobchak 2004: 296). Although she claims that interobjectivity and intersubjectivity are in a necessary relation, I worry that this posits them as separate yet related. The use of the prefix "inter"—meaning "between" or "among"—reinforces that impression: there are two or more units that enter into a relation. Using "trans" instead captures better what beings are as dynamic assemblages that are themselves assemblages and part of larger assemblages as well.

As transjective beings, we are enmeshed in fields of tensions and forces, affects, and material unfoldings that make and unmake us. We are dynamic assemblages of experiences, consciousness, materiality, and so forth, and we exist in an ontological plane in which human exceptionalism is rejected and agency, or rather agentic capacity, is attributed to all beings. Indeed, since all beings are transjective, they all have agentic capacity. And as a transjective being, the human is no longer considered to possess an all-powerful and autonomous agency. The human, like any other being, has agentic capacity and its agentic capacity is modulated by the agentic capacities it encounters and is enmeshed with. The human as transjective is defined as a being that is constituted both transsubjectively and transobjectively, or rather transmaterially. We exist as subjective beings with the very mundane experience of being an individual, of being conscious and having a sense of self, even if this self is much more tenuous than we like to think. We exist as beings that have perceptions, feel emotions, form thoughts, and shape memories as material beings that are material bundles and assemblages dynamically unfolding via multiple relations.

Is the transjective being an "all of the above" notion? Namely, to the question "Which of the following applies to the human?": "The human is primarily a subjective being best understood through the lenses of phenomenology, psychology, and cognitive science" or "The human is primarily a material being best understood through the lenses of biological science, physics, and chemistry." I want to answer "Both" or—in a Deleuzoguattarean spirit of "and . . . and . . . and . . ."—"All of it." The transjective is a subjective and material being and exists as both at all times; one cannot separate these, and we only do so when we seek to explain different aspects or experiences of that being. This is not a facetious move that would be akin to a theory of everything but really an attempt to take seriously all the insights we have achieved on the human and being as a whole and understanding them as in relation rather than separate.

What does it *do* to think of being as transjective? This is not merely a descriptive gesture that offers a theory that allows us to say what is and how it is. Rather, conceptualizing being in one way or another does something to being. We elaborate concepts to allow us to make sense of things and events we encounter or are a part of, but the act of "making sense" is itself an event that serves to categorize, organize, and constitute ourselves, the thing or event conceptualized, and our relation to it/them. Any conceptualization, any creation of concept in that sense, shifts and modulates being. It is part of the transsubjective constitution of being. Claire Colebrook argues along those lines while discussing the rhizome and the immanentist philosophy of Deleuze and Guattari by claiming that the task of philosophy—only philosophy?—is to conceptualize events and to think of concepts as events themselves (2000: 114).

Colebrook pushes this a bit further by arguing that we need to embrace vitalism but not in the way that it has traditionally been conceived, namely taking into consideration how matter as bearer of properties is moved by spirit, which is of a different nature. "The turn to life, the vital, and materialism is therefore also a turn away from the ways in which matter (as a bearer of properties) and the vital (as the spirit that infuses matter) have been defined" (Colebrook 2008: 53). The vitalism she proposes is interested in what animates bodies rather than what they are. Only then can we have a "true understanding" of bodies—bodies in the Spinozist sense, namely any existing thing. Moving away from what bodies are is important but focusing on *what* animates them can be equally problematic. Instead, I would suggest that it is the *animating* we need to consider, that is, the dynamic relating and constitution of an assemblage that occurs and unfolds when bodies enter a relation, but also that creates these very bodies, allows for them to emerge. This is what transobjectivity—transmateriality—is about.

All this discussion of dynamic relations, assemblages, doing and undoing, which are at the heart of transjectivity, may give a sense of fluidity, of ease of flow, exchange, congregation, the sense that membranes let themselves be permeated without resistance, opening their porosity and easing particles through. While this may be the case in some instances—the oxygen we breathe or the water we drink, for example—positing that our entanglements are fluid would be mistaken. For example, Astrida Neimanis argues that we need to think of ourselves as bodies of water and claims that "[a]ttention to water's material capacities informs a new way of thinking about subjectivity in collective rather than individualist terms" (2013: 34). But I worry that such an image—as potent as it truly is—overemphasizes flow and conveys a false sense of a smooth process. Water's fluidity implies an easy flowing of liquids, a continuous movement that accelerates or decelerates but is not interrupted. This ease associated with fluidity seems to ignore the resistance to be found in materiality with which water or any other flowing being is always entangled. The embrace of fluidity has been of service to a certain extent in opening up notions of fixed identity and bodily autonomy. However, as Mary K. Bloodsworth-Lugo claimed, conceiving of the human body as fluid runs the risk of losing sight of its materiality (2007: 60) and the inherent resistance that matter can exercise. Tuana's concept of viscous porosity is potentially more helpful. Tuana's explanation is worth quoting at length:

> *Viscosity* is neither fluid nor solid, but intermediate between them. Attention to the porosity of interactions helps to undermine the notion that distinctions, as important as they might be in particular contexts, signify a natural or unchanging boundary, a natural kind. At the same time, "viscosity" retains an emphasis on resistance to changing form, thereby a more helpful image than "fluidity," which is too likely to promote a notion of open possibilities and to overlook sites of resistance and opposition or attention to the complex ways in which material agency is often involved in interactions, including, but not limited to, human agency. (2008: 194)

Tuana proposes to think of a "complex network of relations" that involves various kinds of beings. An interactionist metaphysics, such as the one she embraces, understands the world and its beings in those terms and moves us beyond the dualistic split between nature and culture, eliminates the debates between realism and social constructivism, and puts us in a position to understand agency in a more complex manner as an assemblage that emerges out of the continuum that flows—or crawls, as a viscous substance might do; think of molasses and the various speeds of its flow depending on how much crystallization has been occurring in it—between beings, beings that themselves are this viscous, albeit dynamic, assemblage.

Another point I would like to bring up is that of the asymmetry of relations. When we discuss the dynamism of relations among entangled beings, whether we refer to them as fluid or viscous, this may lead us to think of that flow as reciprocal and relations as symmetrical. However, there is no such thing as "balanced reciprocity" among beings and this does not necessarily correlate with the level of complexity a being may attain. It is difficult to measure complexity—indeed, complexity in relation to what?—and the complexity of a "single" being does not de facto entail a complexity of relations. A relatively simple being may be engaged in multiple complex relations, thereby rendering it complex. It may also be the coalescence of very complex relations. The asymmetry of relations implies that the agentic capacity of one being may impact another more than that other's capacity would impact it. But how can we even assess that? Can one truly ever fully measure entanglement, the changes that permeability or viscous porosity allow, and the affect that circulates and modulates? Since relations are never simply one-on-one, it may be impossible to determine the level of reciprocity or even if reciprocity exists.

In what follows, I continue to explore interconnectivity and the various entanglements (of) which we are, beginning with a plunge into the world of marine polyps.

MEANDERING 3
CHARLIE AND ME

For two weeks this spring I cohabitated with a persistent bee on my back patio. While this may sound banal for anyone with outdoor space busy with pollinators, there was something unusual with this situation. I always work and sit at the rectangular patio table in the center of my deck. To my right, 10 centimeters away from my elbow, is the table's corner. The bee was flying around that corner. I would wave them away because I did not want to be accidentally stung if I were to move too quick for their liking or inadvertently touch them. They would fly away and come back, hovering around and under the table corner.

I am not afraid of bees even though one day in Salzburg I was stung by one that got caught in the folds of a summer skirt and it hurt like hell, a pain my elderly Austrian landlady replaced by an intense burn as she splattered some herb and alcohol concoction on my thigh to heal it. I occasionally find bees and wasps inside my house. I have learned to pluck them with a towel without harming them and release them outside. I also resist being made afraid by my doctor's warnings and prescription of an EpiPen in case I get stung by a bee. He is concerned given my many other allergies and despite the one incident without anaphylactic reaction. Allergies are unpredictable. Okay.

So, every day the bee showed up despite my presence and persisted in coming back when I waved them away. They were so persistent I named them Charlie. I figured if we were to share this space I might as well name them. I have named other bugs who like to hang out before. Bob the stink bug, who I plucked from my basement and released outside, spent more than a week trying to get back in and crawling on my screen door. Persistence is rewarded by a name. Charlie the bee was incredibly persistent and did not care for me or what I would eat or drink. Charlie was obsessed with the table corner. I looked. There was nothing there but metal and the underside of the resin panel. But Charlie was mostly interested by the metal. I cleaned it with vinegar. I wiped some peppermint oil on it. Charlie always came back. I did not understand why a piece of metal could be so attractive to a bee. And one day I looked closer.

There is a tiny hole right under the corner and it was just the size of Charlie's body. There is one such hole at every corner of the table, but it was that one hole, despite my presence and moving around that Charlie was obsessed with. Once I examined more carefully, I noted that Charlie was sometimes landing on a piece perpendicular to the top and trying to climb upside down toward the hole. Charlie failed most of the time. But finding the hole gave me the explanation for why Charlie sometimes disappeared abruptly. Those were the times they were successful in accessing the hole. But those instances were rare.

After two weeks of this, I figured I would try and help Charlie in their project, whatever that project was. Despite not being afraid, I was not going to be foolhardy and offer my hand. So, I tried offering my phone or a matchbox as a platform for Charlie to land and then access the hole they so badly wanted to get into. That failed. Charlie would fly away and if the proposed platform was still around when they would come back, they would just leave. After a few attempts, I reexamined my vulnerability and decided to open myself to the potentiality that it offered.

As a material feminist, I believe we are fundamentally vulnerable. The openness of our beings and radical interconnections and entanglements that constitute us are necessary for our existence. They are us, and they make us. We most often think of vulnerability as something negative, potentially leading to pain and suffering, something we must guard ourselves against. But it is our vulnerability that allows us to grow and thrive and be the beings we are. This is true of all beings, humans and bees included.

Charlie had been making themself vulnerable for two weeks. I am a much larger being and could have swatted and killed them easily since they intently hovered right next to me for so much time. But Charlie had a project involving getting into that hole and that required making themself vulnerable in my presence. Why could I not do the same?

I started extending my hand and approaching them. Charlie was shy initially or else I did not know how to approach gently enough. After a few tries, Charlie landed on my hand and as I approached the hole, Charlie crawled inside the table corner. I was exhilarated. That initiated a series of interactions that lasted over two days. Charlie came over, hovered, I extended my hand, which was then used as a platform and in we go! Multiple, multiple times. Every five minutes or so. Sometimes I would tell Charlie, "Can't you enjoy the inside a little longer now that you have help getting in there doing whatever it is you want to do?" Off they went and back they came, their hovering a demand and my hand a fulfillment of that demand. Human and bee engaged in a mysterious interspecies project involving a bee crawling into a hole punched in a piece of metal that is part of an object used as a table by a human (Figure 3.1–3.4).

Sometimes, to my surprise, Charlie was shy once again or even refused my hand. Were there more than one Charlie? Charlie the many? How can I tell one bee from another? Was this a collective project, the intricacies of which I could not grasp? I thought I had taught Charlie how to not be afraid of my hand and use it as a platform. Why did Charlie get it many times and not at all a few other times? There must have been more than one Charlie, one more trustful than the others. One more in tune with their vulnerability.

Had I taught Charlie a trick? In my human smugness I thought so. But was it not rather Charlie who taught me how to help them? For the two weeks it took me to decide to help with my hand, was Charlie thinking all this time that I was pretty thick not understanding that they were requiring my help? "Human, why are you waiting to help? Can't you see I can't adjust my flight so I can enter the hole by myself without extreme efforts?" Charlie taught me a trick: using my hand to help them enter the hole and do their thing.

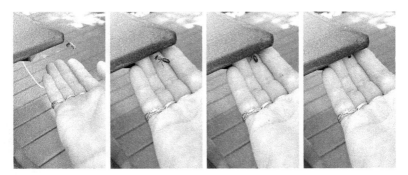

FIGURE 3.1–3.4 Charlie making its way in.

And after two days of interspecies collaboration, Charlie was gone. Whatever needed to be done in there was accomplished and there was no need to return, hover, and request my help. I miss Charlie who taught me that it is okay to embrace one's vulnerability even when one does not understand the project of the other species.

2 OUR POLYP-BEING

To illustrate my notion of transjectivity as it pertains to humans, I contemplate Nietzsche's metaphor and ask: What does it mean to think of ourselves as polyps? Friedrich Nietzsche is part of the philosophical lineage at the roots of posthumanist material feminism. He has offered vehement critiques of the metaphysical-religious tradition, including its long-standing embrace of the notion of a rational autonomous subject. In response to this, he reconceptualizes the human as an embodied consciousness and speaks of the body as the grand reason (*große Vernunft*) and of the spirit as little reason (*kleine Vernunft*), a tool and toy for the body that the body itself created as a hand of its own will. This, of course, is a rebuff of Kant's notions of pure and practical reasons (*reinen* and *praktische Vernunft*).[1] By positing them as no more than little reason, Nietzsche aims to show that there is much more at work in a human being than one's mind and that the emphasis placed on the mind is hurtful and wrong as it makes us feel alienated. The body, as he understands it, is the maker and doer, it is the desiring and willing self that we are, animated by a combination of drives. He thus says that "the way is open for new versions and refinements of the soul-hypothesis; and such conceptions as 'mortal soul,' and 'soul as subjective multiplicity,' and 'soul as social structure of drives and affects,' want henceforth to have citizen's rights in science" (Nietzsche 1989: §12). He also insists that "thinking is merely a relation of these drives to each other" (Nietzsche 1989: §36).

Nietzsche's discussion of drives is (in)famous and often misunderstood as holding on to a hard determinism eliminating the self and its agency. It is not uncommon for thinkers who embrace a materialist position and thereby emphasize the body and material entanglements to face this critique. Indeed, material feminists are also often the target of the same criticism.[2] But, as discussed in the previous chapter, the disregard in which materiality has found itself in Western philosophy necessitates this shift and perhaps overblown attention to it. What is at stake is reaching a more balanced grasp of the human and escaping the traditional overemphasis on the mind and reason. As part of this exercise, Nietzsche offers a thought-provoking analogy that serves as a springboard for my explorations in this chapter. In *Daybreak*, he explains that "[e]very moment of our lives sees some of the polyp-arms of our being grow and others of them wither, all according to the nutriment which the moment does or does not bear with it. Our experiences are, as already said, all in this sense means of nourishment" (Nietzsche 1997: §119).

Nietzsche is not the first to use the polyp to illustrate a philosophical point or even to draw an analogy between the human and this marine creature. Aram Vartanian has traced the use of the polyp in Julien Offray de la Mettrie and eighteenth-century French materialism.[3] He shows that it was Abraham Trembley's 1740 discovery of the animal nature of the polyp, considered to be a plant up to then, that launched this philosophical use and influenced materialist thinking. Trembley observed polyps and noted that they had surprising capacities, such as locomotion, contraction, and extension. This could only mean that they were animals and not plants. But the most prominent capacity of polyps that captured imaginations was their capacity to regrow even after having been cut in multiple parts. This phoenix-like characteristic fascinated the scientific and philosophical community. Vartanian notes that "the polyp became involved in speculations on matters ranging from the nature of the soul to the teleology of organic forms" (1950: 260). It was la Mettrie who first discussed the polyp philosophically in his essay *L'homme machine* from 1748. Fascinated by this regenerative capacity, he inferred from it that since every part of the polyp seemed to contain as much soul and vital principle as the whole—indeed, it had to if it was able to regrow a whole polyp from a tiny part of itself—that meant the soul was divisible and therefore material (Vartanian 1950: 272).

Nietzsche is not so concerned with establishing the materiality of the soul, although he would definitely embrace this notion and was familiar with the work of la Mettrie and Diderot—another French philosopher who also made philosophical use of the polyp in his *Rêve de d'Alembert* (1966) in which he brings up the notion of "human polyps." However, it is not the regenerative capacity of the polyp that intrigues Nietzsche but its mode of nutrition. He sees the polyps' relation to its surroundings as illustrative of how our own interactions with the world constitute us. Importantly, the nutriment we encounter and feed on is "a work of chance:

our daily experiences throw some prey in the way of now this, now that drive, and the drive seizes it eagerly" (Nietzsche 1997: §119). Aphorism 119 of *Daybreak* is titled "Experience and invention." In it, Nietzsche starts off by saying that it is impossible for any individual engaged in self-examination to form a complete image of the "totality of drives which constitute his being" (1997: §119). The section goes on to explain what these drives are and specifies that we are dealing with both physiological and moral drives. It is in this context that Nietzsche uses the image of the "polyp-arms of our being" that grow or wither depending on our nourishment, a nourishment that we depend on but that is contingent. We do not control what comes our way or what does not.

Interestingly, Deleuze and Guattari quote William S. Burroughs's *Naked Lunch* in which he says, "The human body is scandalously inefficient. Instead of a mouth and an anus to get out of order why not have one all-purpose hole to eat *and* eliminate?" This corresponds to the marine polyp I wish to think with here. Deleuze and Guattari bring this up in their introduction to the idea that we are not one body in the traditional sense but rather that we are a, or many, body(ies) without organs (BwO). The BwO is something we are constantly becoming but can never have.[4] We do not possess a body, we exist as it and "it" is multiple and not merely flesh. It is a plateau, not an organism. They claim "the BwO is all of that: necessarily a Place, necessarily a Plane, necessarily a Collectivity (assembling elements, things, plants, animals, tools, people, powers, and fragments of all of these; for it is not 'my' body without organs, instead the 'me' (*moi*) is on it, or what remains of me, unalterable and changing in form, crossing thresholds" (Deleuze and Guattari 1980: 161). This is what I have referred to elsewhere as "Deleuzian traces."[5] Indeed, Deleuze and Guattari also claim that "you have to keep small rations of subjectivity in sufficient quantity to enable you to respond to the dominant reality" (1980: 160). I find it intriguing that Deleuze and Guattari would bring up Burroughs's suggestion in the context of discussing a BwO which exceeds the individual body that "I," or traces of "I," have. But let us investigate further the being of marine polyps.

Marine Polyps

Coral polyps are part of a family of marine invertebrates that mostly live in colonies.[6] They are soft-bodied animal creatures with a mouth that is also an anus and with tentacles that grab their nourishment: the zooplankton floating by.[7] They build for themselves an exoskeleton made of limestone, named callicle, to protect their translucent bodies. While some polyps live as solitary organisms, most live in colonies in which they are all interconnected via their callicles through which they communicate and share nourishment. The colony thereby constitutes one living organism composed of a multiplicity of "individuals."[8] The coral reefs thus formed are multiplicities in another sense as they also host billions of colorful algae that inhabit them. This is what gives the coral reefs their spectacular coloration. Polyps, and the reef they constitute when they form a colony, are highly sensitive to their environment, and fluctuations caused by environmental stress may lead to bleaching of the reefs when the algae inhabitants are evicted in response to pollution or temperature change in the water, for example. Polyps interact with and react to their environment and other beings that color them or nourish them.

In her study of cup corals, Eva Hayward observes that "[c]orals are a composition of faculties, a tuning with environment that can be described as inhabiting what Jacob von Uexküll called an '*Umwelt*'" (2010: 584).[9] They tune with their environment through their material anchoring and communication between the polyps composing them but also through their multiple interactions: with algae, fish, particles that nourish them, water, tides, pollutants, water temperature, and so on. Matter, for cup corals, is not only a dynamic becoming but also a trans-medium mediation—a mediation through which surfaces are not produced as refrains but as lenses. Passing through creates remainders of filterings that result in texture. Boundaries remain refracted interfaces of passage, prepositional orientations. Texture is the unmetabolizable more of animate forces moving across bodies and objects (Hayward 2010: 585).

The coral reef is shaped and textured by the encounters had by polyps and constantly changes as it, and the multiplicity of polyps constituting it, adjusts to those encounters and the beings taking part in them. The reef and its multiple components are exposed, entangled, and transcorporeal beings. They are materially interconnected with one another in the colony, making up one living organism firmly anchored to the seabed after the initial polyp attached itself to a rock and then proliferated. While it is debatable how much consciousness or subjective experience of oneself a polyp may have, specifically due to their lack of a brain, they are acting creatures that relate to other beings they are attached to or host as well as to their overall environment. They act by attaching themselves to a rock and creating a colony. They act by evicting hosts in reaction to environmental change. They act in welcoming them back. Now this agency may not be of the same kind as that of other animals, if only because of its limited scope, and its ensuing subjective existence may thereby be extremely limited. But since we have dismantled the distinction between agents and non-agents and established that agentic capacity is widespread among nonhuman beings, we can definitely speak of an agentic capacity of coral polyps.

Further, I would argue that there is no reason to deny that a polyp may have an experience of itself and that some thinking may be occurring at that marine level. The objection leveled at this claim is that they are brainless creatures. But why would a brain be necessary to "think" or "experience," especially if we embrace the idea that the materiality of bodies and what they experience is the most foundational aspect of our experiences and our selves? It can be argued that the limited agentic capacity of the polyp—one that is limited individually but expanded via the collective action of the colony—is no more limited than that of any other being, including that of our human selves. The agency of a polyp is of the agentic capacity kind and exercises at the very least intentless direction, as discussed in the previous chapter. Its agentic capacity constitutes itself just as much as it constitutes the other beings it is entangled with. And an individual polyp may very well be aware of its own embeddedness. If we consider other marine invertebrates without brains, we find interesting characteristics and behaviors that point to an awareness of one's environment—or at least a proto-awareness—and therefore some form of "consciousness" or "thinking."

Brittle star *Ophiocoma wendtii* is a marine invertebrate animal that has extraocular vision.[10] While most animals can sense light, only those with spatial vision can "see." This requires visual organs, but in the case of *O. wendtii*, "vision" occurs without them and through the use of photoreceptors dispersed on its body. They use dermic vision to go about the world. What this vision is and how the world appears to *O. wendtii* is a matter of speculation. We can only surmise that it would be very alien to what we conceive as vision, especially given the oculocentrism of Western thinking. In addition to enjoying extraocular vision, *O. wendtii* is also a brainless creature like its fellow deep-sea inhabitants such as jellyfish (with the exception of comp jellyfish), sea cucumbers, men-of-war,[11] starfish, sea urchins, sea sponges, clams, oysters, sea lilies, sea anemones, and sea squirts. These animals do not have brains, but most have a nervous system, albeit a primitive one. One of the reasons advanced to explain their lack of brain has to do with survival. Since they all live at deep-sea levels and because it requires a lot of energy to have a brain—energy that may be in short supply in these depths that pose an extra set of challenges for living beings—and since they don't have a particular need for one, then all they have is a nervous system.[12] However, even the animal with the most rudimentary multicellular organism and without a nervous system, the sea sponge, displays some awareness of its environment. Sea sponges sneeze when something foreign gets into their system, thereby demonstrating an awareness of their surroundings. Sneezing is a response to an encounter, to a change in one's entanglement. This awareness may be basic, indeed the most basic there is among animals, but it can be construed as a minimal form of consciousness. This would be the rawest form of embodied and embedded consciousness, and embedded in a radical sense for some of the marine creatures mentioned that live attached to the seabed. It is conceivable that these brainless beings are exercising extracerebral thinking, just like *O. wendtii* exercises extraocular seeing. Extracerebral thinking is that of a body as embedded, the thinking formed through its interactions with its environment, regardless of whether it is as elaborate as we know it and can imagine it. Indeed, we may lack the imagination necessary to conceive of what such thinking might be, which is why we tend to refuse labeling it as such. Our way of thinking is not only oculocentric but also cerebrocentric.[13] However, as Barad suggests, "'mind' is a specific material configuration of the world, not necessarily coincident with a brain. Brain cells are not the only ones that hold memories, respond to stimuli, or think thoughts" (2007: 379).[14] We just need to open ourselves to thoughts that are thought in different ways and that may remain opaque to us all the while we are entangled with them.

    I ask again: What does it mean to think of ourselves as polyps? Another creature briefly mentioned above that I would like to consider in relation to this question is the Portuguese man-of-war. Although it appears to be a single animal, it is in fact a siphonophore, a colony of polyps that live together as one body. They are described as a colony of zooids that are genetically identical even though they are specialized in their activity. There are four specialized parts each responsible for one of four tasks: floating, capturing prey, feeding, and reproduction. The individual zooids composing the colony, what we mistakenly perceive as one animal, cannot survive independently and are connected by tissue. Note that none of the tasks involve locomotion. The men-of-war have tentacles, but these are not used to move. Instead, they are moved by the water currents and winds. The uppermost polyp, a gas-filled bladder (pneumatophore), sits above the water. It is that part of the animal that gives it its name because of its resemblance to eighteenth-century Portuguese warships under full sail. The wind may catch it and push it around in the water, allowing it to move. The man-of-war can also deflate its pneumatophore and temporarily submerge itself to retreat to safety if it is under threat. There are a few interesting things about this animal(s). Just like the sea sponge and other brainless creatures brought up earlier, the man-of-war is aware of its environment and can protect itself, reach out for prey, and capture or sting it. We may infer that it has thoughts since it exists as an embedded and embodied being. Its embeddedness is to be contrasted to that of coral polyps in that rather than being attached to a rock in the seabed, it floats according to currents and winds. Like coral polyps, they exist as a group and can be found floating in groups of up to a thousand or more "individuals." They exist as the embodiment of an entangled multiplicity and as part of a multiplicity floating together. I would say that both coral polyps and men-of-war are equally at the mercy of what floats their way, be they immobile or mobile. Indeed, neither move deliberately and must grab and nourish from what comes their way by chance. With that said, they are both constituted by the environment in which they exist as embedded and embodied.

Despite their simplicity, coral polyps—like the other sea creatures discussed—are transjective beings. They are materially interconnected with one another in the colony, they work together (in the case of the man-of-war), and they display a minimal degree of awareness of their surroundings. There are, of course, incommensurable differences between coral polyps, men-of-war, and humans, but comparing them can serve to emphasize entangled materiality in a generative way. This is especially useful for the human in order to free ourselves from the fantasy of human exceptionalism. Human beings are the same entangled and materially interconnected beings as coral polyps. Like them, we host organisms that may be said to give us our "color," namely our microbiological constitution as a multiplicity. Polyps are attached to a material foundation in a literal way while we are mobile creatures, but our mobility is always and ever grounded in materiality: we are always of a specific location. And like polyps, that grounding constrains and shapes our agency just like it shapes our being.[15] One may want to argue that the materiality to which we attach, as polyps or humans, is not the same because one presumably does not change while the other fluctuates greatly. Indeed, the dynamic becoming of the materiality to which the human attaches unfolds at a great pace, especially given the human's mobility. We are not fixed in a location the way a coral polyp is, and our mobility exposes us to a greater variety of materiality and interactions with other beings we encounter through our movements, at least potentially. Although, as I have claimed above in relation to the man-of-war, being entirely mobile or immobile or even something in between, a transjective being is still embedded and constituted by what surrounds—and permeates—it.

But, further, if one were to believe that the materiality to which the coral polyp attaches does not change, or changes very little, then they would be ignoring the different timescales over which change occurs. The rock to which a polyp attaches undergoes changes on a geological timescale which is, for humans, most of the time unnoticeable. It may take more than a human lifetime to experience a change in a rock that sits in a desert, for example. But is this even true? The activity of microorganisms on the surface of a rock alters its surface constantly. We may, however, fail to pay attention to such microscopic changes. This lack of attention is not a lack of occurrence of change. This all points to intersecting and interconnected agencies, agentic capacities, intentless directions, and temporalities and the dynamic becoming that ensues from encounters between beings. It should also be noted that whether they are attached tightly to their material foundation—like coral polyps—or whether they enjoy mobility on the surface of their material anchoring—like men-of-war or humans—all beings are entangled in a multitude of material encounters. The coral polyp that is attached and immobile, except for its moving tentacles, still interacts with the water it is in, the other polyps it is connected to in the coral reef it forms, the food particles that come its way, and fishes and algae that live in the reef or merely visit it en passant. This is all also true of the human and all other beings. The polyp is a transjective being, entangled with other subjectivities and with objects and materiality. What is notable with the quote from *Daybreak*, cited earlier, and other passages where Nietzsche discusses the self, is that the polyp engages in self-constitution but is also the object of processes of self-constitution that lay outside the scope of its consciousness and are not the outcome of a willful decision or action on its own part.

Bodily Polyps

Marine polyps are beautiful and fascinating creatures. To speculatively compare our being to theirs is thus palatable even if strange. What if we were to push the exercise a little more and examine a less appealing kind of polyp: the bodily polyp. Are we also polyps in that sense? A bodily polyp is a projective tissue growth, usually found on a mucous membrane, that is sometimes referred to as abnormal. Although "abnormal," some are quite common and benign, such as nasal ones (which raises the question of what counts as "normal" if these are so widespread). However, when we think of bodily polyps, our first reaction is to think of cancer. While most colon polyps are harmless, for example, some are precancerous and colon cancer is one cancer with a high mortality rate. The bodily polyps are not individual entities. They are outgrowths, the "product" of cellular division and proliferation gone awry. They are formed of individual malfunctioning cells. We can consider this other very brief passage in Nietzsche's *Thus Spoke Zarathustra* to explore the comparison between humans and bodily polyps: "The Earth (he said) has a skin; and this skin has diseases. One of these diseases, for example, is called 'Man'" (1974: "Of Great Events"). Like bodily polyps, the human being can be considered to be a tissue growth on the Earth's skin. As transjective, the human is materially entangled. This means that its body is made of the matter of the Earth. This is sometimes poetically rendered when the suggestion is made that we are assemblages composed of the inhalation or ingestion of atoms of long-dead dinosaurs and other extinct animals, Gandhi, the person next to us, Greek slaves, deep-sea fishes, plants, minerals, and so on. Our bodies are compounds and as the Earth system lives and changes, the various beings inhabiting it also live and change. Atoms and particles are part of a finite system—or so goes this story—and they enter various assemblages. We are literally stardust as this dust encounters the Earth's atmosphere and we breathe it in (while some metals that have travelled through the galaxy also come to form the bodies we are).

Humans live on the surface of the Earth, on its skin. They feed from its produce and are literally outgrowths of it. Most humans are rather harmless, feeding off the fruits of the Earth without causing major disruptions. Others, however, could be perceived as precancerous—if not outright cancerous—due to their predatory practices. They overextract and exhaust resources; they exercise violence toward other human or nonhuman animals. They seek infinite growth in a system with limited and finite resources. Cancerous cells are defined as such: they divide relentlessly and exploit and exhaust their resource, the organ affected. So, let's take seriously the suggestion that humans are polyps growing on the surface of the Earth's skin organ. I think this allows us to understand ourselves as bodily polyps: mostly harmless but often cancerous. In the Anthropocene epoch—defined as such because of the unprecedented anthropogenic impact on the Earth system—we may indeed be said to have relentlessly developed as cancerous polyps. And just like cancerous cells ultimately bring their own demise by causing the failure of the organ affected and the body it is a part of, we are well on our way to causing our own extinction.[16]

Vegetal and Mineral Extracerebral Thinking

I have no pretension to articulate a philosophy of plants or minerals here. Plants have been the object of inquiry of many thinkers, especially in relation to the effort to build an ontology structured in a hierarchy of beings. Such hierarchies need to be rejected at the same time that we recognize that there can be a plurality of modes of thinking or being conscious, a plurality of modes of existence, of existentiality, and that these are all valuable in and of themselves. This serves to reject human exceptionalism, but it also teaches us a lesson in humility. What we considered in us to be exceptional, our way of life as the kind of embodied consciousness we are, is merely one among many possibilities for being and existing.

There is plant-thinking that considers the possibility of plants being able to think and then there is plant-thinking that is thinking about plants. In his remarkable 2013 book *Plant-Thinking*, Michael Marder traces a history of how plants have been considered in Western thought and opens pathways for thinking the thinking of plants. I want to explore his views at some length here. As he says, plants have been considered liminal beings, at the bottom of any version of the chain of beings.[17] In this regard, it is interesting to consider that Trembley's polyp became all the rage only once it was considered to be an animal: this sudden change in ontological status granted it more value and made the polyp worthy of interest. It climbed the ladder of the hierarchy of beings. According to

Marder, humans are afflicted with the incapacity "to recognize elements of [themselves] in the form of vegetal being," leading to "the uncanny—strangely familiar—nature of our relation to them" (2013: 4). While also acknowledging the contributions feminist and non-Western thought can make, he puts to work Jakob von Uexküll's theory of biology and his notion of *Umwelt* in his analysis. According to Uexküll, all beings make up their environment, their "lived world."[18] As beings perceive, their world of perception shapes itself and, as they act, their world of action also emerges. Combined, the world of perception and the world of action form the lived world. Uexküll invokes the image of a spider weaving its net and says that all subjects build their relations in a web that supports their existence. These lived worlds are subjective: they are woven and generated by a subject. What is key for Uexküll is that it is not only humans who are subjects but any living being constituting a world. With that said, however, it is essential to remind ourselves that "[w]e are always led astray when we want to introduce the measure of our world into the judgment of animal worlds" (2010: 199). This leads Marder to claim that when a human encounters a plant, two worlds meet: "[P]lants are capable, in their own fashion, of accessing a world that does not overlap the human *Lebenswelt* but that corresponds to the vegetal modes of dwelling on and in the earth" (2013: 8). These two worlds meet and even though a great deal of each world remains impenetrable or even unrecognizable as an ontological reality by the subject of the other world, the worlds and their subjects are entangled. The world of the plant may remain inaccessible to us, just like ours remains inaccessible to them, but this is no reason to deny that the plant does indeed have a world.

I find particularly useful Marder's use of Middle Latin etymology to point to the potentiality of plants. As he points out, *Vegetabilis* means "growing, flourishing." The verb *vegetare* signifies "to animate, to enliven," while the other related verb, *vegere*, means "to be alive, to be active." The derived adjective, *vegetus*, points to the qualities of vigorousness and activity.[19] The action of vegetal beings unfolds in a world that is theirs and the entanglements and relations we bring to their world remain part of their world as interpreted from their point of view, through their perception and their action. But there is definitely activity—growing, animation, flourishing. The vegetal world is definitely much more than relatively passive stuff. These living beings build their worlds as they perceive, act, and flourish and their world "makes sense" to them and not to us. Their world makes sense to us only once interpreted as part of our world and therefore not as *their* world at all.[20] Despite all this, there are important things to learn from the world of plants, even if it remains inaccessible to us. First, we need to unlearn the objectifying approach to the world that has been the modus operandi of Western thought (Marder 2013: 71). Instead of considering everything that is inaccessible to us or slightly alien to our way of life as an inanimate object unworthy of attention or care, we must always consider that these beings have worlds and that their worlds are meaningful to them. Likewise, because plants' involvement in their world is so radically different from the way we engage with other beings, we are unable to assess in what ways they relate to their others as "from an anthropocentric perspective it seems that plants are not at all interactive beings, uninvolved in their own existence" (Marder 2013: 132).

Marder wishes to invert Levinas's notion of non-intentional consciousness and attributes nonconscious intentionality to plants.[21] Plants do not have selves that consciously seek to fulfill a goal or purpose and yet their vitality is a form of intentionality. Although, I would say that, if we are to follow Marder's own claim about the inaccessibility of the plant world to us, we must admit that this remains a speculation on our part. Plants may well have conscious intentionality of a kind unrecognizable to us. He explains: "[T]he non-conscious life of plants is a kind of 'thinking before thinking,' an inventiveness independent from instinctual adaptation and from formal intelligence alike" (Marder 2013: 154). Along with this nonconscious intentionality, plants have a nonconscious involuntary memory:[22] they store memories of past physical stimuli in the form of material inscriptions on their bodies (Marder 2013: 155). The phrase "involuntary memory" points to what is missing for plants: the voluntary memories one stores when one seeks to remember past stimuli, encounters, affects, experiences. Voluntary memory would be impossible for a being that is a nonconscious intentionality rather than a non-intentional consciousness. But this discussion leads Marder to conclude: "We are akin to plants in that, like them, we most often act without our heads, without irradiating commands from the central point of consciousness or the brain—and it is by no means evident that the brain itself is subject to this hierarchical centralization—all the while upholding a certain non-conscious logic and consistency in our acts of living" (2013: 160). What is ultimately uncovered through this inquiry into plant-thinking is the thinking of life itself, an "*it thinks*, a much more impersonal, non-subjective, and non-anthropomorphic agency"

(Marder 2013: 165). Plant-thinking and its speculation about what it is like to engage in extracerebral thinking as a plant unearths this *it thinks* which is non-anthropocentric and yet entangled with the anthropos. Humans and plants may each have their own worlds, but these worlds never exist in isolation from one another. There is also much *it thinks* going on within the human, as I discussed in the previous chapter by bringing up Samantha Frost's notion of intentless direction. Dylan Trigg puts it this way: "[T]he human body is never entirely in possession of its own being, neither temporally nor materially" (2014: 74). There is an alien materiality to the body that breaks us away from the self and "the alien within the body is not a departure from the lived body, but a continuation of it" (Trigg 2014: 78). It is the vitality of life that permeates all beings, and this vitality engages in thinking in the mode of *it thinks*, it is part of the affective fabric in which all beings, as transjective, are entangled. Again, opening ourselves to the aliens within and outside us, recognizing their existence and mode of thinking, and acknowledging that these modes of thinking are entangled are lessons in humility and a move away from human exceptionalism.[23] This view of plant-thinking is also a fundamental challenge to those views that relegate plants to passivity.

Another realm of supposed passivity is that of mineral beings. But once we understand and accept that what passes as passivity in our world may in fact be vibrant with activity, to use the evocative adjective Bennett affixes to materiality, we may approach mineral beings differently. It is easier to assign vitality to plants since we can observe their growth and, from there, attribute to them a form of thinking, *it thinks*. But in the case of inorganic minerals, there is no vitality to be perceived. Even if some stones are said to grow and move, such as the trovants of Romania that grow with each rainfall,[24] they cannot be said to be alive and therefore cannot engage in thinking. What is it like to "think like a mountain," as Aldo Leopold entreats us? The mountain of the *Sand County Almanac* is not a single rock, but a whole ecosystem in which rocks and their worlds—if rocks have worlds—are entangled with the worlds of all beings living on or around the mountain. The rocks come alive in this sense, as the foundation of an ecosystem.

Or is this true? What does it mean to say of a being that it is alive? Can inorganic beings be alive in virtue of their entanglement with an organic being's life? Is it because a stone is an integral part of a human story that it gains meaning, and thereby some vitality, or does it have vitality all along? Does life denote "not so much an entity [but] a tendency," (Cohen 2015: 227) a movement forward and in relation? Tim Ingold says, "[t]here are human becomings, animal becomings, plant becomings, and so on. As they move together through time and encounter one another, these paths interweave to form an immense and continually evolving tapestry" (2022: 9). Is each path alive and, key to my questioning here, is each being moving along these paths conscious of itself as such or simply conscious of the movement along the path? Jeffrey Jerome Cohen's study, *Stone: An Ecology of the Inhuman* (2015), investigates our lithic relations and demonstrates that "[l]ate medieval understandings of materiality presumed continuity between rock and flesh" (22). Mineral beings appear radically indifferent to us—indifferent to everything even, without worlds, inanimate. And yet, stone is dynamic and full of potentiality which unfolds at such a radically different pace as to appear to us as nonexistent. As Cohen puts it, stone is an alien presence, "thick with sedimented time" (2015: 36). Stone archives past beings and is shaped by this archival. As Hird and Yusoff argue, an estimated two-thirds of mineral species have been brought about by changes caused by living organisms, bacteria notably. They speak of a mineral-biological system that constantly evolves, but it is one we are ill-equipped to grasp because of our carbon imaginaries.[25] Basically, we are biased against recognizing minerals as life because of a certain conception of life we hold on to. We fail to see that the mineral is alive with past lives, that its being is the outcome of the encounter between the organic and inorganic, rendering this distinction extremely tenuous if at all viable. They invite us to stretch our imaginaries so that we may recognize this conjoined evolutionary path. Cohen shows that medieval thinkers were willing to go even further than this and attribute agency, relationality, temporality, and mortality to mineral beings. The stories we tell with stone, most notably fossils, are very different than the stories stones tell, through their archiving activity. Stone "speaks, when we stop insisting that communication requires words rather than participation in meaning's generation" (Cohen 2015: 192). *Virtus* pertains to stone and designates the great lithic potency, the "creatureliness without anthropomorphism, the life-force of stone" (Cohen 2015: 233). To Cohen, and the medieval thinkers he invokes, it is clear that stone is very much alive, once we recognize its multiple relationalities, agency, and dynamics. Can it think? In virtue of being alive, it seems that it could think in the sense of the "it thinks" put forward by Marder and discussed above. And indeed, why not? What is thinking and is conscious thinking essential to the life of a transjective being, to its flourishing?

* * *

A lot of the above is highly speculative. We simply cannot ascertain that polyps, plants, or minerals think and, if they do, in what way they do.[26] And yet, engaging in these speculations is key to the post-anthropocentric project. Cohen uses the word "anthropodiscentered" to refer to the point of view of stones. To attempt to step outside ourselves, to think like a rock, to think as a rock, leads to this decentering. Cohen quotes Gilian Rudd who says, "to speak [for the nonhuman] risks abrogating it into the human, yet not to speak for it seems to relegate it to the realm of silence and thus render it invisible" (2015: 277, n. 44). To this he adds: "Even if many nonhumans are beyond our grasp and indifferent to our lives, their stories are tentatively imaginable within anthropomorphic narratives that profoundly challenge anthropocentrism" (Cohen 2015: 277, n. 44). Challenging our thinking, engaging in anthropodiscentering, considering whether other beings are transjective in the way we are or asking in what way they participate in transjectivity without being the same as us, is a means to embrace the transjective ethos which I argue is key to our flourishing and that of organic and inorganic others.

MEANDERING 4
FEELING/BEING OUT OF PLACE

This is always *my* place. Indeed, existential phenomenologists claim that as an intentional embodied consciousness, I can never *be* "out of place" since I make my place as I go about the world, giving meaning to the objects and subjects I encounter in the situations in which I am placed. This notion of place fails to explain how one can feel out of place. But is place much more than our intentional conscious construct? Experiences of feeling out of place are due to the sudden awareness of the operations of the world- and self-constitution that are constantly unfolding through our transjective beings. We are always caught up in this process and barely conscious of it, but it can be brought to the surface when we face abrupt changes in our transjective surroundings and being.[1]

To illustrate this, we could use this diagram that indicates that various elements—such as others, place, narratives, the body, and so on—coalesce to constitute our selves (Figure 4.1).

FIGURE 4.1 Self-constitution?

But this seems like too neat of a process. Rather, we are dealing with something like this (Figure 4.2).

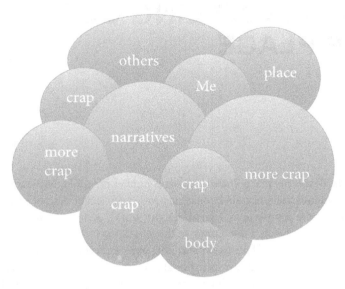

FIGURE 4.2 A messy assemblage.

This sort of looks like an assemblage, and a somewhat messy one, but the individual bubbles indicate boundaries that are in fact nonexistent. All of this is more porous, volatile, fluctuating, and entangled than any diagram can represent. But it still helps to see how place is both constituted by and constitutive of who and what we are and how this impacts the transjective being we are, doing and undoing it in this assemblage of tensions and affects. So how can a transjective being ever feel out of place? If place is a fluctuating thing just as one is, how could a change in one's surroundings ever produce an acute feeling of being out of place?

In September 2011, I presented a paper at a conference that was held at the Queen Mary College of the University of London. This campus is located on Mile End Road in East London. The hotel where I was staying was at Aldgate East tube station. This is at the limits of the center of London about ten minutes east, by foot, from the London Tower. Back then I was still a blissful landline user and did not carry a cell phone with integrated GPS and had to rely on actual maps. However, the university campus was not on any tourist map and I could not find my hotel on one either. A map of cycle paths included where I was staying but not much more to the east. I knew my hotel was at a walkable distance from Spitalfields market to the north. I walked there the day before the conference. I noticed the omnipresence of Indian and Pakistani stores and restaurants. This is London. India was once a colony. Nothing surprising there except for the worrisome absence of pubs.

The morning of the conference, I walked to the university. It was an easy trip to take: just walk along Whitechapel, which becomes Mile End Road, for about 2.5 kilometers and there you go. What I did not know before setting out on my walk that bright sunshiny morning was that that walk would make me abruptly feel like being in the Middle East. Two blocks east from my hotel, my surroundings changed. The concrete world of buildings and streets was familiar enough: recognizable London architecture. However, multiple things and objects transformed the surroundings.

Whitechapel/Mile End Road is a very wide street with those typical wide London sidewalks. Walking on the north side of the road, there were rows of buildings to my left, a wide space in which I was walking, and rows of kiosks on my right on the side of the street. It felt just like Istanbul where I travelled in 1997 and was just as busy. The kiosks on my right were selling the same kind of goods you would find at the Grand Bazaar: cheap gadgets and houseware stuff, spices and exotic snacks and foods, and cheap clothes. There were even a few kiosks selling Islamic clothes including hijabs, niqabs, and burqas—on sale too! I don't remember seeing those at the Grand Bazaar . . . perhaps because I was expecting them there but not here?

Not only did my physical surroundings change two blocks east from my hotel, but my surroundings of people did too. Very few people, including myself, were Caucasian whites (which is the vast majority of crowds west from Aldgate East). Folks of Middle Eastern origin and a few North Africans, East Indians, or Pakistanis populated the street. Some men were dressed in Western fashion but many more were wearing their traditional clothes. Women around me were wearing a variety of Islamic clothes such as hijabs, chadors, niqabs, or burqas.

Walking eastward on that road, I had a sudden and very powerful feeling of displacement, of being out of place. That feeling grabbed my gut and I felt totally uncomfortable, scared, threatened even. My surroundings were no longer friendly and welcoming. This was not *my* place. I thought: "Oh well, I did not know this area was so densely populated with non-whites. But this is London, there is a lot of immigration, etc." I understood the experience, reasoned it, explained it. But my gut did not care: it did not like it, it wanted out, it kept wondering: "Where the hell is this university? How far is it?" and this creeping discomfort/fear, which never became panic, made me walk at a slightly faster than normal pace. I got there, after thirty minutes of walking. A typical Western campus welcomed me. It even felt North American due to the relative newness of the concrete buildings. As soon as I passed its gates, my feeling of displacement vanished. I no longer felt out of place. After all, I am an academic and I completely belong to a university campus, wherever it is. I felt safe again. My gut felt good. To go back to my hotel, which is also *my* place, I took the bus.

Now this experience is very troubling for many reasons. My transjective being came to this experience with a set of assumptions and expectations: having been in London a few times but always in Kensington and in the center except for one brief outing in the area of Brixton tube station, my being naively expected similar surroundings and experiences as the ones undergone before. These assumptions and expectations were challenged and shattered as the London encountered was so radically different. The materiality of the place was radically different than what I had experienced before. The architecture and cityscape were the same, but the materiality of the place was radically different because of the different kinds of beings, humans and not, encountered in it. This place in which I was moving was my place and it was constituting me at the time I was moving in it, but its strange nature made me feel out of place.

Feeling out of place was paired with fear. While my reaction of fear was surprising, and I have sought to explain it to myself, I think what is more troubling philosophically is why a transjective being would ever "feel out of place" since it constantly constitutes its place. I can never be "out of place": my place is made as I go about the world, as I interact with objects and subjects, as I act upon them and them on me. This is my place. Radical and sudden changes in the world of objects and subjects may provoke an equally radical and sudden discomfort: a moment of suspension when one feels "out of place." If I opened the door of the room I am in to write this piece to leave and suddenly found myself at a rave party, I would also experience that moment of suspension. I would feel out of place although it would be my place. But I would not experience fear because nobody warned me against raves, there is no grand narrative portraying rave partygoers as particularly menacing. There is a chance that, with a drink or two or the appropriate pill, I would even feel good about my place, as unexpected as it may have initially been. I wonder if such an adjustment was possible for me in the streets of East London. I doubt it.

In this experience, my place was being done and undone by the narratives I was bringing to it. While the materiality of the place generated an unexpected shift, that shift was magnified by the intermingling of narratives that read the place as menacing, thereby amplifying my feeling of being out of place. "Place" like "transjective being" is a fluctuating notion, being done and undone by the various beings' interactions and the field of affects and tensions. Place itself does not exist. It emerges at various points of encounters between beings and with various degrees of intensities: *my* place, a familiar place, a space in which one feels out of place, and so on. The experience of feeling out of place unveils two things: it unveils the transjective constitution of our selves and of the notion of place (place being much more than one's spatio-temporal location).

In this particular instance, and given the nature of the experience, it unveils the powerful and insidious operations of grand narratives as well as popular mediatic narratives that demonize certain beings with whom we share the world. These have the power to do and undo the transjective being as well as place. On vacation in Cuba one time, I scrutinized the sea surface reassuring myself of the absence of sharks as I was swimming rather far from shore—memory imprints of *Jaws* entangled in the experience. This was not a fleeting moment of irrationality but the sudden operation of a popular cinema narrative that has constituted me and constituted my place at that moment. In London that day in 2011, it was the omnipresent demonizing narrative on the Middle Eastern, quite possibly Muslim, Other that reared its ugly head.

After all, as newscasts, TV series (*24* and others), some movies, and video games tell us, we ought to be afraid since *they* are seeking our demise. For a reasonably smart and enlightened academic who reflects on such things as othering and oppression, this is also the experience of implicit bias becoming explicit in a visceral and uncontrollable way. This instance of ordinary racism and xenophobia is troubling indeed for someone fighting such things. But this is what implicit bias is: the interiorization of narratives that then shape our relation to others and the spaces in which we may encounter them. This *"racisme ordinaire"* like *"sexisme ordinaire"* is constitutive of us and of place.

Place too, just like us and just like any other being, is a "messy, contingent, emergent mix" since its materiality is impacted by its relations to all other beings and narratives. The transobjective and transsubjective can never be disentangled.

3 AFFECTIVE FABRIC AND COLLECTIVE AGENCY

After investigating the life of marine, vegetal, and mineral transjective beings as a means to push our thinking and speculate on more-than-human modes of existence and modes of "thinking" the world, I now want to turn to what it is like to be a human transjective being. Human transjective beings are material beings entangled in webs of materiality, and they are also subjective and intersubjective beings that are entangled in webs of subjectivity. As described in Chapter 1, those two types of entanglements are themselves entangled, producing dense meshes of material constitution and experiences, all material through and through, and also all subjectively and intersubjectively experienced and rendered meaningful as the transjective navigates life.

I, who am writing these lines, am the precarious and soon to be undone transjective being that is constituted by: the banana and nuts oatmeal I had this morning and the digestive processes currently unfolding in my body; the onset of summer temperatures in Southwestern Ontario; the blooming crabapple and cherry trees next to my house; the vibration of cargo ships travelling the canal between Lake Ontario and Lake Erie, which is only 165 meters away from my house; the side conversation I have been having with a friend on Messenger; the consultation of my day planner and reflections on how to meet my manuscript submission deadline; my appointment later today; the chirping birds populating my yard and the sparrows who are nesting on top of one of my doors; the recent decision to include a very significant meandering in this book; the neighbors that have returned from months in Florida making it now impossible to walk naked or even in underwear by the window on that side of the house; the fact that this house that was empty for months now provides a vantage point on me working at this standing desk which I am using right now to type these lines; the tickle in my legs; the lower back pain that I have been dragging around for years; the anticipation of a pre-lunch run; the action of the mouthwash I used fifteen minutes ago and the desire to drink that glass of water next to me but not for another fifteen minutes; thoughts of what to make for dinner which caused me to escape writing this paragraph for a few minutes to look at my bank of recipes; my books and notebooks containing the research, notes, and thinking processes I have engaged with in the last few years and that are on my desk; the two big sips of water I just took and the refreshing feeling of it going down inside my body; the brief Google search for the English word for "*gorgée*" which my bilingual brain was failing to retrieve at this exact moment; the device I am using to type these words; the knowledge, in the background, that someone will be reading these words—on screen or on paper—and that it matters a great deal which words I choose to express my ideas so that clear communication happens; the professional pressure to write a book a certain way but also the freedom a full professorship gives me to write it in the way I want; more water; more tickling legs (the run will do me good) . . .

At any moment we can take pause and engage in this exercise and reflect on all the elements that come to constitute the "I" that we believe we are, this entity, this individual to whom we attach a name and pronouns, a status perhaps, various roles, duties, projects, memories, and so on. I stopped myself in the previous paragraph from continuing to describe items on the endless list of things that constitute my everchanging being, but there is much more to that freeze-frame than I can even articulate or grasp. Even if I were to continue listing everything that I am aware of or can think about, many processes, unknown to me, are unfolding and permeating me, allowing me to exist but also maybe—or perhaps most certainly—hurting me and limiting my long-term capacity to exist.[1] It would be impossible to include those in a list that one compiled about oneself. Many memories, past experiences, training, learning, and interpersonal engagements shape my thinking right now, whether I bring them forth in my conscious thought process or not. They are part of the manifold entanglements constituting me. Not all elements of the assemblage that emerges as "me" are constitutive in the same way or to the same extent. But they all matter.[2] And since we do not exist as freeze-frames, the next moment encompasses new elements that inflect the being I am. This is why I will say again and will reiterate a few times in this book: we are constantly done and undone.

In this chapter, I consider Spinozist affect theory as developed not only by Spinoza himself but also by Deleuze and Guattari, Massumi, and Bennett. Jane Bennett's now famous analysis of her encounter with debris in Baltimore has been an inspiration for me in writing the above paragraph. Bennett uses her description of encountering a particular arrangement of debris to attract attention to "thing-power," to the vital materiality that animates this seemingly random assemblage of things: "Glove, pollen, rat, cap, stick" (2010: 4). What strikes her in this encounter is the fact that these objects, dead and discarded and contingently gathered in the gutter, become things with meaning attributed to them by the human encountering them but also meaning that exceeds their current occurrence (the action of the person who put out rat poisoning, the other that threw away the bottle cap, etc.). Not only that, but these objects animate each other in the encounter, one attracting Bennett's gaze and then directing that gaze to other elements of this urban tableau.[3] They are vibrant with "*Thing-power*: the curious ability of inanimate things to animate, to act, to produce effects dramatic and subtle" (Bennett 2010: 6). This view resonates with Chen's (2012) notion of animacy, Hayles's (2017) concept of the cognitive unconscious, Tsing's (2015) views on assemblages, and Sobchack's (2004) interobjectivity, as well as with the action of *zoe*, as per Braidotti (2019). Adding to this Ahmed's (2006) views on orientation and Manning's (2014) bodying gives us the ground for a fruitful reflection on what I call the affective fabric of life. However, I am not treating those like pieces of a puzzle which, once assembled, will give us the complete and accurate view of what it is to exist as transjective human beings. I do not think such a picture is possible. What we can think through, though, are the dynamic processes at work, what one might be tempted to call "structures of experience." But, importantly, there is more than "experiences" because even things we do not consciously experience are constitutive elements of the assemblage. So, using a phrase like "structures of experience" is inaccurate. In what follows, I am not aiming at providing a full exposé or in-depth critique of the views I am approaching. Instead, I consider the generative power of the proposals I find in these works to illuminate the processes by which human transjective assemblages are made. This chapter will itself be an assemblage of these views, offering what I hope is a fruitful encounter between affect theory and phenomenology that deals with the body in its manifold manifestations.

Affect

What supports and "holds together" all the elements of the assemblage that constitutes a transjective being—in the case I am contemplating here, a human—is not a preexisting substance like an "I" but the field of immanence, the affective fabric that life is, the flow and intertwinement of affect that entangles different bodies. "Body" here needs to be taken in the broad Spinozist sense of any entity—including abstract bodies like concepts—and not in the narrow sense of human body or any other biological body, the everyday meaning we attach to this word. It is important to discuss the biological body and how it is experienced phenomenologically, but we first need to clarify the notion of affective fabric. The transjective being is materially entangled in a dynamic web of relationality, in a messy field of tensions. What this involves, or rather what constitutes this field of tensions, is affect, which operates and unfolds among human and nonhuman beings and is "non-intentional and indifferent" (Brinkema 2014: 33). It is radically material or grounded in materiality. As Chen puts it, "affect is something not necessarily corporeal and . . . potentially engages many bodies at once" (2012: 11).[4] Affect itself may not necessarily be corporeal, but it is always that which flows among bodies or, as Claire Colebrook puts it, "the world is a dynamic network of interacting, affectively attuned, responsive and self-maintaining bodies" (2011: 23). Spinoza posits that we do not know yet what a body can do. This is the case because of the infinite ways in which bodies can be affected and can affect other bodies. The empirical space is that of a subject that has experiences but affect lays in the plane of immanence with intensities and tensions between different bodies and those bodies are any kind of body, "human, nonhuman, part-body, and otherwise" (Seigworth and Gregg 2010: 1). One can posit that "[a]ffect is in many ways synonymous with *force* or *forces of encounter* [however] affect need not be especially forceful" (Seigworth and Gregg 2010: 2). It can be the gentle, subtle interaction of a warm breeze and skin but it can be very forceful, as in the violent slashing and cutting open of skin through assault. These examples relate affect to the human and may lead to think that there is affect where there is a human to be affected. That is not the case, however: transjectivity and the affective unfolding of life are to be found in and among every being.

N. Katherine Hayles's approach takes this in a slightly different direction by focusing on cognition and considering both human and nonhuman "cognizers" (including machines and AI). She examines the "unthought," which is "a mode of interacting with the world enmeshed in the 'eternal present' that forever eludes the belated grasp of consciousness" (Hayles 2017: 1).[5] Simply put, according to Hayles, there are multiple cognitive unconscious processes performed by human and nonhuman cognizers. Consciousness makes sense of life by creating narratives, what appears to be a deeply human need, but cognition is broader than consciousness (Hayles 2017: 9). Hayles explains that "most human cognition happens outside of consciousness/unconsciousness; cognition extends through the entire biological spectrum including animals and plants; technical devices cognize, and in doing so profoundly influence human complex systems" (2017: 5). Biological and technical cognizers process information, recognize patterns, make connections, enact decisions at a speed unmatched by consciousness. And these processes are essential to consciousness—in fact they can be said to support it. The cognition of biological and technical cognizers is of a similar nature and performs similar functions without being the same since the particular systems in which it unfolds provide its context.[6] Structurally similar but not the same, biological and technical cognition are also intertwined (Hayles 2017: 11; 13).[7] Hayles offers a "tripartite framework of (human) cognition as a pyramid" (2017: 40) with modes of awareness at the top, nonconscious cognition in a middle layer, and material processes forming the base. While this may be reminiscent of Plato's tripartition of the soul, one needs to keep in mind that the two bottom layers are not confined to one body but rather deeply intertwined with nonhuman nonconscious cognition and material processes. Also, and since I want to invoke phenomenology's insights about experience, we can complete this topology by further differentiating the top of the pyramid into three layers: the self-reflective consciousness, reflective consciousness, and pre-reflective consciousness.[8] What I take from Hayles is this further understanding of entanglements and dynamic processes that are widespread, similar yet not the same, and animating all that is, contributing to the affective fabric of existence, to its constant modulation and shifts.[9] Hayles's model also connects phenomenology and materialism in a very useful way.

I have said above that a human experience of affect is not needed for affect to unfold. As Braidotti puts it, "[a]ffect needs to be de-psychologized, and to be de-linked from individualism in order to match the complexity of our human and non-human relational universe" (2019: 45). However, humans are also permeated by affect and there is definitely a relation between affect and the emotions transjective humans feel, although we need to be careful not to confuse one for the other. One may say that affects are the ineffable support of emotions. In some ways, emotions can be defined as the contamination of the phenomenological by affect. As Massumi explains, "[a]n *emotion* or *feeling* is a recognized affect, an identified intensity as reinjected into stimulus-response paths, into action-reaction circuits of infolding and externalization—in short, into subject-object relations. Emotion is a contamination of empirical space by affect" (2002: 61). The affect experienced through the lived body of phenomenology and which manifests as emotion or becomes conscious perception and thinking is grounded in the immanent affect put forward in the very simple formula proposed by Spinoza: "The human body (Posts. 3 and 6) is affected by external bodies in a great many ways and is so structured that it can affect external bodies in a great many ways" (E2P14). Spinoza further says: "By emotion [*affectus*][10] I understand the affections of the body by which the body's power of activity is increased or diminished, assisted or checked, together with the ideas of these affections" (E3D3). We have to keep in mind that when Spinoza talks about bodies he has in mind any kind of body, even though Part II of the *Ethics* focuses on human bodies and their affects, or rather emotions. His philosophical monism posits that the soul and the body are "one and the same thing, conceived now under the attribute of Thought, now under the attribute of Extension" (E3P2S). And again, we do not know yet what a body can do. The reason for this is that bodies are entangled in this affective fabric, being affected by other bodies and affecting them, doing them and undoing them, being done and undone, without pause, in dynamic flux. The possibilities are indeed manifold and even more so when one considers that "the human body is composed (Post. 1, II) of very many individual bodies of different nature, and so (Ax. 1 after Lemma 3, q.v. after Pr. 13, II) it can be affected by one and the same body in many different ways; on the other hand, since one and the same thing can be affected in many ways, it can likewise affect one and the same part of the body in different ways." (E3P17S)[11] This leads Hasana Sharp to say that, as per Spinoza, we are "constituted by our constellations of relationships and community of affects" (2011: 8).[12]

The affective fabric permeates the human transjective but also exceeds it.[13] Affect traverses all transjective beings: "Impersonal affect is the connecting thread of experience. It is the invisible glue that holds the world together" (Massumi 2002: 217).[14] And, as Elena del Río points out, the "[c]apacities for affecting and being affected lie at the heart of any body's existence, thereby performing a radically leveling function across human, and even non-human beings" (2012: 211). As she also notes, and as I will tackle later, this has important ethical and political implications.[15]

The Body, with or without Organs

Western thinking has taught us that we are a mind in a body. Our body carries us around and allows us to accomplish whatever project we set our sights on. Existential phenomenology has unearthed the inseparability of consciousness and the body: consciousness only exists as embodied, as full of world. That body exists in a situation which comprises its geographical, cultural, political, and social location. As Beauvoir (2011) and Fanon (1967) have forcefully demonstrated, the type of body one is—of one sex or another and of one skin color or another—impacts one's insertion in that situation, how one's body is perceived and construed, and thereby how one's consciousness, as this particular embodied consciousness, is shaped. This existential-phenomenological approach opens the way to think the various entanglements of consciousness.[16] But despite its emphasis on embodiment and rejection of the notion of a transcendent or transcendental consciousness that could exist separate from a body, it still remains somewhat steeped in a dualistic approach that I seek to overcome here. This takes me to Deleuze and Guattari and their answer to dualist modes of thinking. Instead of thinking of the body in terms of a substance, albeit a material one, one should think of it as an event. As Nathan Widder puts it, "[t]he body as an event [just like its dispersed ego] is Deleuze's answer to the problem of traditional dualisms that his ontology of sense invites. . . . It connects two multiplicities through a disjunctive synthesis and, as such, includes a difference that exceeds identity and representation. The body is the expression of this sense of difference, of the being of sense itself" (2011: 111).[17] While Widder refers only to Deleuze here, it is clear that both Deleuze and Guattari embrace this view, especially if we consider their concept of the body without organs (BwO). This is a notoriously complex concept and one that has often been misunderstood, including by me and potentially again here. The concept is a contested one and I have no ambition to settle it—here or elsewhere—but I do like Mel Y. Chen's characterization of it which is worth quoting at length:

> The body without organs is that body that actively refuses its own subjectivity by engaging the dis-ordering of its "organs." In the body without organs, no given organ has merely one functionality, and the organism itself cannot be represented as an ordered system. Instead, the body without organs makes impossible any coercive systematicity by affirming an infinite functionality and interrelation of the "parts" within, "parts" that can only be individuated by one of an infinite number of permutations of a body into "parts." Deleuze and Guattari's body without organs essentially describes a condition of animate transubstantiation. (2012: 151–2)

One can establish a minimal self, a tenuous trace of the self, with the help of the BwO and *haecceities*, those processes of individuation that we are. That tenuous self is a precarious and always rearranging collective assemblage. I return to this in the next chapter. But the question for now is: What can the BwO do for us? I take the concept, as discussed in *Anti-Oedipus*, to serve the important purpose of provoking us to think the notions of body and desire apart from the body itself (*le corps propre*). The BwO "has nothing whatsoever to do with the body itself, or with an image of the body. It is the body without an image" (Deleuze and Guattari 1983: 8). The BwO is the surface upon which events unfold and inscribe. The affective fabric of a self? It can be defined as a force, "an uninterrupted continuum of intensities in the field of immanence" (del Río 2012: 100). It is a "process that dis-organ-izes the organs/affects of the body; through such a process, the organs multiply connections with each other and with the organs of other bodies in ways that defy the systematicity that keeps them bound to the slave morality of representation and majoritarian behavior" (del Río 2012: 11). The BwO is a disruptive concept that opens up the space for bodies and subjects that are non-fixed, in flux, never consolidated. The only subject—or rather "something on the order of a *subject*"—that is possible is the one that emerges from this recording surface but

> It is a strange subject, however, with no fixed identity, wandering about over the body without organs, but always remaining peripheral to the desiring-machines, being defined by the share of the product it takes for itself, garnering here, there, and everywhere a reward in the form of a becoming or an avatar, being born of the states that it consumes and being reborn with each new state. (Deleuze and Guattari 1983: 16)

Leaving aside the notion of desiring machines (another complex Deleuzo-Guattarean concept), we can still understand what the concept of a BwO performs with regard to a decentering of subjectivity and a rejection of dualistic conceptions, which allows for the unearthing of the "processual rhythm" (Massumi 2002: 217) that moves the affective.

If, as mentioned earlier, the BwO refuses its own subjectivity, dismembers itself, and dis-organ-izes itself, it remains that something like a body and something like a subject emerge from the field of relations of the affective fabric of life. What emerges, however, is a body that is always an assemblage of many other bodies, always interconnected: "Our bodies retain traces of the changes brought about in them by the impinging of other bodies" (Gatens and Lloyd 1999: 18). This body can be conceived in terms of an "event" that is dynamic and alive (Massumi 2002: 5), but that only exists as in movement (Manning 2014: 163) and through its perceivings, which is to say through its complicated entanglements with its objects of perceptions (Massumi 2002: 95). However, just like there is not a substance waiting to be affected—something like an "I"—the body "never pre-exists its movement" (Manning 2014: 164). Manning rejects the notion of embodiment in favor of "bodying" (Manning 2014). The body bodies itself as it moves about: "Movement goes a-bodying" (Manning and Massumi 2014: 39). It is through a process of dynamic becoming, relationality grounded in affect, and movement that a body emerges as the movement of thought. Manning and Massumi explain that "[t]he body itself, with its rhythmic milieu, *is* a motional-notion: a movement of thought" (2014: 45). But there is no "we" or "I" doing the thinking: the thinking happens in the movement and every experience amounts to a worlding, a making of worlds as thinking unfolds and bodies and thoughts coalesce for a fleeting moment to engage in the acts of perceiving and making sense. Thought literally occurs in the act, as per the title of Manning and Massumi's book, *Thought in the Act*. It is also playfully evocative of the expression "caught in the act," which conjures up the idea of a chance happening, an impromptu encounter with an event that is unfolding. The dynamism of the course of action is captured in the moment, it is caught in thought. A fleeting moment of coalescence. This is grounded in Whitehead's process philosophy whose force "lies in its ability to create a field for experience that does not begin and end with the human subject" (Manning 2014: 164).[18] The body that emerges through this movement, the bodying, can be present only in the mode of dissolve: "out of what it is just ceasing to be, into what it will already have become by the time it registers that something has happened.... A body does not coincide with its present. It coincides with its potential. The potential is the future-past contemporary with every body's change" (Massumi 2002: 200). And yet, one experiences oneself as a body. The phenomenological descriptions offered to explain consciousness's embodiment, its experiences of existing as body that has feelings and perceptions, resonate with experiences most readers will be familiar with. The point is not to reject this mundane everyday experience but rather to point out that it only exists on the surface of relationality and movement that unfold in the affective fabric.

Bodying-Orientating-Worlding

What of that experience of embodiment then? Here I want to invoke Vivian Sobchack's[19] and Sara Ahmed's analyses. Sobchack points out that as embodied consciousness, the subject is always thinking as a being that experiences the world through its senses but most importantly, the body "makes meaning before it makes conscious reflective thought" (2004: 59). It does so as this bundle of senses that work in a synesthetic manner.[20] There are no clear boundaries between the senses for her and no one sense operates in isolation from others. This is what leads her to argue that cinema is not merely about the visual: "seeing a movie can also be an experience of touching, tasting, and smelling it" (Sobchack 2004: 70). Phenomenologically, "in the theater (as elsewhere) my lived body sits in readiness as both a sensual and sense-making potentiality" (Sobchack 2004: 76). Our material presence in the world lays at the heart of our sense-making. Inspired by Merleau-Ponty,[21] she conceives of the encounter between consciousness and the world as occurring via the intentional arc that originates in and is constituted by our sensory presence as material beings. This intentional arc in which consciousness not only perceives but also interprets, that is, "makes sense" of what it encounters, is made possible because of our bodily existence. It is as embodied consciousness that we encounter the world and have experiences that we shape and that shape us. This allows Sobchack to claim that the film experience is meaningful "*because* of our bodies" (2004: 60, my emphasis).[22] She also posits that it is because we are embodied, material beings that we experience the world through the joint perception of our senses and can "make sense" of the images we encounter. And, as a sense perception apparatus, we can literally be touched by the films we watch. She identifies melodrama and horror movies as good examples of this encounter as they exacerbate the sensory perceptions through their particular style.[23] According to her, contemporary film theory, and its inclination to connect cinema with vision and looking, seems unable to explain how one can be "touched" by a film: one *watches* films. However, "vision is only one modality of my lived body's access to the world and only one means of making the world of objects and others sensible— that is, meaningful—to me" (Sobchack 2004: 64). Sobchack offers that our "making sense" of film happens at the pre-reflective level while we, as "subjective matter," encounter the moving image with our bundle of sensory perceptions intertwined and responding to the stimuli, via the intentional arc. We sensually experience the film in a prepersonal, global way (Sobchack 2004: 80). But this is also true of any and all experience we have as transjective beings. Sobchack speaks of interobjectivity as the "[c]omplementary co-constitutive experience we have of ourselves and others as material objects" (2004: 296). This interobjectivity is in necessary relation—intertwined—to intersubjectivity. That relation, however, is both complimentary and contrary (Sobchack 2004: 311). In saying this, she remains a phenomenologist who deals with separate entities that enter in relations that intertwine but never fully permeate one another to the point that we cannot disentangle them which is what we are dealing with with the transjective. Nevertheless, Sobchack's analyses of interobjectivity are illuminating of what happens in sensory experience. In this regard, what she proposes about objectification is also helpful for my reflections.

As a transjective being, the human experiences its presence in the world in various and varying kinds of ways as the affective fabric shifts and modulates. Let us consider the experience of objectification.[24] It is very common to encounter a negative take on objectification, and this is not an entirely unfair stance. Indeed, objectification has served as a foundation and justification for many oppressive and violent dealings with humans. A human that is considered as devoid of subjectivity, that is made into a mere object in or by the gaze of another, is a being that can be treated in whichever way one wants. Slaves have been objectified, concentration camps prisoners were objectified, and women are objectified in patriarchal regimes that take their bodies to be mere vessels for reproduction and sexual gratification for men. If I am objectified, there is a whole essential part of my being that is not being recognized and this is a destructive experience. Oppression is harmful because it entails objectification and the devaluation of oneself as a subjective being, in fact the eradication of a portion of oneself. With that said, and recognizing the harmful impacts objectification can have and has had, one could argue that since one is both a subjective and a material being, it can be good and valuable to *also* experience oneself as an object: also, not merely. Sobchack, for example, explains Merleau-Ponty's account of objectification as a process wherein the body-subject suffers "a *diminution of subjectivity* and, in this diminution, comes to experience—within subjectivity—an increased awareness of *what it is to be a material object*" (emphasis in original) (2004: 288). She objects to the notion that this constitutes a diminution of subjectivity and contends instead, as we saw in Chapter 1, that "[t]he body-subject experiences not a diminution of subjectivity but its *sensual* and *sensible* expansion—and an enhanced awareness of what it is *to be material*" (emphasis in original) (Sobchack 2004: 290).[25]

This can happen, for example, through experiencing the gaze of another. In his analyses of being for-others, Jean-Paul Sartre argues that the encounter with the other is alienating because it makes the self into an object for the other. The other encounters me as an object in their world. Concrete relations with others are fraught with difficulties because of that initial objectification that takes place and that the conscious being-for-itself suffers. The look one sheds onto another is objectifying and alienating.[26] However, the experience of being photographed, taken as a model for drawing or painting, or being filmed is one type of positive objectification. The attention that is directed to one's body as object in such circumstances is one that is pleasurable to experience, making one most fully aware of one's material being, via the attentive approach of an other, one in which one is not oppressed or dismissed. Rather, the materiality of one's being is precisely what is valued by the other that is directing their attention to it. There is a way in which one's whole being tickles and literally feels the gaze, the objectifying attention, on one's skin. Being looked at as a model for a painting or photograph is a radically different experience than being looked at as a being that ought to be recognized as both subjective and objective but denied the experience of subjectivity. The body is reduced to its materiality rather than embodied. It looks like this, like that, it must strike this pose or that. The light must hit it this way or that. And the gaze that examines it pays attention to material details about it rather than to the person. When one is at the receiving end of such attention, one experiences objectification but of a kind that expands one's possibilities rather than squishing and limiting them. Further, attentive objectification can also be felt via the attention given to one's material possessions or the objects one engages with frequently, in particular the space that one inhabits. I was surprised to experience this when my cleaners came to my house when I was present. They were cleaning the inside of the house as I was working on the back patio and yet, I could feel on my skin the same kind of tickling attention I had received before while posing! The house and its objects were like an extension of my self, which is no surprise given the amount of time spent entangled with these objects through my presence inside my home. This is just one of many examples of how the flow of affect can shift and thereby impact one's emotions or perceptions. Seigworth and Gregg explain:

> Cast forward by its open-ended in-between-ness, affect is integral to a body's perpetual becoming (always becoming otherwise, however subtly, than what it already is), pulled beyond its seeming surface-boundedness by way of its relation to, indeed its composition through, the forces of encounter. With affect, a body is as much outside itself as in itself—webbed in its relations—until ultimately such firm distinctions cease to matter." (2010: 3)

The body that we are is in relation with objects—animate or not, human or not—and this shapes our experiences and specifically how we experience our bodies as embodied consciousnesses. That body bodies as it goes. It is not merely made into the body that it becomes, as we saw above, but it makes itself that body that bodies itself. It does so through its relations with others but also with its surroundings. It is in the context of thinking about orientation that Sara Ahmed explores the impact surroundings have on self-constitution. Ahmed is proposing a queer phenomenology, one that considers the materiality of bodies and their surroundings insofar as they shape the embodied consciousnesses.

In her attempt at queering phenomenology, Sara Ahmed thinks through the impact our surroundings have on self-constitution. For example, she says,

> [t]he "here" of bodily dwelling is thus what takes the body outside of itself, as it is affected and shaped by its surroundings: the skin that seems to contain the body is also where the atmosphere creates an impression; just think of goose bumps, textures on the skin surface, as body traces of the coldness of the air. Bodies may become orientated in this responsiveness to the world around them, given this capacity to be affected. In turn, given the history of such responses, which accumulate as impressions on the skin, bodies do not dwell in spaces that are exterior but rather are shaped by their dwellings and take shape by dwelling. (Ahmed 2006: 9)

Ahmed's famous notion of orientation rests on this responsiveness to surroundings. Such a phenomenological approach, queer as it may be, still maintains a dualistic split between the self and its surroundings, the body and its surroundings. She thus says, "the orientations we have toward others shape the contours of space by affecting relations of proximity and distance between bodies" (Ahmed 2006: 3). In explaining things in this way, Ahmed retains the distinctions posited by classical phenomenology. Regardless of these limitations, I think it is useful to think about the impact surroundings have on self-constitution in literally shaping the body itself, as we live it. The material surroundings shape the body that encounters them just as much as the body shapes the surroundings in an intentional encounter. That encounter is also unfolding both as intentless directionality, as per Frost,[27] and as willful and conscious orientating of oneself toward others and objects. Indeed, as I stand in my office right now, typing at my standing desk, a number of bodily processes allow me to do so and are animated by an intentless direction. These allow for an orientation to the space, pre-reflective or reflective: I prefer to work at a standing desk now that I have moved away from my sitting habits. But there is a chair behind me in the back corner of the room to my right that I know I can pull to sit on, should my legs get too tired. This assemblage of wood pieces is made into a potential sitting device as I exist as my body in this room. And its material composition, the vibration of particles constituting the object, will support that bundle of vibrating particles that I am, should I choose to sit on it, or it will continue to be part of the blurry background to my current activity, should I carry on standing. But Ahmed also claims that disorientation is as vital as orientation is. Moments of disorientation may be powerful or quite ordinary fleeting and recurring feelings throughout a day, but we can learn from them (Ahmed 2006: 157).

Disorientation occurs when we become objects (as per the alienating gaze described above) or when the space in which we are is rendered unfamiliar, "when we fail to sink into the ground, which means that the 'ground' itself is disturbed, which also disturbs what gathers 'on' the ground" (Ahmed 2006: 160).[28] Moments of disorientation give us glimpses of the multiple entanglements, animacies, vibrancy, and dynamic becoming that forms the affective fabric in the midst of which we emerge as tenuous embodied selves. Orientating is the way in which a self holds things together: itself, its body, objects, and others. Orientating is a bodying, is a worlding, is an objectifying, is a subjectifying, is an orientating—It is itself a dynamic process whose interruptions or hiccups, as in disorientation, are themselves contributors to the orientating, the bodying, the worlding—We do not experience ourselves as the fleeting beings we are. Our bodying is also a process of self-ing. We are constantly involved in efforts to make sense, to consolidate, to establish a self, some kind of unity grounded in a body that we also work to consolidate.[29] This ever-ongoing project can be made more exhausting or challenging when undergoing disorientation or traumatic experiences, but this "self," whatever it comes to be, appears to be essential at least as a practical tool—a helpful pragmatic illusion—that allows us to navigate the affective fabric in which we exist. I turn to this self-ing in what follows.

MEANDERING 5
INOCULATION

April 20, 2021. It is 9:00 p.m. and I am having a conversation with Jack Daniel's. My goal is to finally completely unwind and bring my blood pressure down. Jack Daniel's is the best remedy for me, despite my family doctor's skepticism. I measure my blood pressure regularly and each time I have had a chat with Jack, it is very low (well, low for me, in the realm of 110 over 60). On April 20, I peaked in the afternoon while at the vaccination site in Helsinki's Jätkäsääri district. Who knows exactly how high it got but, some thirty minutes after my shot, systolic pressure was still well over 180—I forgot the exact number as well as the number for the diastolic. The on-site doctor was concerned but reassured when I showed her my tracking history saved on my phone. What brought this about?

I had early access to Covid-19 vaccination because I belong to what Finnish authorities considered a lower high-risk group due to bronchial asthma.[1] When I found out about early access, I called the booking service immediately to set an appointment. I had been eager to be vaccinated and participate in the global effort to curb the pandemic. My asthma was also making it likely that I would suffer from a more severe case of the disease, were I to become infected, making vaccination highly desirable even if I am otherwise healthy. Booking my appointment was done expediently and I was set for the following week. I asked which vaccine I would be receiving but they could not confirm; they said it would likely be the Pfizer but that this would be determined on-site. Knowing of previous reservations on administering mRNA vaccines to allergic people, I mentioned my history of allergic reactions and said I would make sure to have my EpiPen with me. They said the location they were sending me to was the one for allergic people and that a doctor was on-site and I would be monitored closely in case of an anaphylactic reaction. All I had to do was explain things to the people there.

It was a five-day wait between booking my appointment and receiving the shot. Five days is a short period of time—and, as I am writing this, many people are still waiting and will likely have to wait for months, so I was lucky—but it was also a sufficiently long period of time for ideas, memories, and anxiety to begin to spiral. Reading about the shots and their side effects, assaulted by clickbait headlines on the few thrombosis cases potentially caused by the AstraZeneca and Johnson & Johnson produced vaccines was causing some worry. Despite being fully aware that the risk of thrombosis associated with the vaccine is still much lower than the risk I incurred for years while on oral contraceptives and now on hormone replacement therapy, I was still concerned but not enough to not get vaccinated. My worries were much more severe with the Pfizer vaccine because what I knew about it and the few cases of severe allergic reactions brought back very unpleasant and scary memories of suffering through one.

I have a few allergies and most of them are mild and non-life threatening. Some are more annoying than others, like my allergy to a few strands of antibiotics, leaving only very little wiggle room to treat infections when I get them. But the way I discovered my allergy to shellfish was rather brutal—this was in my pre-vegan life when I would happily consume fish and shellfish. I often had gastric issues after those meals but I would often attribute those to other factors such as the occasional super-abundance of garlic. In March 2014, a restaurant dinner that included lobster tail did not pan out well. Back home, two hours after the meal, I had delayed anaphylaxis. The reaction was sudden and extremely violent. The experience was one of completely losing control over my body as it violently rejected the allergen. At one point I started to think that I was dying. The severity of the reaction required a trip to the hospital where I finally stabilized and mostly slept in the waiting room out of sheer exhaustion. Yet, I did not know if it was an allergic reaction. At first, we thought it might have been food poisoning but given that my partner at the time had had the same meal and was fine, it was unlikely. The doctor eventually declared it an allergic reaction—though I never got tested for it, simply staying clear from fish and shellfish after that. In any case, but not because of that, I became vegan a year later, so it is no longer an issue.

The memory of that experience, revived because of the remote possibility I might have a similar reaction to vaccination, did not leave me for the five days I had to wait to get my shot. I could almost feel again what it had been like for my body to react in this violent way and the exhaustion that followed. I also recalled the few instances where I understood an antibiotic I was taking was not doing its job because I was allergic to it, trying to breathe through the wheezing and counting the dots of the hives covering my skin. Or that other time I discovered a food allergy by developing angioedema: my whole torso turned bright red, itched and burned, and only calmed down after ingesting a strong dose of Benadryl. With this history of allergic reactions, my family doctor prescribed an EpiPen that I am to carry with me everywhere and the pharmacist gave me a full-on training on how to self-administer. I remember thinking then: "I guess I truly am an allergic person now!"

Truth is, I never really think about these experiences unless there is a discussion about allergies. I know what foods and medications to avoid and have been stung by a bee before without anything more than the initial pain from the sting. I take my seasonal allergies medication each spring and fall. I know what to do, what to avoid, what to ingest. However, the real, albeit very small, possibility of suffering a severe allergic reaction, because I was going to open my body to an mRNA vaccine, was on my mind for a few days. It was on my mind as I walked over to the vaccination site (Figure 5.1). It was definitely on my mind as I explained to the nurse what my low-risk condition was followed by my allergy history. He took me to the on-site doctor who had her own curtained-off area with a bed and all kinds of medical instruments and devices. I had imagined that I would be sitting with all others receiving the vaccine and that maybe someone would keep a closer eye on me and, if anything were to unfold, they would fetch the doctor. I had not imagined this and being placed under the doctor's immediate supervision made the possibility of anaphylaxis even more real. I was asked every possible question about past allergic reactions and their causes and asked to explain my symptoms and if I could recognize them, were they to reappear. I then said, "Oh, by the way, I am also taking this antibiotic right now. . ." Uh oh! A tooth had had the good idea of getting infected the week before and I was being treated for it. The doctor got on her computer and searched the Pfizer package leaflet to see whether it was contraindicated to administer the vaccine with me on the antibiotic. I looked at the nurse and my eyes must have said it all. He said: "Now you regret mentioning it, don't you?" After

FIGURE 5.1 No selfie for me, busy as I was handling my fear and trying to not completely collapse out of sheer anxiety. So, this is my only souvenir.

an intensive search it was determined that if I had no fever, I was good to receive it. A thermometer poked into my left ear informed everyone that my temperature was at 36.3 Celsius.

So, there I was. Ready to be jabbed. Anxiety on full throttle. Racing heartbeat. Deep breathing to control the urge to hyperventilate (it turns out a yoga practice is really helpful with that). The nurse reassured me: "Don't worry, I am very good at what I do." And in it went, the 3.5 centimeter needle inserting itself into my deltoid to deliver the dose of mRNA vaccine to protect me from Covid-19. About 0.3 milliliters of liquid carrying the necessary message to teach my cells how to make a protein, or even just a piece of protein, triggering an immune response that in turn generates antibodies protecting me from the virus. My cells are learning and doing their assignment as I write this. It is a process that unfolds over a few weeks, and it has been only one week and a half since that moment of opening myself to an exterior agent that could protect me but also very well kill me. Nietzsche once wrote, "What does not kill me makes me stronger." I wish I had thought of that as I was reacting to the shot emotionally, yet not physically. Both the nurse and the doctor bent over me as I was hyperventilating and sobbing in my hands, covering my face: "Are you okay?" "Is everything good?" Trying to make me speak to snap me out of this freakout I was having. I nodded and whispered I was going to be okay. I was offered a glass of water. The nurse wondered about my fear of needles and my numerous tattoos. I had to explain it is absolutely not the same. Also, it was not the needle I feared, although truth be told, I don't particularly like them. But talking about this and explaining things took my mind off the experience. Good strategy, nurse who is really a paramedic in "normal times." I wondered about the physical intimacy involved in his job, getting into the inner physical bubble of people at their worst moments of being wounded or dying, intervening on and in the body, and doing what they have to do to save a person. Professional deformation at work: me philosophizing all the while looking for signs of anaphylaxis. I had to stay there for thirty minutes. The doctor was doing things on the computer but stopping every five minutes or so to check on me. The nurse came and went. I was calming down and reading news off my phone.

After the thirty minutes and before releasing me, the doctor turned away from her computer and toward me and said: "You look all relaxed! Let's check a few things." She checked my oxygen levels and they were at 99 percent, even after wearing the mask for so long and the bit of hyperventilating I was doing—or maybe that helped? My pulse was perfect. She took my blood pressure with the outcome I mentioned at the start of this meandering. There was no other possible outcome given the accumulated worry of the past few days, my white-coat syndrome, the setting, the real—albeit small—possibility, not of dying (I knew I would not die because treatment was readily available if something went amiss), but the possibility of having to suffer through an anaphylactic shock. I said to her I would have a conversation with Jack Daniel's later in the evening as it has proven the most effective at bringing my blood pressure down. "That's fine," she replied, "but try to keep that conversation short!" She smized (Figure 5.2).

FIGURE 5.2 Blood pressure's best friend.

Revisiting these memories as I write about my experience of the inoculation, I feel a mix of compassion for myself—it is no fun to be an allergic body—but also amusement: how could I be so silly?[2] But, of course, I know how, I know why. And all the while I have been writing this meandering my chest has felt tight and in reliving the anxiety I have felt a little wheezy and I now contemplate the hive on my chest and think that the antibiotic might have taken care of my tooth but has also triggered an allergic reaction to it after all. I will talk with Jack again tonight.

4 OF SELVES AND AGENTS

What kind of self is a transjective one? What kind of self does a transjective being have? How does a transjective being exist as a self? While a reader might think an authorial or editorial choice ought to have been made between these three formulations of what appears to be the same question, I wish to retain them to start this chapter by exploring how we can even ask the question of the "self" or the "I" and to ask ourselves what it is we are looking for in selfhood. Is a self the totality of a being as it experiences its self/itself (first formulation)? Is selfhood something a being acquires/constructs/inherits and then possesses (second formulation)? Or is selfhood the sum of experiences a being has, the continuum of experiences connected by memories, consciousness, and anticipations/projections (third formulation)? These questions are asked in an attempt to define that entity we claim to be when we say "I." What indeed does "I" stand for? Is claiming "I" of any value for a being defined along the lines of transjectivity, namely as a dynamic unfolding assemblage amid affective fabric? What is the content of the claim and what purpose does it serve?

It is interesting to call to mind the traditional opposition between a rationalist and an empiricist view of personal identity at the outset of this discussion. For Descartes, the I is a thinking substance, the one thing of which we cannot doubt exists. I must exist as a thinking substance, I who doubt at this very moment. The claim "I think, I exist" is the one thing that resists radical doubt and the foundation upon which knowledge can be established. David Hume instead proposes that the I is "a kind of theatre, where several perceptions successively make their appearance; pass, re-pass, glide away, and mingle in an infinite variety of postures and situations" (1985: 301). The catch of Hume's position? There is no stage as such, no blank slate upon which these perceptions would inscribe themselves, as his empiricist predecessor Locke would have it. Discussing Hume's proposal, Deleuze and Guattari refer to the "I" as a habit (1994: 105). As they explain, the brain says "I" "but *I* is an other" (1994: 211)—a claim Arthur Rimbaud made as a pun in a letter to Georges Izambard from May 13, 1871.[1] The "I" that the brain claims to be is an identity separated and yet related to it, a kind of concretion of various experiences, thoughts, affects, and so on, a sedimentation perpetually on the verge of fracture because it is itself a collection of fractures, of additions, of relations that are within the individual but also exceed it in myriad ways as we have seen. This individual is more properly referred to as a dividual. Deleuze and Guattari claim, "we are sick, so sick of our *selves!*" (1983: xxi). There they mean the philosophical concept of selfhood and not the mundane feeling of being or having a self that (in)dividual human transjective beings experience or even what they understand as a self: the residue that emerges alongside the desiring machines and body without organs. Indeed, we continue to refer to ourselves using the pronoun "I." *I* am the person writing these lines. *My* reader is thinking "*I* am the person reading this book." But what is this "I" that is both a habit and a cause for sickness? As we will see later, it is important not only to define that "I" but also not to lose the self and its agency. Indeed, the fluctuating self that I have described generates anxieties not only for the individual whose efforts at consolidating as a self are at risk but also for philosophers of different stripes that resist the elimination of agency for fear or ethical and political nihilism. The stakes are high.

Philosophical Anxieties

Is the "I" an addiction? Addictions are diseases and difficult to break. One way in which this addiction presents itself is in the resistance put forward by some to a posthumanist critique they often misunderstand. In many ways, Seyla Benhabib's reaction to what she refers to as strong or hard postmodernism paves the way for the current reaction to posthumanism, especially in feminist circles. Troubled by the potential elimination of the subject that would ensue from embracing positions such as Butler's— positions that insist on the linguistic construction of subjects through structures of power—Benhabib equates such a position to the risk that a hard materialism poses to the subject: the subject ends up being a puppet at the mercy of forces external to it. However, she considers the free self who can exercise agency as essential to the ethical and political feminist project. To her, a hard postmodernism in which the subject has been replaced by "a system of structures, oppositions and différances which, to be intelligible, need not be viewed as products of a living subjectivity at all" (Benhabib 1992: 209) makes the pursuit of this project impossible. This view of the subject makes it incompatible with a social movement such as feminism. Because the subject becomes "yet another position in language," key ethical and political concepts such as intentionality, accountability, self-reflexivity, and autonomy disappear. And this is the worry: if we dismiss the subject, we dismiss an agent to whom we can ascribe moral responsibility. We also dismiss an agent who can undertake to bring about the social changes on the feminist agenda. Benhabib also worries that this rejection of the subject entails the undermining of "the discourse of the theorist herself" (1992: 216). Of course, this is an important worry and if the end result of the posthumanist critique is the impossibility to ascribe responsibility, then we may have thrown the baby out with the bathwater.

The worry of humanists reacting to the posthumanist critique can be summarized by adapting Benhabib's concerns with "hard postmodernism": by radically challenging the humanist subject, one may lose the ethical and political agent to whom we can ascribe responsibility and who can carry an agenda to effect the sociopolitical changes we are aiming for. Beauvoir scholar Sonia Kruks expresses this reaction while contemplating potential affinities between posthumanism and Beauvoir's thinking. To her, the alignment is impossible: Beauvoir may share certain critiques of the subject but is unwilling to do away with it. Kruks explains that Beauvoir "did not embrace the troubling erasures of 'the human' that poststructuralism and posthumanism would often advocate or invite" (2012: 26). Beauvoir is proposing instead an ambiguous humanism which takes seriously the posthumanist challenges to humanism and "[y]et, it should not consent to erase or indefinitely to deconstruct, decenter, or defer 'the human'" (Kruks 2012: 32). For Kruks, this would even amount to nihilism. She continues: "To erase 'the human' from consideration is to cut from under our feet the grounds on which we may contest certain practices and situations as oppressive. In spite of the violence that may be—and has been—done in its name, even the most flawed humanism still secretes an opposition to what *dehumanizes*" (Kruks 2012: 32). I see a few problems with Kruks's claims, the most important being that her assertion that both movements erase the "human" is overstating what the thinkers involved are seeking to achieve: not a complete erasure or dismissal of the "human" but rather a radical reconceptualization. The subject of posthumanism is posthuman in the sense that it is a posthumanist human: still human but not in a humanist sense. To claim that poststructuralists and posthumanists dismiss the human, the subject, is caricaturing what is in fact a much more complex project of dismantling the humanist construct and proposing instead a dynamic, fluctuating subject that is perpetually done and undone but never entirely done away with. In more recent work, Kruks remains suspicious of the posthumanist new materialist project which she sees as stripping the human from any specificity. To her, new materialists "collapse the human into the material world writ large to such an extreme degree that they obscure what still remains ontologically distinct to human life: namely, the qualities particular to human agency that should be called 'freedom'" (Kruks 2019: 254). She reads the new materialisms as "inattentive to specific social contexts and power differentials" and is concerned that "because 'agency' is said to be so widely and fluidly distributed among diverse 'intra-acting' material entities, human responsibility for harms—which are alone those harms that we might and should endeavor to ameliorate—become difficult to identify" (Kruks 2019: 255).[2] I think this critique misses the point.

According to Susan Hekman, a core sense of self is necessary to social life, and we need to be able to theorize it. She makes this claim after having examined the linguistic turn and why feminists are suspicious of it. As she puts it, the linguistic turn has taught us that language does construct our reality but that this is not the whole story. "What we need is not a theory that ignores language as modernism did, but rather a more complex theory that incorporates language, materiality, and technology in the equation" (Hekman 2008: 92). She explains the feminist resistance to linguistic determinism by pointing out their fundamental political commitment. They want to "be able to talk about the reality of women's bodies and their lived experiences in a patriarchal world. Extreme linguistic determinism precludes such discussions" (Hekman 2008: 107). Furthermore, she explains that "feminists want to assert the truth of their statements regarding women's status in that world. Embracing social constructionism and the relativism that it entails makes it impossible to make such truth claims" (Hekman 2008: 107). I agree that this is what renders feminists suspicious, as we saw with Benhabib and Kruks. Hekman points out that the subject as one element of the social world has been a heightened object of attention in recent decades. The part of her argument where she discusses the relation between the individual and the collective, the subject and the society it lives in and through which it acquires an identity, is interesting to consider. She says:

> defining the individual is a fundamental element of social organization. The definition of a subject in any given society provides individuals with the possibility of an identity. Those who do not meet the definition of the subject extant in society, or those who challenge that definition, lose their identity as subjects; they cease to be subjects altogether. . . . Either I become a subject or I do not. If I am excluded from subjecthood, I am deprived of an identity that can provide me with a possible life in my society. Having a viable identity, being accepted by my society as a subject, is necessary to social existence. Without it I am, quite literally, no one. (Hekman 2008: 113)

To her, an ontological perspective on the subject allows us to understand the necessity of identity and its social function. Hekman's analysis is helpful to understand the feminist reticence to the linguistic turn—or the posthumanist turn for that matter, when misunderstood—but this analysis seems to me to conflate different things. To not be a social subject, that is, a subject as defined by a certain social setting or collective,[3] is to be no one. However, I think it is important to keep in mind that while one may not be recognized as a subject, it does not mean that one does not exist as a self. That self simply does not fall within the definition of who qualifies as a subject. Now, this is what rightfully motivates the feminist critique of humanist patriarchy: its subject is the white, hetero, cisgender, able-bodied male. The subject of modernity is an exclusive one. If one is not recognized as a subject, one falls outside the political, the ethical, and the legal. One has no duty toward a nonsubject and such nonsubjects cannot claim any rights. But this "nonsubject" still has an experience of itself as a self, as having an identity, albeit not one that matches that ordained by the social setting. It seems to me that this is what an ontological perspective allows us to also uncover, and it is indeed a key understanding. It also allows us to capture the inner and expansive multiplicity of the transjective.

The Subject as a Trace

At the close of the posthumanist critique, there is still a subject, an agent, albeit a minimal one which amounts to traces of the humanist subject. In fact, the concern about the loss of the subject, and the associated attempt to establish the minimal locus of agency we need and which a subject position allows for, is shared by many posthumanist thinkers, including myself. Rosi Braidotti, for example, says that we need to "devise new social, ethical and discursive schemes of *subject formation* to match the profound transformations we are undergoing" (2013: 12, my emphasis). And this subject formation, this "I" that is a fluctuating assemblage, is certainly grounded in the material world but not collapsed in it just as much as it does not reduce to what a social organization devises as a subject. It is one thing to say that we are material beings like any other beings, but this claim does not amount to saying that this is merely what we are, just like we can say we are linguistically or socially constructed but not merely that. The concept of transjectivity actually captures that really well. We are material through and through but we are also transsubjective beings and, as such, we can exercise the agency and freedom Kruks and others are attached to all the while recognizing that these may be much more limited than we have previously thought. Limiting is not eliminating.

Conceiving of the self as a dynamic assemblage of beings that exercise their own agentic capacity both maximizes and expands the notion of agency—more agents act—and restrains the agency of the one being that continues to concern us most, namely the human. Here I want to turn to another potent Nietzschean metaphor. In aphorism 12 of *Beyond Good and Evil* encountered briefly in Chapter 2, against the Christian soul atomism which conceives of human beings in dualistic (opposite) terms and as having a soul that is immortal, indivisible, and monistic, Nietzsche posits that we need to open ourselves to new interpretations of the soul. The idea is not so much to dismiss the soul. Rather, he says, "the way is open for new versions and refinements of the soul-hypothesis; and such conceptions as 'mortal soul,' and 'soul as subjective multiplicity,' and 'soul as social structure of drives and affects,' want henceforth to have citizen's rights in science" (BGE §12). Nietzsche's individual is more properly a dividual, a community of selves, a multiplicity, an assemblage. It is also an assemblage of material bodily affects, affects which are intertwined with thinking. In an entry to his notebooks from the fall of 1885, written at the time he is finalizing *Beyond Good and Evil,* Nietzsche posits: "*Man* as a multiplicity of 'wills to power': each one with a multiplicity of means of expression and forms*" (emphasis in original) (2003: 58).[4] This is the multiplicity of drives, of affects, he has been uncovering and which I have been discussing while elaborating my concept of transjectivity. It generates the subjective multiplicity that he sees at work. He further notes: "Thoughts are signs of a play and struggle of the affects: they are always connected to their hidden roots" (2003: 75).[5] The Nietzschean self is a complex structure and using any one word or concept to refer to it is merely a means to simplify what is in fact a manifold. While this use of a single term or concept may be a strategy to think about such things, one needs to remain mindful that it is a distortion of what is actually happening within this subjective multiplicity.

We can use this to answer the questions posed at the beginning of this chapter. What does the "I" stand for? A "subjective multiplicity." But more, it stands for a *transjective* multiplicity. It is an assemblage of subjective multiplicity, intersubjective and transsubjective multiplicity, and material multiplicity. The multiplicity contemplated by Nietzsche is even more multiple than he thought. This is not to say that the dividuals we are are fooling ourselves about our selves, at least not completely. The "I" claim captures—or rather approximates—a real experience. The statement "I exist" is true as experienced by a self but that self is not the be-all and end-all of itself; it does not exhaust itself. As N. Katherine Hayles puts it, "we can no longer simply assume that consciousness guarantees the existence of the self. In this sense, the posthuman subject is also a postconscious subject" (1999: 279). The self is not limited to what one is conscious of. As enthralling as existential and phenomenological theories of consciousness may be, they only give us access to a very small part of our self, one that is entangled with all other parts and never separated from them. That consciousness which we tend to associate with the self amounts to the subjective that is entangled in the transjective, as discussed earlier. It is not to be thought in isolation. It is entangled with itself, with others, and with materiality.[6] We will discuss in the next chapter how this makes us ontologically vulnerable as affectable.

The self relates to itself. I am other to myself. There is a relation between "I" and my consciousness which I can contemplate and question, which I seek to understand. This is a fundamental inner multiplicity that we deal with at every moment.[7] It is further complicated by memories and pre-reflective or subconscious parts of our conscious selves, as well as our temporal unfolding: our past remembered self and our future anticipated self. The self also relates to itself as this body that it is. The perceptions, emotions, affects, and all material biochemical and physiological processes unfolding in, through, and as my body form a dynamic multiplicity that intertwines with the subjective multiplicity that I am. This (in)dividual multiplicity then encounters the multiplicity of intersubjective relations and material entanglements with other bodies—human or not. This is why it is impossible to conceive of the self in isolation, as Gatens and Lloyd point out in their reading of Spinoza. The self depends on its continuing dis/engagement with other selves "in changing structures of affect and imagination. Selfhood arises within a complex affective framework in which emotions circulate through systems of social relations" (Gatens and Lloyd 1999: 65). But these social relations encompass more than other human (in)dividuals. The economies of affect they refer to also comprise the affect generated by the agentic capacities of all beings. The multiple dividual is multiplied via its multiple entanglements. This is what the transjective is: a collective agent.

Massumi speaks of collective individuation (2015: 123). By this, Massumi does not mean a process whereby an individual would give itself the task of making itself. Rather, "[e]very time there is a thought, there has already been activity in the body. Every time there has been activity in the body, there has been activity in the environment" (Massumi 2015: 154). This preindividual and entirely relational field is that upon and from which subjects emerge, as we saw in the last chapter. In an interview, Michel Serres explains, "[t]he thinking subject is changing, but our way of being together is also shifting. . . . Two things are changing: the thinking subject and the community as subject" (Obrist and Cohen 2013/14: np). What Serres is suggesting here goes back to what he established in *The Parasite* where he explains that living systems are ongoing pieces of work since all life is at work. "My body is transformer of itself" (Serres 1982: 86). The body is a quasi-object and, as such, it requires a subject, otherwise it is dumb, without function or value (Serres 1982: 225). However, I would claim even though it requires a subject to give it meaning, that does not mean it is not vibrant with vitality without a subject. In any case, and as we have already seen, the anxiety generated by an egoless or subjectless dividual might be too much.

In *Difference and Repetition*, Deleuze says, "[w]e are made of contracted water, earth, light and air—not merely prior to the recognition or representation of these, but prior to their being sensed. Every organism, in its receptive and perceptual elements, but also in its viscera, is a sum of contractions, of retentions and expectations" (1968: 73). The idea of a sum here could be misleading. It is not to be understood as a "sum total," whatever we would arrive at once we add all parts of the dividual and, having identified them and brought them together, declare it to be an "individual." I cannot insist on this enough: there is no stable unity to the collective agent, to the transjective as multiple. Any impression of such stability is bound to be challenged the next instant, the next affect, the next thought. Deleuze says we are a "sum of contractions, of retentions and expectations." Contractions allow for affects, agentic capacities, thinking, and so on to bundle together. Retention encompasses internal as well as external affects, whatever relations that entangle us and become part of "who" we are. It relates to the expansivity of our beings and provides some mode of crystallization or sedimentation. Expectations are also expansive in that they are projections into a future, be it inward or outward—and by the way, it is the second time now I use this distinction but we know from earlier in this book that such demarcation is impossible: the inward is the outward is the inward. The sum is multiple and is not ever fixed: it is in perpetual movement, perpetually summing up again, a flow.

That flow contains moments of coalescence, of concretion, of sedimentation that allow for a self to emerge, for an "I" to be proclaimed—the "sum" in question. These moments are substantial enough for us to think of ourselves as selves with a relative unity despite the multiplicity/ies that we are. To think of the self as sedimentation seems to be problematic. Sedimentation is a process whereby matter settles at the bottom of a liquid body to form a solid layer. Insofar as those moments where the self emerges are brief and the self itself precarious—in a reprieve, waiting to be undone again, being undone as it waits—it cannot be referred to as sedimentation because this concept entails a degree of stability and permanence that a self can never attain. Indeed, sediments may be disturbed through drilling and digging—I am obviously thinking here of geological sedimentation—but they also may be left undisturbed for very long periods of time. By themselves they don't change. The self, however, is undone almost immediately after having emerged and does not require the intervention of an external agent for this. The change can be triggered by the inner multiplicity that it is or any and all of the entanglements it is a part of. Concretion or coalescence do not fare much better than sedimentation as they too seem to indicate stability over time. Sedimentation, coalescence, and concretion all seem to be processes through which a body of matter stabilizes and retracts from the multiplicity of entanglements of which it is. How can we then refer to those moments of emergence of the self?

Each "individual," each self, exists as a transjective being. Various elements of our experiences as bodies that are also conscious are incorporated and become part of our being. As Massumi puts it,

> The intensity is experience. The emptiness or in-betweenness filled by experience is the incorporeal dimension of the body. . . . The conversion of surface distance into intensity is also the conversion of the materiality of the body into an *event*. . . . It is a relay between its corporeal and incorporeal dimensions. This is not yet a subject. But it may well be the conditions of emergence of a subject: an incipient subjectivity. Call it a "self-." The hyphen is retained as a reminder that "self" is not a substantive but rather a relation. (2002: 14)[8]

All we can say about the self is that it is a relation. It is essential to reiterate this as we run a constant risk of reverting to discussing the self, the subject, the "I" as if they were discrete entities that enter in relations. This is not the case as I have discussed in previous chapters. As Rick Dolphijn puts it, "*all is relations within relations.* Spinoza's individual [which informs the notion of the transjective as we saw] is 'that which is united in one action' or 'that which functions as one' (again see, for instance, E2D7) and changes its reality (actively and passively) according to the way these relations change (i.e. it is not dependent upon particular 'things')" (emphasis in original) (2021: 12–13).[9] The notion of relationality as the foundation for a self-, for an "I," as it is put forth in the theories I have been exploring here and in previous chapters, has the advantage on many theories of the self—including the narrative theories of Cavarero and Brison which I discuss in the next chapter—to incorporate the ineffable, to render it as powerful as it is in the self's constitution all the while being unable to fully articulate it. That portion of the affective fabric is hinted at, gestured to, without being articulated because it cannot be put into words and yet it is as impactful as what can be put into a narrative, a story, a complex thought process. That ineffable is as much an active player as anything else in the doing and undoing of the transjective. A transjective being that is constituted by the affective fabric as described, is, as already said, a body that is "as much outside itself as in itself" as Seigworth and Gregg put it (2010: 3). To which they add: "Because affect emerges out of muddy, unmediated relatedness and not in some dialectical reconciliation of cleanly oppositional elements or primary units, it makes easy compartmentalisms give way to thresholds and tensions, blends and blurs" (Seigworth and Gregg 2010: 4). This makes it extremely difficult to talk about a self, a subject, an I, or an agent because our very use of language, which tends to define and compartmentalize words that want to relate to specific entities or phenomena, contributes to the blurring of the blurs. This takes us back to the anxieties expressed earlier and the need for us to cling to some notion of selfhood or agency. To say the least, "[t]he subject is not a straightforward matter," as Guattari claims (2000: 35). He goes on: "Rather than speak of the 'subject,' we should perhaps speak of components of subjectification, each working more or less on its own. . . . Vectors of subjectification do not necessarily pass through the individual" (Guattari 2000: 36). However, nothing here seems to alleviate our anxieties much.

Perhaps a better question is why we feel a need to hang on to selfhood and agency. Even when we believed in such a thing as the subject as unitary agent we had great difficulties defining it or living by its definition whenever we thought we arrived at one. Theories abound as to how a self is constituted. The theory of the narrative constitution of the self will come up in the next chapter as one potentially helpful one. However, be it narrated by itself or itself and others, or even itself, others, *and* social and power structures, the self that is envisioned by such theories—or rather more precisely aimed at in the cases we will discuss of reconstructing oneself following traumatic experiences—that self is construed as much more unified and stable than what the transjective can ever be. What is interesting is that there is a shift in anxieties about the self. From a humanist perspective according to which a self exists and we only need to apply ourselves to uncover it, understand it, and become it—a project that can generate enough anxieties especially when pursued under the guise of moral and religious diktats of authenticity or faithfulness to oneself—we have now moved to a perspective that uncovers the self as radically multiple, thereby generating even more anxieties about that self, especially from the point of view of trying to determine how this self is also a socio-politico-ethical agent. How is a transjective collective agent to be understood? Can we ever fully grasp it? If figuring out the mechanics of a single self *qua* agent was hard, it may very well be impossible to understand fully a multiple self as collective agent. I would say, though, that this increased anxiety about the self and agency is precisely what makes the question of understanding that self and agency even more pressing. It may also just be the case that we understand it well but that it is really with the consequences of that conceptualization that we struggle.

What if the precarious assemblage that the transjective is amounts to a subjectless bundle of subjectivities, a Deleuzian haecceity? Elena del Río discusses this concept and defines it in terms of "singular becomings disengaged from human egological agency" (2012: 6). del Río argues that this weakening of the notion of subjectivity in Deleuze opens the way for the body and the power of affects which serves as a foundation for her analysis in her book. Discussing the concept of haecceity—this singularity stripped of subjectivity—she also analyses the body without organs and points out that "[t]his kind of desubjectifying process ... such evacuation of subjectivity ... entails a seemingly paradoxical proposition the more unstructured bodies become, the more they gain in intensity" (del Río 2012: 94–5). This is because once freed from the constraints of the subject as construed in humanist terms, the multiple agencies and agentic capacities of the body and the bodies it is intertwined with through affective relations can manifest themselves. However, the complete disappearance of the subject is not desirable, not if we are to cling to a feminist ethico-political agenda which I am intent on doing. I do think that the transjective being I am proposing comes close to what Deleuze and Guattari propose as haecceity, the point at which latitude and longitude intersect (materiality and affects). In the plane of immanence, multiple interactions unfold and the body emerges as that "sum total of the material elements belonging to it under given relations of movement and rest, speed and slowness (longitude); the sum total of the intensive affects it is capable of at a given power or degree of potential (latitude)" (Deleuze and Guattari 1980: 260). As we have seen, the body is caught in this realm of immanence where forces interact and are in tension, and it is therefore itself a fluctuating thing and the "self" that may emerge is even more tenuous. Haecceity is a mode of individuation that is not to be confused with that of a thing or a subject. In fact, "[t]here are only haecceities, affects, subjectless individuations that constitute collective assemblages. ... Nothing subjectifies, but haecceities form according to compositions of nonsubjectified powers or affects" (Deleuze and Guattari 1980: 266). This makes us fleeting beings—never fixed or stable—that exist at the point of encounter of affects and tensions, beings that emerge and disappear as quickly through an encounter of relations because "pure affects imply an enterprise of desubjectification" (Deleuze and Guattari 1980: 270). As del Río puts it, even the body, which is often conceived as the grounds for establishing individual subjectivity, "is never a fixed or unified entity, but, instead, an open and unstable whole" (2012: 27). A self cannot achieve any permanence. Subjectivity is an illusory concept and yet, we still exist as some kind of subjects. Braidotti explains that we are rhizomic subjects, not arborescent ones. She says:

> Subjects defined as transversal relational entities do not coincide with a liberal individual, but are rather a "haecceity"—that is to say a degree of power in the affirmative sense of potential, which means an event of complex singularities or intensities (Deleuze and Guattari 1994). Subjectivity is thus both post-personal and pre-individual, relational and hence in constant negotiation with multiple others and immersed in the conditions that it is trying to understand and modify, if not overturn. (Braidotti 2019: 42)[10]

How does such a post-personal and preindividual subject become an agent? What type of agency can it exercise?

Agency—Individual as Collective

Everything I have discussed thus far moves us away from any notion of agency that would be the expression of an autonomous discrete entity's desire or will.[11] There is no such entity and as a dividual, its desires and wills are fueled by the multiplicity of affects constituting it. Agency is collective because of the multiplicity/ies any agent is. It is also collective temporally as one integrates into the assemblage past iterations of that self and future orientations for it. It is also collective in that it bundles intentless direction with affective desires and with conscious practical deliberation and intentional decision-making guiding action. It bundles the unthought, the affective fabric, the moments of coalescence that form proto-subjects that engage in courses of action or thinking. Importantly, "[a]gencies exist all along this continuum of nonconscious, conscious, human, animal, and technical cognitions, but the capacities and potentials of those agencies are not all the same and should not be treated as if they were interchangeable and equivalent" (Hayles 2017: 67).[12] Collective agency is not a collective of agencies with equal power or impact, which complicates the matter of determining the degree of agency any assemblage may have.

Here I am returning to the discussion of the notion of agentic capacity that was brought up in Chapter 1. Diana Coole's view on this is illuminating and I embrace it. She wants to speak of a spectrum of agentic capacities and claims from the onset that "a subjectivist account of agents . . . is no longer tenable" (Coole 2005: 124). She sets out the problem in the same terms I have identified earlier: eliminating agency altogether renders political—and one could add ethical—life impossible (Coole 2005: 125). Taking a first step in a phenomenological conception of embodiment, which already deflates the notion of a rational discrete reflective and disembodied agency, she further proposes to break down "the notion of agency into a series of contingent phenomena in order to describe their provisional emergence, as well as to reflect upon the agentic propensities of a variety of processes as different levels of (co-)existence" (Coole 2005: 128). Somatic agency operates alongside subjective, and transsubjective, processes that shape reflective conscious agency and we end up with "agentic constellations where agentic capacities manifest a provisional concentration and integrity" (Coole 2005: 132). This is the case for social or political collective agents, such as groups, but I argue it also applies to the self- as assemblage, as a collective agent. This passage is worth quoting at length:

> [political agents] emerge as provisional concentrations of agentic capacities that acquire more or less coherence and duration, depending upon their context. But . . . the appearing of these singularities can only be grasped as moments within the whole spectrum of agentic properties. For on the one hand political agents emerge from, and are motivated by, diffuse experiences that are lived and communicated by the body and on the other, they emerge within and into a field of forces that incites, shapes and constrains their development while subjecting them to a transpersonal logic of collective action. (Coole 2005: 135)

But again, while this applies to groups of individuals such as citizen collectives, pressure groups, unions, and such, it also applies to the transjective human being as the multiplicity that it is. When Coole is using "transpersonal"[13] she is talking about the transsubjective intertwinement of "individuals" that I have discussed again and again. The action of an individual is the expression of the collective that it is and of the collective of which it is, that shapes it and makes it the agent it is. Each agent is internally a collective that is permeated by the collective in which it exists. The fleeting moments of coalescence that we are and that allow for us to act, to affect and be affected, are at best collective agentic capacities, and not anything like an agency. The self- is tenuous and always in flux as is its agentic capacity. As I will discuss in Chapter 7, even such a tenuous notion of agentic capacity still allows us to ascribe ethical responsibility and duties to transjective beings.

* * *

So, we need a self and an agent, albeit a fleeting one. This can occur through a self-reprise that a conscious part of ourselves can effect. And this might be the human specificity that Kruks is looking for, as I brought up earlier. But we know that other species also have a sense of self and so this may not be special enough for those who are unwilling to let go of humanism. However, I am not concerned with rescuing human exceptionalism. Rather, I am concerned with the retention of a concept of agency, albeit a radically reconceived one which is what transjective agency, or rather agentic capacity, is. The self we have uncovered is tenuous and always in flux. It can be further shattered and rendered even more unstable through extreme experiences such as the ones I discuss in the next chapter. As we will see, focusing on trauma and how one may recover via narrative reconstruction of the self points to some interesting strategies.

MEANDERING 6
INOSCULATION

In September 2020 in Hietaniemi district in Helsinki, I encounter an ash and a birch who embrace tenderly. The ash trunk swirls around the birch at their shared base. The birch sprouts out of this swirl. The ash hangs on to the birch as it leans away from it.

"Hold me! Don't let me fall!" says Ash to Birch (Figure 6.1).

Two trees dancing the tango, holding onto each other while moving away and closer to one another. Branches mingle in this incredible proximity, in this intertwinement of bodies. No room for crown shyness here, that interesting phenomenon whereby individual trees keep their canopy from touching that of other trees. Two trees growing and sharing the same soil resources, the same air, sunlight, wind, each other's shadow. The base of their joined trunks is covered by grass and moss. Some tiny plants cheekily grow between the ash's trunk swirl and the birch's trunk. An ecosystem of shared bugs and birds and plants, and minerals.

Ash and Birch giggle: "It tickles!"

The difference one letter can make. Inosculation . . . inoculation . . . inosculation. Add an *S* to a word that has carried so much anxiety and triggered embodied reminiscences of extreme vulnerability and you are faced with an entirely different phenomenon with a whole set of different connotations.

Inosculation is about two trees embracing each other through their branches, trunks, or root systems. This evokes harmonious fusion, joyful thriving. Inoculation, which sees a needle enter a muscle to inject a vaccine, is not the same. It evokes vulnerability, the need for strengthening

FIGURE 6.1 Ash and Birch embrace.

to face disease. Not a closing off of porosity but building inner defenses should porous membranes be assailed by a threatening element. But is inosculation really a beautiful, loving, harmonious embrace? Could it not also be the way for trees to join forces, to gain strength by growing together, sharing resources and nutrients, potentially avoiding collapse while hanging onto another that maybe grows a little straighter, a little stronger? Or is inosculation perhaps the choking of another tree, a fusion that is more like a sucking of energy and resources, a vampiric embrace?

"Let me grow!" entreats Birch, "You are squeezing a little too tight!"

"I am hugging you lovingly," comforts Ash.

And both trees thrive. For now. Their branches are loaded with healthy leaves. They look happy, whatever happiness may be for trees. Ash seems older than Birch. What will happen when it dies? Or will Birch go before Ash? Ash trees' life expectancy is much longer than that of birches, 200–300 years compared to about 100 years maximum for birches. When Birch dies, will it fall off and leave a gaping wound like the one Ash already has? Is this a trace of a past embrace? Does Birch know? Does it confront Birch with its own mortality? To Ash's seeming

FIGURE 6.2 Ash and Birch embrace.

immortality? Do Ashes mourn? Did this one mourn in the past and is getting ready to mourn again? (Figure 6.2).

Will Birch stay standing and welcome other plants and fungi in the embrace, like this other birch tree I encountered in Lauttasaari in April 2021, dead and yet alive with so many beings, flowering with mushrooms living off it, covered with moss, and bugs and critters (Figure 6.3).

Dead Birch giggles: "It tickles!"

The tickle extends the life of the birch that once was thriving as birch and lets it thrive as dead birch that hosts those beings and allows them to thrive. Dead but very much alive.

Life: a tickling.

FIGURE 6.3 Dead tree very much alive.

MEANDERING 7
4:00 A.M. BY THE TRAIN TRACKS

A night bus home from work at the bar. Not enough money for a cab. The bus stop, two long blocks away from home.
    Walking up the street. Empty warehouses. Desert industrial urbanscape. Old train tracks in the middle of an urban field, crossing the street ahead. Noise behind. The distant silhouette.
    Quickening pace, no running. A look behind. The man closer on the other side of the street. Quicker. Quicker. Get to the still open factory past the tracks. A grab. From behind. Pulled off of the sidewalk. Thrown into the tall grass. 4:00 a.m. By the train tracks.
    Face down in the grass. The man on top searching the purse for money. A reassuring "I won't hurt you." Almost soothing.
    The ordeal. Dissociation and sobbing. Observing, from some distance up high, this intertwining of bodies. Forceful. Violent.
    It's over. More sobbing. Re-association. Laying flat in the tall grass. 4:00 a.m. or a little after. By the train tracks.
    Laying. Sobbing. Laying. Sometime after 4:00 a.m. By the train tracks.
    No energy to stand up. Must go home. Seek shelter. The open factory nearby, on the other side of the train tracks. Sometime after 4:00 a.m.
    "Help me please!" A confused foreman calls the cops, from a phone in the factory on the other side of the train tracks. Sometime after 4:00 a.m.
    Police pickup. Hospital rape kit. "I apologize," says the ER doctor. Home. Shower. Curling up in bed. Cat cuddles. The sun now out. 4:00 a.m. by the train tracks has passed. But . . .
    Months and years of hypervigilance. Insomnia 'til dawn. It is always and ever 4:00 a.m. By the train tracks.

5 VULNERABILITY

The previous chapters have established that we exist as transjective beings that are constituted transsubjectively and transobjectively. We are permeated through and through by all other beings we encounter just as much as we permeate them through and through. All beings are radically entangled and open to these entanglements, whether they wish to be this open or not. This openness of our being, the outcome of our porous entanglements, is what renders us vulnerable. Vulnerability is ontologically grounded in transjectivity. "Vulnerability" is commonly taken to be something negative, something we must remedy. Public discourse on vulnerability is most often in terms of finding ways to protect vulnerable individuals. For example, a lot of the discourse on animal rights revolves around the idea that humans have a moral duty to protect nonhuman animals who are vulnerable to us. Simply put, vulnerability is considered to be an undesirable subject, or even simply body, position to find oneself in. Furthermore, to make another vulnerable and to take advantage of one's power position to exploit this vulnerability is considered a moral flaw. However, I argue that we need to change how we approach the concept of vulnerability and stop trying to guard ourselves against it. This, as we will see, does not entail dropping our ethical obligations toward others. In fact, it is quite the opposite. The view I offer strengthens the ethical duties toward others and toward oneself. Simone Drichel rightfully points out that "[i]n seeking to defend ourselves, we—perversely—come to violate ourselves, or, to put this differently, what we preserve in 'self-preservation' is what makes the self 'inhuman' rather than human" (2013: 22). Sara Ahmed points out that "vulnerability involves a particular kind of bodily relation to the world" (2006: 69), one in which the body retracts in fear of the danger that it faces. But this is impossible, for the transjective being that is always and ever entangled, one cannot retract oneself. In an effort to protect ourselves and become invulnerable, to retract from perceived potential pain and injury, we do violence to ourselves and dehumanize ourselves.[1] Drichel is not making this point from a posthumanist material feminist perspective, but adopting it like I do provides a solid ground for arguing that vulnerability is an ontological fact about our beings and that it can be expressed as either negative or positive depending on how we relate to it. In fact, for us to even be able to thrive, we must embrace this vulnerability and, as Alaimo would put it, perform the exposure (2016).

A lot of the literature dealing with vulnerability has focused on trauma, and trauma theorists have offered important insights, but these need to be supplemented. Indeed, the focus has been on the subjective aspect of traumatic experiences and how they are suffered by a self who is shattered by them even when such trauma is experienced in the flesh. We must supplement the phenomenological analyses that emphasize intersubjectivity, embodiment, consciousness, and the relational self—understood as intersubjectively relational—with a posthumanist material feminist conceptualization of vulnerability, which takes into account our material, interobjective, and transobjective entanglements. Putting together the notion of transjectivity put forward in Chapter 1 and the theories of affect that further flesh it out—pun intended—we can better grasp how traumatic experiences function just like any other experience. What differentiates traumatic experiences from everyday ones is their intensity, not their structure. In that sense we could say that experiences of extreme happiness—such as Teresa of Avila's ecstasy perhaps—ought to be as telling since they represent significant departures from ordinary daily experiences. All experiences, all events, all encounters are ontologically impactful and transformative, but the particular intensity of traumatic experiences provides an important lens through which we can understand how our material entanglements impact us just as much, if not more, than our intersubjective relations. It also shows that one cannot disentangle the material and subjective impacts. They remain intertwined.

This chapter is a step backward for me in some ways since it was my thinking about narrative theories of the self and theorizations about the experience of rape from a phenomenological perspective focused on the relational self that reinforced my view that material entanglement required much more attention than it had been receiving. Two works by philosophers who provide poignant accounts of the trauma of rape written from the perspective of the victim have been of great interest in this regard. Susan J. Brison's *Aftermath: Violence and the Remaking of a Self* (2002) and Karyn L. Freedman's *One Hour in Paris* (2014) each gives an account of their respective horrendous rapes and their processes of recovery, offering important insights into the level of disruption such violence imposes on a being.

The Undoing of Selves

Brison (2002) argued that her rape was self-shattering and that, as a result of undergoing such an attack on one's self, one stands in need of self-reconstructing. However, the reconstructed self can never be the previous one: there is no going back to who and what one was since that being has been radically altered. Likewise, Freedman explained that while the trauma of her rape left permanent traces that have altered her and her behavior, referring to it as a "chronic condition" (2014: vii), one may still recover by directing one's consciousness and memory. Brison and Freedman both acknowledge the fact that the trauma is "held in the body" (Freedman 2014: 95),[2] but they do so from the point of view of a self that is seeking to regain itself via conscious processes, such as giving an account of the trauma, narrativizing one's self-reconstruction.[3] Because "[a] traumatic experience impacts our physiology, our emotions, and our neurochemistry. . . . [Because i]t changes us" (Freedman 2014: 108), it is essential to understand and come to terms with it. Freedman adds that "[t]raumatic events like rape can change our neurobiology, but they can also change the way we see ourselves, and our place in the world, by calling into question some of our core assumptions about our fellow human beings . . . when you are subjected to interpersonal violence your worldview is prone to change, because experiences like this teach us something about human nature" (2014: 109). Both Brison and Freedman end up focusing on how the bodily material trauma impacts the interpersonal and social. They think that with a good degree of conscious attention to the trauma and how it has impacted a self, one can control how one relates to the trauma and thereby reconstruct oneself, even though this reconstruction is not a full return to who or what one was prior to the trauma. As Freedman says, "a traumatic experience does not have to be a place of pain forever" (2014: viii) and the goal is to acknowledge the trauma and infuse it with new meaning through the reconstructive process that one can engage in. Brison's and Freedman's approach provides key insights. However, like most accounts and dealings with trauma, they emphasize how a self subjectively relates and deals with the trauma. They gesture to bodily impact but are interested in it only insofar as it allows for an explanation of how a subject can understand, accept, and/or control one's response to that bodily inscription of trauma. This, however, fails to take into account how we may be altered in our being in ways that far exceed our possible conscious grasp. What I am referring to here is the way in which our whole being is materially constituted through the manifold interactions and relations we engage in, and this can happen in unsuspected ways because we fail to grasp ourselves as transjective beings. Acknowledging that such material inscription and alteration occurs through all of our experiences is key to approaching our ethical relations to all other beings, including ourselves, differently and potentially more fruitfully.

Ultimately, accounts like Brison's and Freedman's, as well as many others in the literature on trauma, appear to maintain a traditional mind-body dualism according to which the mind can have a hold over the body and its trauma. The attention both Brison and Freedman pay to the inscription of trauma in the body points to our ontological vulnerability but fails to capture the extent to which this material inscription has its own agentic capacity. The agentic capacity of the material aspects of trauma pointedly illustrates how any experience and interaction with other beings impacts the self and acts upon it. About vulnerability, Brison claims that "the self is both autonomous and socially dependent, vulnerable enough to be undone by violence and yet resilient enough to be reconstructed with the help of empathic others" (2002: 38). The violence perpetrated on her that fateful day shattered the social bond of trust as well as her own self. Since the self is conceived as relational, the process of piecing it back together, as she puts it, requires a reinstatement of the social bond. It requires "a process of remembering and working through in which speech and affect converge in a trauma narrative" (Brison 2002: x). The self will rebuild itself narratively but only if that narrative is heard and acknowledged by others. This is not an individual process but one that occurs at least between two. The implication is that this is the process that is always at the foundation of self-constitution.[4] The violence done to the self disrupts this process and tears the intersubjective fabric of which we are made. The other is no longer to be trusted. After surviving an act of violence, one must rebuild oneself through rebuilding this intersubjective bond.[5] What this will mean for each and every instance of reconstruction will be specific to the entanglements—material and subjective—of which one is comprised. The same act of violence will not have the same impact on each person, and the way to "recovery" will therefore also not be the same. Nonetheless, a heightened alteration of oneself will have taken place.[6]

Adriana Cavarero discusses the narrative constitution of the relational self in her book *Relating Narratives* (2000). It is interesting to consider the original title of the book: *Tu che mi gardi, tu che mi racconti*. Literally, this translates as "You who look at me, you who tell me." "*Racconti*" means to narrate or recount, so the interlocutor who looks at "me" is the one narrating their self or story to me. But what the title is really meant to capture is that the person looking at me, "You who look at me," is really telling me about myself, unveiling my self to me through them. Another possible translation of the first part of the title, although not a literal one, and one informed by the ethical implications of Cavarero's positions on the relational self explained in the book, would be "You who look after me." Indeed, because the relational bond is fundamental to the self's constitution, there is a duty to look after each other, to open oneself to the other's narrative.[7] According to this view, human lives are fundamentally disjointed and fragmentary and only consolidate into a self or at least attain a "fleeting and unstable unity" (2000: xxii)—as Paul A. Kottman states in the "Translator's Introduction" to Cavarero's *Relating Narratives*—by giving a narrative structure to one's life through one's life story. This implies a relation to at least one other to whom the story is told. Memory has a spontaneous narrating structure, which is constantly active and productive of the self. However, this process remains internal to consciousness and is not sufficient for the self to truly consolidate. For this, there needs to be a relation between two where one gives their life story and the other receives it. For Cavarero then, "the ontological status of the *who*—as exposed, relational, altruistic—is totally external" (2000: 89). This, of course, points to an inherent vulnerability of the relational self: I depend on an other and their good will toward me to hear my account and acknowledge it and therefore, acknowledge my self. If that other reduces me to a thing by assaulting me, refusing to hear my narrative or to acknowledge me as the self I narrate, this amounts to the erasure of the self. There are many violences that can be perpetrated onto a self: rape, racism, psychological abuse, and so on. Indeed, in a later book, Cavarero says "the human condition of vulnerability entails a constitutive relation to the other: an exposure to wounding but also to the care that the other can supply" (2009: 38). Both outcomes are always possible. She also points to the fact that such wounding or caring is experienced corporeally as well as subjectively.[8] However, and just like Judith Butler who works with Cavarero's texts in *Precarious Lives, Frames of War* and *Giving an Account of Oneself*,[9] the mention of the body and bodily trauma remains unsatisfactorily investigated because material entanglement is not discussed as such. Furthermore, and as Tuija Pulkkinen has pointed out, Cavarero's and Butler's use of "vulnerability" differs insofar as Butler would reject "the focus on the foundational, transcendentally understood subject" from the phenomenological-existential tradition Cavarero is working with (2020: 152).[10] Butler's post-phenomenological position takes into consideration the subject as always in relation.

Judith Butler's work on precariousness is extremely important and provides them with a solid foundation to criticize contemporary issues, as in their most recent work *The Force of Non violence* (2020). However, it seems that Butler always talks about the body but never of its very materiality. This is because, for them, the body is mostly social. Let's examine carefully what they say about this. To them, "[l]oss and vulnerability seem to follow from our being socially constituted bodies, attached to others, at risk of losing those attachments, exposed to others, at risk of violence by virtue of that exposure" (Butler 2004: 20). They agree that the body is vulnerable, but this vulnerability is rooted in its sociality. They explain that

> [t]he body implies mortality, vulnerability, agency: the skin and the flesh expose us to the gaze of others, but also to touch, and to violence, and bodies put us at risk of becoming the agency and instrument of all these as well . . . the very bodies for which we struggle are not quite ever only our own. . . . Constituted as a social phenomenon in the public sphere, my body is and is not mine. (Butler 2004: 26)

The vulnerability they are discussing then is that of the body at the mercy of others and of the social. It is the social body and not the material body or, rather, it is the materiality of the body insofar as it is socially construed. Importantly, the body in relation, which is Butler's focus, is in relation with not only other human bodies (as per Cavarero) but with the more than human. They explain: "What each depends upon, and what depends upon each one, is varied, since it is not just other human lives, but other sensate creatures, environments, and infrastructures: we depend upon them, and they depend on us, in turn, to sustain a livable world" (Butler 2020: 16).

So, Butler is also talking about entanglement but their focus is on intersubjective entanglement along with the entanglement of power and the social with individual self-constitution. "We are at once acted upon and acting," they say but that does not absolve us of responsibility since it is at the point of articulation between the two that it is grounded: "Being acted upon is not fully continuous with acting, and in this way the forces that act upon us are not finally responsible for what we do" (Butler 2004: 16). They then claim something similar to what material feminists and I want to propose: "Let's face it. We're undone by each other. And if we're not, we're missing something" (Butler 2004: 23). They add that we are "constituted by our relations but also dispossessed by them as well" (Butler 2004: 24). However, we cannot "will away this vulnerability. We must attend to it, even abide by it" (Butler 2004: 30). In their more recent work they say that we are never fully individuated since we are always entangled in the conditions that make our lives possible, we are always relational and therefore vulnerable (Butler 2020: 46). Since there will always be a potential destructiveness at the heart of our relations (Butler 2020: 61), we need to act ethically and politically toward generating conditions where such destructiveness will be minimized. The political task is to pay attention to the material conditions, understand in what way they may be harmful, and work to improve them. "When the infrastructural conditions of life are imperiled, so too is life, since life requires infrastructure, not simply as an external support, but as an immanent feature of life itself. This is a materialist point we deny only at our own peril" (Butler 2020: 198). Butler's insights are important but I think we need to further expand to the materiality of bodies, to the material processes that unfold beyond their social construction and interactions. Susan Hekman has rightly pointed out that Butler's work is key for addressing politics that rests on the exclusion of some subjects. Determining who does and who does not count as grievable and, most importantly, on what basis is essential to rectify inequities. But in order to be fully equipped to do this, one must consider expanding one's inquiry into the strictly material and into the nonhuman as well.[11]

Braidotti, who inspires a lot of my thinking, is very critical of Butler's take on vulnerability. In an earlier essay discussing her ethics of affirmation, she positions her views as incompatible with those of Butler (Braidotti 2006). What she is concerned about is what she sees as the necessary containment of the other that Butler's view on precarious life entails (Braidotti 2006: 239). She sees Butler and other theorists of vulnerability as preoccupied with a minimization of pain and suffering, while her "[n]omadic ethics is not about avoidance of pain; rather it is about transcending the resignation and passivity that ensue from being hurt, lost, and dispossessed" (Braidotti 2006: 243). Embracing a Spinozist perspective, Braidotti wants to focus on the activity/passivity distinction rather than that between the self and the other or good and bad (2006: 241). Passivity hinders life as *potentia*: it prevents life affirmation and thriving, the desire to become. She says: "In a nomadic, Deleuzian-Nietzschean perspective, ethics is essentially about transformation of negative into positive passions, that is, about moving beyond the pain. This does not mean denying the pain but rather activating it, working it through" (Braidotti 2006: 247). Dwelling on the pain, on one's vulnerability, and trying to protect oneself from the suffering, actual or foreseen, means that one cuts oneself off from others, from interactions that may foster growth. "Negative passions are black holes" (Braidotti 2006: 247) and while one need not look the other way, one needs to approach them with the desire to transform them. In fact, knowledge of pain and vulnerability is useful as "[i]t forces one to think about the actual material conditions of being interconnected and thus being in the world" (Braidotti 2006: 249). Having said all this, one may be puzzled as to why Braidotti is so critical of Butler's position. It may be the case that Braidotti's early critique has been one inspiration for Butler to clarify their positions on vulnerability as a fundamental condition (Butler 2020). Recognizing our shared vulnerability does not entail closing oneself to it but instead, as said earlier, it compels us to inquire into the conditions that render us vulnerable and work toward improving them. This is not an individual enterprise in Butler since all individuals are in relation. And it is an affirmative and transformative approach to vulnerability of the kind Braidotti is calling for. As Katharine Hoppe puts it, "[a]n affirmation of vulnerability is, thus, at the core of Butler's project. Neither do relations of vulnerability have to be neglected, and nor does the notion describe merely negative relatings" (2020: 131). Braidotti appears to take Butler as relating vulnerability to violence, a threat posed to one and to which one must react, an acute situation, a moment of crisis. On the contrary, according to Hoppe, Butler offers a view of vulnerability as ontological (2020: 132). I agree that Braidotti and Butler are closer than Braidotti thinks in her early essay. In any case, I wish to put them to work together in my thinking about vulnerability as ontological but also as something we must embrace and affirm.

The Ineffable

For both Brison and Cavarero, and ultimately for Butler as well, we are dealing with singular discrete entities that interact in either a positive or negative way, related to others in various ways. The nature of the interaction impacts the self either by strengthening it or dismantling it or, as Butler would have it, we are always undone by each other, which gives way to new processes of subjectivation, new assemblages, new selves-. To be fair, Brison indicates that the self is not a single, unified, coherent entity but she still holds to a notion of interaction between two or between one and others that implies boundaries between beings and entities that interact. Moreover, her account focuses on the subjective experience of the shattering of the self and its intersubjective reconstruction. However, her account of her own rape indicates that there is also material inscription of trauma in the body even though she does not emphasize that. She says that the material is also operative in the disruption and in the reconstruction of the self via narrative. However, as she indicates, it is impossible to recover in the sense of going back to the pretraumatic self. The best one can do is reconstruct oneself by relating to the trauma, narrating it for oneself and for others. To a great extent though, a large part of the trauma remains ineffable. That ineffability is telling of the transobjective entanglements that are integral parts of self-constitution.

What we see with the theorists examined thus far is that if the mind can overcome the bodily trauma, it can do so only through an intersubjective relation. Indeed, we never make our selves by ourselves, as we already discussed. But, there is more than the rupture of the intersubjective bond that occurs through such traumatic experiences as the ones suffered by Brison and Freedman, and the too numerous victims of rape and other horrendous violences. Trauma is never merely subjective or intersubjective nor is it ever merely bodily.[12] I break a little toe. There is trauma in the toe as the bone needs to heel and this takes time. It is aggravated by the fact that there is no way to cast such a small limb to help it heal, and it is almost impossible to not use the limb at least very minimally as one moves around. One can try avoiding putting pressure on the toe by walking with one's foot sideways or stepping only on one's heel, but one easily forgets and the inevitable happens regularly and serves as a painful reminder of the injury. This impediment to one's way of existing as one's body and going about the world impacts our subjective experience of ourselves. Very active people's sense of their selves is challenged as they cannot engage in their various strenuous activities and might even need assistance for every day little tasks. This affects their relations with others and therefore their transsubjective self-constitution. A broken toe sounds like a very banal occurrence that should not cause any subjective trauma. It may also appear to be a frivolous example to use in the context of such a serious discussion about rape and the trauma it inflicts. Far from me to put on the same footing a broken toe and rape. They both disrupt self-constitution, but it is clear that one does so in much more dramatic and fundamental ways than the other. But my point here is that trauma such as rape is a heightened mode of reorganizing self-constitution and that there are various degrees through which we are constituted as transjective beings: in very banal ways and in profoundly traumatic ways. All imply entangled transsubjective and transobjective relations.

In the case of rape, the body is penetrated by another body without consent. Indeed, it is the lack of consent that is considered to be the key defining element in rape. In some cases, the body remains "intact." If the rapist did not ejaculate and leave a physical trace of their own body with semen, hair, or skin cells, or did not cause any lesion to the victim's body the integrity of the victim's body would appear to have been maintained. But to construe rape in this way is to fail to see how the bodily encounter cannot be disentangled from the subjective. A bodily interaction may leave no visible trace—such as a scar, infection, or in the case of rape, a pregnancy, a sexually transmitted disease, or lesions to the genitalia—but even when it does not, other traces are left. Let us consider the lyrics of the song "Lucie" by Québec singer Jean Leloup. The song is the story of a young girl who hires a hitman to kill her family whom she despises. In the CD booklet of the album *Milles Excuses Milady* (2009), Leloup explains that the inspiration for the song came from observing an eleven- or twelve-year-old girl at a garage sale in a driveway, sitting there with her dolls and bicycle, surrounded by her parents. They all appeared scruffy and dirty, and Leloup's impression of the parents was that they were drunk and violent, with the father potentially being vicious. Thinking the family life must have been horrible, Leloup thinks the young girl must have wanted to burn these ignoble parents. This is the inspiration for

Lucie's hiring of a killer in the song. Her only possession is her body and she offers her virginity as payment for the deed. The man kills the family, lighting the house on fire, while Lucie waits in the shed. She then fulfills her promise.

The song claims that, through this deed and payment, Lucie has become a hitman. She has fun and travels, thanks to a small inheritance, but the song also claims that she will end up in prison. The whole song is sung by a chorus with two or three predominantly female voices to a funky tune. At two minutes forty-nine seconds, the music changes to a sad, quiet lullaby with the single male voice of Jean Leloup, sounding increasingly unhinged, singing and growling. The "I" of the hitman hired by Lucie tells her, in a repetitive and angry manner, that he will age with her, rot within her, and will be her.[13] What these lyrics illustrate is the impossibility of disentangling the subjective and bodily inscriptions of the trauma or, in this case, the agreed upon sexual encounter *qua* payment for murder. Lucie's being is constituted by the sexual encounter at the moment the killer penetrates her. But the sexual organ of the killer penetrates her not only at this point in time but forever. It is an everlasting penetration, one which will last as long as Lucie's being will. It also transforms her: she is done and undone by the encounter. The killer and the deed that led to the intercourse will stay with her, it will grow old with her, rot within her, and it will be her. She is a killer even if she stayed in the shed while the deed was done. She can travel and have as much fun as she wants, but she has been made a killer, in fact made herself one, and that interaction, the deed, the penetration of her body by the killer, will forever stay with her and constitute her.

Another example, taken from a different register of violence and trauma, is interesting to consider. In 2010, photographer Lalage Snow documented the deployment experiences of soldiers sent to war-laden Afghanistan. She took a close-up picture of their faces before, during, and after their deployment. The exhibit that ensued presented the images as triptychs and was titled "We Are the Not Dead." Each triptych was accompanied by a statement by the soldier photographed about their experience in Afghanistan. When asked in an interview whether she noticed a significant difference in the young men and women each time she visited them, she answered: "On a personal and psychological level, yes. Having got to know them so well through training, the change was even more marked and poignant. I didn't notice a change in their faces until I put the three [photographs] together, though, and that was a revelation" (Noorata 2013: np).[14] These changes are not to be attributed to lighting or post-production manipulations and "trickery," as she puts it. The "before" and "after" photos were taken in the same Scottish barrack and the "during" were taken in Afghanistan with natural light. Nor should the changes be attributed to aging as these pictures were taken over a period of eight months. What we are confronted with in these pictures is the material inscription of the trauma experienced while being deployed at war. One notices a particular kind of intensity in the "during" pictures that contrasts with the calm neutrality of the "before" images and the haunted faces of the "after" portraits. One could say that they are very mild modern forms of the *gueules cassées* (broken faces) from the First World War. Soldiers often returned from the First World War trenches severely wounded and those with wounds to the face and the head presented a particular kind of challenge. Sometimes left with a face missing large chunks or severely disfigured with dropping eyes, open jaws, and entirely torn noses, these soldiers needed facial reconstruction and sometimes masks and prostheses to cover their disfigurement. In their cases, the material trace of the trauma was very obvious and the trauma was due to a direct injury to their faces or heads. The soldiers' faces in "We Are the Not Dead" bear the material inscription of their traumatic experience without having been physically injured to the head, which makes the power of these images even more potent from the point of view of my analysis.[15]

One may want to contest whether material inscription of trauma is as important as I claim and propose that it only matters once it surfaces in the subjective realm through symptoms of post-traumatic stress disorder (PTSD), for example. I would argue, on the contrary, that this precisely points to the importance of material inscription, one that sticks with the individual being regardless of whether that being pays any attention to it. It is not unusual for trauma victims to live happily after having recovered only to find themselves experiencing the trauma or part of the trauma all over again years after the fact or to come to the realization that they were suffering from it all along. And what are psychosomatic diseases in such cases but ways for the material inscription of the trauma to manifest itself without the individual's subjectivity recognizing that this is what is going on. The body and its biochemical processes carry the burden of the trauma just as much as consciousness or the subconscious. These things go both ways as psychological trauma may express through bodily ailments. What the examples I have brought up illustrate is that an existential-phenomenological analysis that focuses on the (trans) subjective is not sufficient. One needs to also take into account the (trans) objective at the same time that one acknowledges they ought not to be considered in isolation from one another. They are always intertwined.

Vulner—ability

We are permeated by the world we are in as much as we permeate it. The permeability of our being, the fact that we are transformed in our core by the experiences we have and the others involved in these experiences— the other bodies encountered, other humans, nonhumans, living or nonliving beings—all of this renders us vulnerable. Thus far I have been talking about vulnerability without really defining it but what is a vulnerability grounded in transjectivity? Rosalyn Diprose points out that the Latin "vulner" means "to wound" and the usual meaning we attach to "vulnerability" is "to be susceptible to physical or emotional injury. [This understanding of vulnerability] assumes that the body is normally well-bounded and should remain so" (2013: 188). Such an understanding of vulnerability cannot apply to the transjective being. I think we need to take vulner—ability in a different sense. And here I choose to strongly hyphenate the word to emphasize each component of it and their distinct and powerful meanings. The transjective being is vulner—able since it is a body that does and undoes what it interacts with. It has the ability to wound, to affect. Being entangled in the affective fabric I discussed earlier, it is not only on the giving end of "wounding" but on its receiving end as well. It should also be understood that "ability" here does not point to any kind of strong willful agency. This ability is that of a being which is an intensity that emerges out of the dynamic flux of forces and tensions in which it exists. It is the ability of a transjective being radically entangled with a myriad other abilities driven by agencies and agentic capacities. The ability of the human transjective being is therefore mostly driven by intentless direction and not willful autonomous agency. This makes us, through and through, vulner—able as affect—able.

This vulner—ability is not to be understood negatively since it is generative of a new type of ethical responsibility, one that may lead to enhanced flourishing of life in all its instances. Indeed, as Jane Bennett puts it, from a Spinozist perspective, "in a knotted world of vibrant matter, to harm one section of the web may very well be to harm oneself"

(2010: 13). The acknowledgment of one's manifold entanglements is a precondition of this realization. Let us recall Spinoza and his understanding of affective bodies as having the potential to affect and be affected. Hasana Sharp explains that the "politics of renaturalization" depends on an accurate ontological understanding of ourselves and our active embrace of it. As she says, and as I have partly cited in Chapter 3, "[o]nly when we consider ourselves to be constituted by our constellations of relationships and community of affects can we hope to transform the forces that shape our actions and characters" (Sharp 2011: 8). This includes the material entanglements of which we are. As she points out, there are multiple agencies at work, including what she refers to as "impersonal politics," that which allows for the conscious and personal processes to unfold. Making ourselves aware of the existence and operation of these processes is key to not only a better understanding but an active embrace of a better ethos, a transjective ethics, one that immerses us in these processes rather than distinguishes us from them. As Sharp puts it, this requires "an affective orientation toward joy, which indicates an augmentation in one's power or agency" (2011: 14). It is only through such an orientation that we may take delight in our vulner—ability and thrive ethically. The ethics we need is not a set of rules but rather the embrace of an ethos, the adoption of an orientation toward being, whereby one understands oneself as a transjective being. Acknowledging and nurturing our ontological vulner—ability is an essential part of this. I return to this in Chapter 7.

It would be best to accept and embrace our vulner—ability and seek a multitude of experiences, recognizing that a number of them will lay in the intensive field of affect that we may or may not recognize as emotions—depending on whether the affects contaminate the phenomenological, as we saw earlier—but that are still constitutive of our being. Claire Colebrook also thinks that to ignore the kind of being we are is very problematic. She identifies the denial of our vulnerability, or our constant attempt to protect ourselves from it, with humanistic thought. She says, "[t]he fact that we forget our *impotentiality*—that we treat humans as factual beings with a normality that dictates action—has reached crisis point in modernity, especially as we increasingly suspend the thought of our fragility for the sake of ongoing efficiency" (Colebrook 2014: 13). In *Frames of War*, Butler says "the ontology of the body serves as a point of departure for . . . a rethinking of responsibility . . . precisely because, in its surface and its depth, the body is a social phenomenon; it is exposed to others, vulnerable by definition" (2009: 33). As we have seen, the transjective being presents itself as even more vulnerable than what Butler is offering here. And importantly, transjective vulner—ability is also equally potentially positive, something we ought to cherish and nourish rather than try to guard ourselves against. One may say that this transjective vulner—ability is an ambiguous potentiality, one we need to understand as and keep ambiguous.

My proposal for a transjective vulner—ability does not amount to a rejection of phenomenological accounts as wrong. In fact, I think these help a great deal to conceptualize the transsubjective. But they do fail to capture the affective constitution of experience that I have discussed. Eve Kosofsky Sedgwick says, for example, that "[i]f texture and affect, touching and feeling seem to belong together, then, it is not because they share a particular delicacy of scale. . . . What they have in common is that *at whatever scale they are attended to*, both are irreducibly phenomenological. To describe them in terms of structure is always a qualitative misrepresentation" (emphasis in original) (2002: 21). However, theories of affect that inscribe themselves in the Spinozist lineage deal with affect in a non-phenomenological way that moves us away from the centrality of a subject and its experiences. This is a posthumanist move that serves to defeat human exceptionalism as well. A phenomenological approach that focuses on a self's experience and relation to other beings remains caught up in the subjective. As Massumi puts it, "there is no 'raw' perception . . . all perception is rehearsed. Even, especially, our most intense, most abject and inspiring, self-perceptions" (2002: 189). However, as material feminism and Deleuzian theories of affect show, whatever a self experiences is the outcome of multiple happenings in the affective fabric of life, it is the expression of its vulner—ability. Paying attention to the transobjective and the operation of affects offers a more comprehensive understanding of the multiple layers of relationality in which we are always entangled.

The task, therefore, is to recover ourselves as transjective and vulner—able. Alaimo calls for the performance of exposure, namely for the embrace of our permeability, and explains that "exposure entails the intuitive sense or the philosophical conviction that the impermeable Western human subject is no longer tenable. . . . To occupy exposure as insurgent vulnerability is to perform material rather than abstract alliances. . . . The exposed subject is always already penetrated by substances and forces that can never be properly accounted for" (2016: 5).[16]

We must actively seek what has been construed as our "undoing" in the humanist worldview since only then will we be thriving as beings that are constantly and dynamically done and undone. As Erinn Gilson points out, "[v]ulner*ability* is not just a condition that limits us but one that can enable us. As potential, vulnerability is a condition of openness, openness to being affected and affecting in turn" (2011: 310). To exist is to be done and undone. Performing the exposure does not generate or increase it. The experience of post-traumatic stress disorder (PTSD) is characterized by the resurgence of the feeling of loss of control and the distress this causes that one experienced during the trauma. The emotions resurface, often quite uncontrollably, due to a sensory or psychological trigger and can cause intense psychological and physiological discomfort. What we understand from the analysis that precedes, however, is that we are in fact never quite in control of anything and the traumas we have experienced are always present and active within and through us. We are done and undone at every moment of our lives. Understanding this and embracing it, performing our exposure, is the radical affirmative embrace of our being as exposed, as vulner—able, as transjective.

MEANDERING 8
WORLD IN TURMOIL

October 15, 2019. I am sitting in the theater as credits are rolling on the screen. I just watched *Joker* (2019) directed by Todd Phillips. I am gutted. I am angry. The kind of deep anger that knots your gut. On my fifteen-minute drive home I ask myself why I am so angry. It comes to me in a flash: we all live in Gotham. We are all Arthur Fleck in the making. The world is in turmoil and everyone is caught in this whirlwind of social, economic, political, and environmental challenges. Adding to this mix the pandemic caused by SARS-Cov-2, there is little space for anyone to evade the toxic fabric of the world. We may be living in the Anthropocene but we are also living in the Anxiocene and, just like its counterpart, it is difficult to pinpoint exactly its cause and start date. That we are living at a time in which anxiety is rampant and at an all-time high is hardly debatable. *Joker* delivers the punch to the gut that lets one's long-contained anxiety loose.

Joker is a deeply disturbing movie. The viewer is nailed to their seat, transfixed by the exceptional performance offered by Joaquin Phoenix. This spiraling into the depth of mental illness along with its intense pain and suffering is riveting. But there is much more to this than mental illness. Joker says it best to an increasingly alarmed Murray Franklin, a late-night talk show host who ridiculed Arthur Fleck's failed attempt at being a comedian: "What do you get when you cross a mentally ill loner with a society that abandons him and treats him like trash? I'll tell you what you get! You get what you fucking deserve!" Most essays analyzing the movie have focused on the claim that Joker is a mentally ill person. But Arthur points to the society that has failed him. In his second meeting with his social worker, who displays a heightened level of indifference and distraction, he pauses and remarks, "You don't listen, do you? I don't think you ever really hear me." The problem is not mental illness alone and how one could be precipitated into it but a society that lacks fundamental empathy. That society has lost its humanity. Gotham is an inhuman city in which, as Joker tells Murray, "Everybody just yells and screams at each other. Nobody's civil anymore! Nobody thinks what it's like to be the other guy." However, one person does among Arthur's acquaintances and it saves their life: Gary, the little person who worked as a colleague at the clown agency at the beginning of the film. When he and another coworker, Randall, visit him to convey condolences, things take a violent turn. Randall mentions that two policemen have been asking questions. Randall had offered a gun to Arthur after he was attacked at the beginning of the movie but then lied about it, causing Arthur to lose his job. Arthur assaults Randall and kills him but he lets Gary leave unharmed saying: "You were the only one who ever was nice to me." He then kisses him on the forehead and lets him out of the apartment.

One of the reasons why the movie is so disturbing is its heightened level of violence. And yet, there is very little graphic violence when one compares it to mainstream action flicks. *Joker* displays extreme social, psychological, emotional, affective, and economic violence. This is not to say that there is no physical violence whatsoever. There is. Arthur gets beaten up by kids who have stolen the sign he was holding while in clown costume, working to advertise for a store about to close. "Everything must go!!" says the sign. Following that incident, Arthur engages in a few violent acts: he shoots and kills three young men who are bullying and attacking him on the subway, he chokes his mother to death with a pillow at the hospital, he kills his former colleague who visits him at his apartment by stabbing him with scissors, and finally kills Murray on the late-night talk show, although he initially appeared to prepare to shoot himself while being interviewed. While Arthur perpetrates the most gruesome physically violent acts in the movie, he is also the victim of violence: we see him beaten up twice—merely for being different—and Thomas Wayne punches him in the face when Arthur confronts him. We also find out that Arthur was abused as a child and that his own mother let the abuse take place. His mother's favorite saying was: "You must put on a happy face." That disconnect alone, of a mother allowing the abuse on her child while advising the child to put on a happy face, was bound to make Arthur unstable. We are led to conclude that this, and the severe head injuries he suffered during the abuse, is the root cause of his condition: the uncontrollable laughter he has when placed in a stressful—or unfair—situation like when he is on the bus and starts engaging with a child in front of him, making faces that make the child laugh until the mother curtly orders him not to bother her child.

Arthur Fleck is mentally and socially ill and we are too. We all live in Gotham City. And as the sign Arthur holds up at the beginning of the movie, "Everything must go!!," claims, everything indeed must go in a society that rests on injustice, inequity, oppression—financial, social, racial—and on a general lack of empathy. The penultimate sequence of the movie shows Gotham City on fire as protesters in clown masks or makeup are disrupting the social order that crushes them and acclaiming Joker who is standing on top of the police car hood in which he crashed a few moments before. He "puts on a happy face," drawing a smile with the blood filling his mouth. From there, we move to the next and last sequence in a psychiatric hospital, with Arthur laughing uncontrollably while smoking a cigarette, handcuffed, across the table from a woman interviewing him (one is left to wonder whether she is a detective or therapist). "What's so funny?" she asks. Arthur mumbles it is an old joke and when she asks him to tell it to her, he replies, shaking his head, "You wouldn't get it." The movie ends with Arthur walking out of this room into a corridor, leaving a trail of bloody footprints and then being chased presumably by hospital personnel.

In a podcast discussion with Michael Moore on *Rumble* (Ep. 6 "Everything Must Go" [feat. Todd Phillips], December 31, 2019), the director of *Joker* claimed that the movie is not political but rather "humanist." He explains it is about the power of kindness and a cry for empathy and resistance. He also says that even if it is set in the early 1980s, it is a movie about our contemporary period. I could not agree more. Our world is like Gotham, lacking empathy and lacking genuine interconnections. It is a world in which everyone is made into a loner and made to suffer from mental illness, whether one was born healthy or not (what an ableist statement to make, by the way, as if there was an ultimate health that one can measure up to or not). This is why I was feeling gutted and so angry after viewing the film the first time, and every time I have watched it since. How can one feel otherwise when the very fabric of our existence is permeated by so much hatred, violence, heightened individualism, inequities, and other disregard for human and nonhuman thriving and well-being?

If one were to proceed like annalists of old, there would be multiple entries per year noting horrendous events of varying nature. I offer a small sample:

- September 2, 2015. Three-year-old Syrian boy Alan Kurdi lays face down on the beach. Alan is dead. The waves come washing over his head and lifeless body. The picture captures all the sacrifices, pain, and crushed hopes of migrants seeking to reach Europe for a better life, putting their lives at risk in overcrowded rafts and boats led by smugglers taking advantage of them. The picture becomes viral.

- October 1, 2017. A lone gunman is on the thirty-second floor of the Mandalay Bay Resort and Casino in Las Vegas. He aims at the crowd assembled for an outdoor concert at the Route 91 Harvest Festival, fires over 1,000 bullets, kills sixty people, injures 411 with a few more hundred being injured by the panic that was created on site. The shooter is later found in his suite, dead by self-inflicted gunshot. Images and interviews of attendees become viral.

- Fall 2019. Raging fires from the Australian bush. Unprecedented in their extent and intensity (as per the New South Wales Department of Planning, Industry and Environment), the bushfires of the 2019–20 season burned a total of 5.3 million hectares, destroying homes and natural habitats, killing an estimated one billion animals (an estimate many consider "conservative"), bringing many species closer to extinction, destroying plants and ecosystems. Screens filled with images of fire as the Australian bushfires found their echo in the California wildfires. Flaming virality.

- May 25, 2020. "I can't breathe, Mama. I can't breathe!" George Floyd was lynched in the streets of Minneapolis. Derek Chauvin pressing his knee in Floyd's neck for 9 minutes and 29 seconds, pressing and pressing and staring with an empty gaze at Darnella Frazier, the courageous young woman filming the murder, holding her phone steady, and bearing witness to yet another act of police brutality against Black people. The video goes viral.

- April 2021. Open-air cremation of the bodies of patients who died of Covid-19 in India. Images of individuals in despair. Pleas from medical personnel. Family members devastated and crying. Imploring for international help. The need for oxygen is pressing. Images become viral.

- May 2021. Israel attacks Gaza. Rockets, fires, destroyed buildings, howling adults holding their dead children, living children with a horrified gaze, suffering. But, also, obscene rejoice at suffering: shocking images of Israeli settlers dancing and cheering at the Aqsa Mosque set on fire. Images take a viral round.

- March 6, 2022. A video of the shelling of the city of Irpin as civilians try to evacuate. A family and church volunteer killed on the spot. Their surviving dog, in a green crate, howling, crying, and barking. Another viral video, one among many from the horrendous war waged on Ukraine by Russia.

- May 14, 2022. A livestream on Twitch. A self-proclaimed eco-fascist eighteen-year-old heavily armed and wearing tactical gear opens fire at a Buffalo supermarket in upstate New York, killing ten and injuring three others. Eleven of the victims are Black. The shooter drove some 320 kilometers to this area because of its high density of Black population. A 180-page manifesto details his belief in the "white replacement" theory. The racist violent attack is on every newsfeed.

Pain, joy, pain, joy overcome by pain, more pain, some joy, here is a cat video to make you feel better, or an image of a squirrel smelling a flower, the video of a baby sleeping while cuddling Samson the goldendoodle from Westport, Connecticut. Varying affective modes of virality. Moments of peace, cuteness, and grace . . . on one's phone, in one's news feed. Not in the far distance, a reality one does not read about in the newspaper or hear about through a newscast. A reality that is part of one's intimate sphere. Pain, joy, pain, all in one's hand, a swipe away.

But these are not mere images that one can choose to ignore and remain indifferent to. They make us present to the events recorded. We are witnesses and cannot remain indifferent, even if we try. Those images and events shape us as they permeate the transjective beings we are. And this carries on. War in Ukraine and the rise of strong (or wannabe strong) men and women (Le Pen). Governments at odds with the social good and public health, for the sake of the economy, reopening and lifting health protective measures while the pandemic is still raging. Ottawa's occupation by the so-called "freedom convoy" to protest mandates (or so they claimed), polarization of public debates, conservatives legislating women's bodies and reintroducing laws against abortion in increasing numbers, IPCC 2022 report sounding the alarm, again. . . . This makes for a distressing mix of emotions and affects. As hard as we may want to ignore it all, we must pay attention through our news feeds or in the stories we tell ourselves in fiction such as *Joker*. The world is in turmoil. An affirmative ethos must find a way to also affirm the unbearable because it is never really "unbearable": we always bear it, whether we like it or not.

6 MANIFOLD TOXICITY

I have discussed quite extensively the ways in which we must understand the transjective being as radically entangled and thereby fundamentally vulner—able as affect—able. I have discussed certain types of disruptions that shed light on this ontological fact. As transjective beings, we are exposed to the various toxicities with which we are in relations. In her *Staying with the Trouble* (2016), Donna J. Haraway offers multiple variations on Marilyn Strathern's claim that "[i]t matters what ideas we use to think other ideas (with)" (12).[1] These variations are like a refrain throughout the book and remind us of our multiple entanglements. Indeed, "[s]taying with the trouble requires making oddkin; that is, we require each other in unexpected collaborations and combinations, in hot compost piles. We become-with each other or not at all. That kind of material semiotics is always situated, someplace and not noplace, entangled and worldly" (Haraway 2016: 4). Haraway's trajectory from the early cyborg to the recent child of compost Camille[2] shapes and reshapes the companions and our modes of being-with. Kin becomes oddkin—odd because they may not appear to be kin—and ethical political obligations modulate accordingly. Those who are at the table together, *cum panis*, are companion, and they are kin and infect each other.[3] The use of "infect" is interesting as it also draws attention to the unintentional ways in which we affect others. Affecting is infecting and vice versa. And those others who infect us as we infect them, as we have seen and as I will continue to explore here, are many many more than we recognize at first glance. We exist as humus in a compost pile[4]—a pile that contains different types of toxicities and different types of beings, themselves entangled in myriad ways.

Here I want to tackle these entanglements by considering the multiple ways in which we exist, "'We'-who-are-not-one-and-the-same-but-are-in-this-convergence-together" (Braidotti 2019: 182).[5] The posthuman convergence that Braidotti points to is the target of my investigation here. This convergence has always existed in one form or another, depending on the various elements of webs of entanglements, but we are discovering it now, in our posthuman moment. As transjective beings, we are entangled dynamic assemblages, which are also modulated via the types of entanglements that transpierce and constitute our existence. Félix Guattari proposes that we consider the three complementary ecological registers of social ecology, mental ecology, and environmental ecology as comprising the "vectors of subjectivation" that constitute us (2000: 41).[6] The self is not a given but rather emerges as the precarious coalescence of these vectors. These ecologies capture the life of a self with itself (mental), with other humans (social), and with nonhuman others (environmental). N. Katherine Hayles and Rosi Braidotti each also propose a tripartite mode of subjectivation that we can see as variations of Guattari's proposal.[7] Hayles (2017) speaks of the human as species-in-common, species-in-biosymbiosis, and species-in-cybersymbiosis. Each of these terms emphasizes a type of entanglement among beings: humans, living beings, living and nonliving beings.[8] In a similar vein, Braidotti offers to speak of the subject as zoe/geo/techno framed, namely as shaped by life, which "is not exclusively human: it encompasses both bios and zoe forces, as well as geo- and techno-relations that defy our collective and singular powers of perception and understanding. Posthuman subjects establish relations on at least three levels: to one's self, to others, and to the world" (2019: 45).[9] This is a reprise of Guattari's ecologies that incorporates the technological. But the way Braidotti puts it here indicates that beyond these three ecologies, or rather within them, one also relates to oneself, to others, and to the world. This also entails a "transversal alliance [which] involves non-human agents, technologically mediated elements, Earth-others (land, waters, plants, animals) and non-human inorganic agents (plastic buckets, wires, software, algorithms, etc.)" (Braidotti 2019: 164). This alliance is new and forms a new people.[10] Within and across each sphere of our experiences, there is a multiplication of relations and entanglements. In addition, we must add the temporal unfolding of beings and how it also serves to multiply and complexify entanglements. In their discussion of Spinoza, Gatens and Lloyd note that

> Our bodies retain the traces of past modification; and those modifications in turn reflect the effects of modifications of other bodies, in chains of causal determination going back to the distant

past. . . . In understanding how our past continues in our present we understand also the demands of responsibility for the past we carry with us, the past in which our identities are formed. We are responsible for the past not because of what we as individuals have done, but because of what we are. (1999: 81)

I have alluded to the temporal aspect of the constitution of the transjective self in my analysis of trauma in the previous chapter. As I explained, any and all experiences leave traces—material and subjective—and these traces consolidate in this dynamic assemblage that constitutes us and our selves. Selves are as precarious and dynamic as the beings they are attached to. This multiplication of vectors of subjectivation, subject framing, and symbioses that entwine the temporal, spatial, material, subjective, social, and environmental in the mesh that we are and exist in can only be understood via an expanded notion of intersectionality. We are dealing with a transjective intersectionality that goes well beyond the intersection of gender, race/ethnicity, and dis/ability.

In the attempt to understand this intersectional transjective reality, we should not make the mistake of trying to "make sense." Rather, making sense can take different forms and include healthy portions of uncertainty, unresolvability, opacity, strangeness, and perhaps even monstrosity. In his *Necropolitics*, Achille Mbembe argues that modern modes of knowing that seek to make sense through rationalizing are problematic:

> Using algebra to model nature and life [a seventeenth century mode of knowledge], a modality of knowing thus gradually imposed itself that consisted essentially in flattening out the world, that is to say, homogenizing the entirety of the living, rendering its objects interchangeable and manipulable at will. A good part of modern knowledge will thus have been governed by this centuries-long movement of flattening out. (2019: 165)

This modern algebraic pursuit of knowledge is really a way to tame the unknown, or at least our fear of it. Through it, we seek to make the strange familiar, the opaque clear, and the monstrous human. Rendering the uncanny canny again. A modern motto from which we continue to suffer.

We seek to come up with theories and formulas that capture the beings we are. Because of our inner/outer multiplicity, we will always fail to do that—no formula will ever work. And when we live under the illusion that we have theorized ourselves and then erect our ethics and politics on such flawed foundations we end up multiplying relations and affective threads and impacting ecological registers in ways that are damaging and do not foster thriving. The further we do so, the more we are confused and uncertain about our beings, that of others, and the world. If we were to pause this race for a full, rational, algebraic knowing that would shed light on every single aspect of life—a race that is run in a spinning wheel—a world of wonders, ambiguities, and teras would emerge. As Patricia MacCormack indicates, "[m]arvelling opens up the witness; meaning closes off the monster" (2016: 93). The act of making sense, of theorizing and rationalizing the world and its beings, is an exclusionary one. It sets up standards and identities that relegate to the realm of monstrosity any being that does not fit into those contrived categories. MacCormack discusses a teratological connectivity, one which recognizes that the human is a fabrication and that we are always already monstrous (2016: 94; 98).[11] We are such because we are this constellation of relations and entanglements—threshold subjectivities, betweenness, assemblages (2016: 119)—that we can only approximate in any attempt at understanding what they are. We can say that they are but what they are and how they function is only very partially accessible to us. There is a high degree of uncertainty, opacity, and monstrosity in every being. For the being that has dreamt itself transparent and rationally conceivable, this understanding is a lesson in humility, a key value for a transjective ethos.[12]

In Chapter 5, I discussed how individual crises unveil to us the inner multiplicity of our selves. Any humanistic understanding of the human as rational and autarkic fails to fully explain how a self can be affected in the multiple ways it is by negative experiences. Moreover, what this teaches us is that any and all experiences impact us in ways we often do not understand or cannot even capture. The societal and environmental crises we live through—continued social unrest cultivated by populist far-right racist and fascist modes of thinking, the pandemic that launched in 2019, the advent of the Anthropocene and Sixth Extinction—continue to teach us about our own monstrosity. The world, like our bodies and those of others we are entangled with, also resists our attempts at making it fully meaningful: it just does not fit the neat mechanistic explanations and theories that we long for in our desire to assuage our anxieties and feel in control. Instead, the world reminds us of the turbulences out there. Our bodies do the same as do others we interact with—human and nonhuman animals, cyborgs, AI, minerals, and so on.

Social Toxicities

A profusion of memes and Twitter quips have labeled 2020, 2021, and now 2022 as the worst years ever (it seems the bar keeps getting lower for a year to be better than the previous one, and yet . . .). It is true that many disruptions tore the affective fabric of which we are a part and comprised of. The social unrest that erupted in the first half of 2020 in the United States is a good example of this. Triggered by the lynching of George Floyd on May 25 in Minneapolis, the Black Lives Matter (BLM) movement launched into unprecedented widespread action with protests across the United States and abroad in cities of all sizes. BLM was not new to 2020, but the convergence of events, their worldwide mediatization, and the participation of protesters from all walks of life and ethnicities—including a large portion of non-racist white people who were not previously engaged in active protests—was new. The seventeen-year-old bystander Darnella Frazier who filmed the murder with her phone felt an urge to document this instance of police brutality—not a novel or surprising occurrence—putting herself at risk of being arrested or similarly assaulted by the officers on-site, but also not knowing what the final outcome of the violent encounter she was witnessing would be. She was left deeply traumatized by what she saw and recorded but also by some of the criticism she received after posting the video and accompanying images on social media. Indeed, some called her out for not doing enough and limiting her intervention to the recording. And yet, it is this patient and painful recording that allowed the world to witness, yet again, police brutality toward Black people. This video, which captured the utter disregard for Black life in the expression and actions of Minneapolis police officer Derek Chauvin—the main but not sole perpetrator[13]—shocked the world and served as a powerful affective reminder of the severe inequities faced by people of color in the United States. Floyd's murder occurred only two months after the killings of Breonna Taylor and Daniel Prude, which were equally shocking, but its mediatization—the recording and its posting on social media which allowed for its virality—made it the catalyst for the sudden amplification of the BLM movement.

As a Twitter user, I almost immediately was alerted to the horrendous act. My phone's notifications and banners were drawing me to Minneapolis and in close proximity to the murder. But I did not watch the video, I only read the stories. I stopped watching videos of violent assaults, beatings, and killings of Black people a few years back. I have seen many and when they come up in my feeds, thanks to the many human rights activists I follow, I read the story. This is not a case of ignoring what is going on or trying to pretend it does not exist. I know it does and it is important to spread such stories and images. But the fact of the matter is I no longer need (Did I ever?) to be exposed to such images in order to be outraged and to want to act to bring about change. But many others do need to be exposed to this. Susan Sontag's insightful analyses in *Regarding the Pain of Others* (2003) come to mind here. She begins with a discussion of Virginia Woolf's critique of war. Woolf sets up for her readers a thought experiment in which they are viewing photographs of individuals maimed by war. Sontag says, "[t]he photographs are a means of making 'real' (or 'more real') matters that the privileged and the merely safe might prefer to ignore" (2003: 7). These images have the power to elicit responses, but these may be in opposition to one another: a call for peace, a call for revenge, "[o]r simply the bemused awareness, continually restocked by photographic information, that terrible things happen" (Sontag 2003: 13). However, there is always the risk of emerging indifferent. When exposed repeatedly to similar kind of shocking images, the shock may wear off (Sontag 2003: 82). There is also the possibility that "[p]eople can turn off not just because a steady diet of images of violence has made them indifferent but because they are afraid" (Sontag 2003: 100). But when the risk is not immediate, when the threat does not concern us, fear is not what drives our indifference. The interiorization of the affective load generated by the photographs might be too painful and traumatizing. And while images themselves do not necessarily help us understand—"Narratives can make us understand. Photographs do something else: they haunt us" (Sontag 2003: 89)—they have the power to trigger a reaction in viewers. One of their roles is to trigger witnessing and remembering. As she puts it, "[r]emembering is an ethical act, has ethical value in and of itself. Memory is, achingly, the only relation we can have with the dead" (Sontag 2003: 115). The empathic act of taking in the violence via the image, be it a photograph or a video, and the affirmation of this reality, the acknowledgment of the violence—perpetrator(s), suffering, and victim(s)—amounts to a form of the affirmative empathy I argue needs to be at the core of our transjective ethos.

For many people, this exposure to the images of George Floyd's lynching brought about the sudden and full realization of their entanglements and their responsibility to intervene, albeit in a post-mortem manner, to put a stop to the unequal treatment of the people they are related to in a fundamental fashion. Judith Butler argues that "[t]here is a sense in which violence done to another is at once a violence done to the self, but only if the relation between them defines them both quite fundamentally" (2020: 9).[14] What they mean by that is that we need to recognize the other unto whom violence is done as grievable. Grievability is a key Butlerian concept and one I have alluded to while defining vulnerability. Butler works with the notion of relationality and emphasizes that beings are interrelational and, therefore, we always depend on others as they do on us. They explain:

> Equality is thus a feature of social relations that depends for its articulation on an increasingly avowed interdependency—letting go of the body as "unit" in order to understand one's boundaries as relational and social predicaments: including sources of joy, susceptibility to violence, sensitivity to heat and cold, tentacular yearnings for food, sociality, and sexuality. (2020: 45)

For that interdependency to be "avowed," however, one may need to be confronted with images such as those documenting the lynching of George Floyd. There is power in being told about violence and severe inequities, but there is also power in the affective relation that is triggered by viewing images, allowing one to be a witness, to hear and see the actual violence, to feel the violence in one's body. As I said, the viral video allowed the deed to be brought into close proximity with even those who were very far from it. Recognizing the assault on equality, the assault on life, triggered reactions in locations far remote from Minneapolis. People from across the world could literally be in Minneapolis as witnesses through the viral video and choose to react in their own locality.

In a world currently permeated by various toxicities, from the new coronavirus to resurgent fascist and racist modes of thinking, we are constantly exposed to toxins—and made sick from them. The pandemic has certainly taught us this lesson: we are interconnected in ways we often don't suspect—yet one of the measures taken to combat the spread of the virus was to try to minimize this interconnection via lockdowns and physical distancing. However, can one really cut oneself off from the violence in the world, and the discourse and ideologies of those perpetrating it? Is it desirable to turn oneself into one of the three wise monkeys, or all of them at once? If one does not see, does not hear, and does not speak evil, then evil does not exist . . . does it? As users of media—traditional, digital, social—we are constantly exposed to the evil in the world and cannot cut ourselves off from it. It can be argued that we all suffer from at least a mild case of PTSD as a result, since we hear about, read, or even see the beating and killing of humans on a daily basis because of their race, their creed, or their objection to the dominant political and economic powers. I have been exposed to the violent assault and killing of many American Black people via my Twitter and Facebook feeds. I have been exposed to racial and religious intolerance taking the form of violent assaults on Muslim communities such as the Québec City mosque shootings of January 29, 2017, and the Christchurch mosque shootings of March 15, 2019. I have been exposed to the pain and suffering undergone by the victims of war in Ukraine since February 2022. I have been regularly—and unfortunately will continue to be regularly—infected by this toxicity. What matters is how I respond and how I "take it in." Now, as said, one cannot escape this "taking in" since we are always and ever entangled, infected, but we can choose the mode through which we are.

I have described elsewhere the affective load of waking up to a phone loaded with banners detailing the Christchurch events.[15] This affective load is possible because we are transjective beings. Exposure to events, facilitated by the various technologies we use, transports us to distant locations and makes us into witnesses of atrocities, feeling the violence in our bodies and minds as it is perpetrated onto those others we are entangled with. These assaults on life that we witness, assaults on life that we share, life that we are, are assaults on us but also on life itself, on the transjective fabric of our existence. Any such assault alters the assemblages and transjective web of relations. Any assault, big or small, leaves a trace that impacts all entangled beings. However, and as painful as this can be, the violence needs to be exposed so that we may resist it, so that we may change how we insert ourselves in the world and how we exist as life. Each and every exposure is a punch in the witness's gut, it is itself violent and destabilizing, but I argue it is necessary. I will pick up this thread again in the next chapter and have hinted to it in the previous one: I want to claim that we must transform the ontological fact of our vulnerability into an ethical stance through which we embrace this vulnerability, open ourselves to violences and assaults on life so that we may convert the pain into growth, suffering into thriving. This openness may lead to the affirmative empathy we need and can exercise only once we have understood transjective vulnerability.

Lessons from Virality

Granted, coming to this realization may be a difficult thing to do given how pervasive humanist modes of thinking are. 2020, 2021, 2022, and possibly 2023 may have been the "most disastrous years ever" but for whom? For people living in war zones or parts of the world ridden by famine or severe diseases, the hardships of the pandemic years were hardly new.[16] To the developed West, however, the Covid-19 pandemic that started to unfold in the fall of 2019 and exploded in the early months of 2020 is a paradigm-shifting event. 9/11 has been described as an event that made North America, and more specifically the United States, lose its innocence. Even though it had been attacked on its soil in 1941 at Pearl Harbor by the Imperial Japanese Air Service, the United States had clung to a notion that it was safe from any foreign attacks. The distant location of Pearl Harbor on the island of Hawaii in the Pacific Ocean allowed the continental United States to continue to feel safe. Almost sixty years later, the attacks on iconic New York City and the Pentagon by a terrorist group from the Middle East defied the imagination. That a relatively small group from such a remote location could strike a blow of this proportion on American soil meant the sudden realization of a vulnerability that had always been there, but not felt. The feeling of innocence that was lost was the understanding, through violent action brought home, that one was always open to such mortal danger. In many ways, the Covid-19 pandemic struck a similar blow and signified a second loss of innocence. The so-called developed world had been sheltered from epidemics of this scope and deadly diseases at least since the 1918 Spanish Flu epidemic. Fantasizing about its own scientific and technological power, the developed West lived under the illusion of being protected from anything like that not only because of its high levels of sanitation but also because of its distance from the usual locations where outbreaks occur. The typical reaction until the early months of 2020 was "There is a new deadly disease? Must be occurring in Africa, Asia, or South America." Leaving aside the latent racism animating such reactions, Ebola, HIV, various strands of flu, and the Zika virus were always a threat, especially in the globally connected world in which we live.[17] This time, in a matter of a couple of months,[18] the Covid virus spread to the whole world, reaching remote locations like the Amazon rainforest but also every European and North American country. More than 100 years after the Spanish Flu epidemic, no one was left with memories of what it was to live through such conditions. The sudden discovery of our manifold entanglements, incited by our unavoidable entanglement with a virus emerging at the other end of the planet, has meant a shocking and distressing realization about our vulner—ability.

As we go about our lives, we engage in a balancing act of sorts, juggling our various entanglements, and orientating ourselves to the world in certain ways. As we have seen, this is what allows us to achieve some levels of stability in the midst of the dynamic and constant reconfigurings of our selves and the world. When a global event like the pandemic disrupts this already precarious balance, when our *zoe*/geo/techno entanglements are shifted quite dramatically, and when certain types of entanglements are not possible or reduced significantly—via social distancing or severe lockdowns as experienced in some regions of the world—our mundane everyday experience of our selves, others, and the world is deeply affected. We no longer share the same spaces in the same ways, the same smellscapes or soundscapes, and the actual presence of others. Their presence is no longer perceived in the same ways due to their being potential threats to our health, embodying a newer type of affect—ability. An important shift that has been prominent throughout pandemicity—the experience of living through a pandemic, which seems to overly prolong itself to many people's dismay—is our use of digital technology to engage in various activities. From attending virtual school, to online shopping for essential goods, to Zoom parties to reconnect with family and friends, widespread availability of digital technologies has compensated to a degree the isolation potentially felt due to sanitary protective measures. While availability or reliability of such technologies varied greatly—sometimes unearthing existing deep inequities within communities in the West—it remains that this mode of connection opened up new potentialities. As Puig de la Bellacasa put it before the pandemic forced our increased use of them, "[c]omputers are more than working prostheses; they are existential companions for people trying to keep in touch with dislocated networks of loved ones" (2017: 107). However, she continues, "these new forms of connection produce as much copresence as they increase absence. They do not really reduce distance; they redistribute it" (Bellacasa 2017: 109). This has been felt in a heightened way throughout the pandemic. And yet many affordances that we would have otherwise ignored have expanded our entanglements and inflected the dynamic assemblages we are.[19]

The pandemic has also taught us in what ways we are entangled with place—the place we inhabit as well as the remote shadow places that support our existence in our own familiar places. The concept of shadow places is discussed by Val Plumwood as she examines the global economy and culture in which we live. Indeed, our ways of living are sustained by "many unrecognized shadow places that provide our material and ecological support" (2008: np). We exist as intertwined with them and the people inhabiting them and our actions and consumption impact these people and places, and vice versa, economically, socially, and health-wise—especially since many workers are forced to labor in unhealthy conditions. We continue to talk about communities, countries, and continents as if these were contained and discrete entities when in fact borders are as permeable as a body's skin. In fact, the traffic through these borders is essential for the thriving of all. Let us recall Frost's claim that life depends on the traffic that occurs through membranes, discussed in Chapter 1. The same applies here. Plumwood says, "[c]ommunities should always be imagined as in relationship to others, particularly downstream communities, rather than as singular and self-sufficient" (2008: np). Her concern, however, is that the type of traffic that takes place in our consumer culture is one which impacts negatively and disproportionately on some communities. These shadow places "that produce or are affected by the commodities you consume, places consumers don't know about, don't want to know about, and in a commodity regime don't ever need to know about or take responsibility for" (Plumwood 2008: np). An ecojustice approach to dwelling in the world would tie together the land of the economy with the land of attachment, care, and responsibility. While this would require a fundamental overhaul of how economies and trade are structured locally and globally, I am not sure it would eliminate this interdependence and reliance on places that are not our immediate ones. Would the point instead be to drag these places out of the shadow in which we are currently relegating them? Has the pandemic's impact and the lesson it taught us about our proximity in a global world brought the necessary incentives to do so? And further, if we conceive of place as intimately tied with thinking,[20] if we posit ourselves as entangled with the materiality of our place and also posit that immediate place as also entangled with a distant place, possibly cast in the shadows, then is our thinking not also inflected by these distant locations? What does distance even mean in such a view?

Distance is bridged rather quickly as our bodies are permeated by the various toxicities that surround us. Via global trade, we are exposed to foods and goods produced in remote, shadow places. These may come with various pesticides, herbicides, pollutants, and plastics that add on to those already present in our immediate places and constitute our bodies as toxic. In the Wasteocene—a variation on the term Anthropocene coined by Marco Armiero (2021)—societies with high instances of consumerism and wasting ship their waste to remote locations and dump it on those others that are deemed less worthy. The environmental injustice and slow violence imposed on the less privileged also inflect the degree to which their bodies are exposed to toxicities. The extra burden on bodies that are already toxic as entangled often means a significant impact on the health of individuals but also of the communities of which they are a part, local and global. Until we fully come to grasp with our manifold entanglements, we will not realize that health, well-being, and thriving are global pursuits before it is an individual one. Myra J. Hird argues that landfills and their incessant geo-bacterial activity illustrate the asymmetry of relations between humans and nonhumans, but also points to the fact that "nature relentlessly flows, but not in ways that are necessarily compatible with human flourishing" (2013: 115). This activity—that we do not know about, that we do not fully comprehend, activity that sustains us but that also may be transforming the world in ways that will render it increasingly inhospitable to humans, activity that far predates us and is radically indifferent to us, this activity or rather the unfolding of this myriad of powerful agentic capacities—is also us, permeates us. We are entangled with it.

Anthropocenic Anxieties

Opening their introduction to the special section of *Environmental Humanities* on "Toxic Embodiment" they coedited, Cielemęcka and Åsberg explain, "[t]he cumulative exposure to endocrine disruptors, neurotoxins, asthmagens, carcinogens, and mutagens comes with everyday life today, making us all toxic bodies" (2019: 101). Indeed, "the trans-corporeal transits of toxicity seem to spare no place and no body" (Cielemęcka and Åsberg 2019: 102).[21] But they rightfully question the concept of toxicity, asking: "How are we all complicit in who and what gets to count as toxic and in toxic existence at large, with our consumerist lifestyles and dependency on intoxications of all kinds?" (Cielemęcka and Åsberg 2019: 105). But toxicity is not the same for all beings. Certain foods that are edible for humans will be toxic for some nonhumans, and vice versa. Degrees of toxicity will also vary depending on other entanglements constituting a being. But also, their question draws our attention to the various agentic capacities of toxins and whether some toxic products may be generative of new life when they encounter nonhuman beings. Myra J. Hird and Kathryn Yusoff, for example, have pointed to the generative and transformative power of bacteria, pitching them as the "superagents of earth" (2018: 274). They want to move us away from our ongoing anthropo- and biocentric focus and recognize what creative interactions, what they call the "mineral-microbial chatter," actually shape the world we are in and all beings that inhabit it. In fact, as Hird explains, the success of bacteria in shaping the places and environments in which different beings exist is due to their symbiotic relations (2010: 59–60). She explains that "[b]acteria may be generating new life forms not registered by humans and . . . this is what the microcosmos has been doing for the past 3.5 million years" (Hird 2017: 264). Bacterial agentic capacities are extremely impactful. As Heather Davis (2015) points out while discussing the "plastisphere," we need to flip the narrative about plastics and pollution: From the point of view of the nonhuman, they are incredibly generative as they allow for bacteria to thrive and create microbial progeny. We can go so far as to say that humans are living in a "bacterialized" world in which there are important shifts in biodiversity. The future may be bacterial and not human.[22] In any case, the intertwinement of agentic capacities and their impact, across distant space and across multiple species, needs to be acknowledged. Again, and I cannot say it enough, we are entangled in ways that we have yet to uncover. Yusoff, for example, discusses our entanglements with the inorganic. Our way of life, exploiting resources such as coal or oil, has generated another type of entanglement between the living and nonliving, or rather the no-longer-living. She questions whether "this 'life' that we call our own [is] just a vehicle for one last Carboniferous plant ride?" (2015: 212). As we consume the energy produced by burning inorganic life that once was organic, releasing anew potentialities and agentic capacities, our present is literally fueled by the past and projects us into a future in which "[f]ossil fuels make 'ourselves'" (Yusoff 2015: 213). And just as the waste and dead bodies from distant pasts allow humans to exist as they now do, it is imaginable, and anxiety-generating, to think of ourselves as the fuel of future beings. Our waste is already allowing for this to begin unfolding. Our contemporary Anthropocene anxiety has to do with proliferation(s) that may lead to extinction. "Proliferation and extinction mutually subtend each other" (Hird 2017: 252). As Hird puts it, a "discourse of proliferation—of too much muchness—may be articulating this anxiety [named by the Anthropocene]" (2017: 255). It is not so much that life will disappear, leading to a barren Earth that should trouble us. What is most troubling, and which we realize once we contemplate our geo-entanglements, is that life will continue without us and that we will have been responsible for our own extinction.

The proposal that we now live in the Anthropocene, a new geological epoch in which the human being has left a global mark on the Earth system, seems to reinforce our anthropocentric perspective that deems the human to be a superagent. However, we are not such a superagent, despite the fact that anthropogenic activity has been extremely damaging. The human species can be considered to be a toxin[23] insofar as it has had this extensive impact on ecosystems and the whole Earth system. Humans are also toxic to nonhuman animals, their activity being also responsible for the onset of the sixth mass extinction event—the first event of this scope to occur due to non-natural events. But let us pause here and clarify: Which human? All humans?[24] What does it mean to call a new geological epoch after ourselves? The ultimate hubristic act of the most damaging species? As Neimanis et al. put it, "calling an epoch after ourselves does not necessarily demonstrate the humility we may need to espouse" (2015: 68). However, and as Dale Jamieson puts it, "[w]hat makes the Anthropocene a moment of crisis is the recognition of humanity's collective power that is oddly and perhaps paradoxically matched with a widespread feeling of powerlessness" (2016: np). Naming the new epoch in this way points to the crisis and may serve as the recognition of anthropogenic responsibility, the political purpose behind the naming as acknowledged by Crutzen and Stoermer (2000). But again, are all *anthropoi* responsible in the same way? In the last few paragraphs, I have made an abundant use of "we" and "us." While the notion of radical multiple entanglements that I propose with the concept of transjectivity entails that responsibility cannot easily be ascribed to a single unitary agent, it remains that the agentic capacity and impact of individual humans, or some human collectives, do not match that of others. It is a certain wasteful consumerist way of life "enjoyed" by some to the detriment of others—other humans, other species, other spaces, shadow places, past and future lives—that has driven the increase in anthropogenic change and the advent of the Anthropocene along with the sixth mass extinction. That is why we have seen a proliferation of terms proposed as alternatives to "Anthropocene"—such as Capitalocene, Thanatocene, Androcene, Plantationocene, and the already mentioned Wasteocene[25]—which are meant to capture what human activity or which humans are specifically responsible for the new geological epoch but mostly for the overall ecological degradation and bleak futures that lay ahead.

* * *

Are futures necessarily bleak though? For what and for whom? What must we do with the knowledge we can acquire about our transjectivity, manifold entanglements, toxicities, and overall degradation? Again: degradation for whom? Bacteria seem happy! Choosing to revel in the description of how much damage we cause, the toxicities of our entanglements, the magnitude of each toxic entanglement along with the number of those for any individual being, without thinking of how we can move forward is a form of nihilism. What is needed instead is for us to reckon with our entangled beings, the nature of these entanglements, the potential pitfalls—we have encountered and created many—and orient ourselves differently. We need a new ethos. So, while I sympathize with Patricia MacCormack's provocative views in *The Ahuman Manifesto* (2020), I still think there are some futures possible for humans as long as they embrace their entanglements. Just like the death of God opens up new horizons, as Nietzsche eloquently proposes in *The Gay Science* (see Aphorisms 124 and 125), so does the death of the human. But the human we need to see go extinct is the humanist concept of the human, not the human itself. This would amount to a joyful extinction, one that would open up bright futures.[26] What these futures might be and what shape they will take is unclear. So much still needs to be worked out. But one thing is certain: a joyful extinction of the humanist human to take place and for the bright futures to be possible necessitate doing things extremely differently. An affirmative transjective ethos is needed. Indeed, for, as long as we continue to adhere to damaging worldviews and views of ourselves, we will only come up with solutions and changes that are temporary fixes and never quite move us toward these futures; in fact, they will continue to move us closer to the bleak futures that the actual extinction of the human species represent, a future bleak for us but potentially quite bright for all nonhumans. Nevertheless, embracing an affirmative transjective ethos will open up futures in which all beings can thrive and not only the human.

MEANDERING 9
COHABITATING

I live in a small town and my house is on a rather large lot with lots of vegetation and, of course, many nonhuman critters. Squirrels, mice, opossums, raccoons, occasional foxes, groundhogs, rabbits, chipmunks, and skunks come and enjoy my unruly yard which provides them with good shelter and food. In recent years, due to urban development taking over natural spaces, coyotes have been heard and seen in the area, although I have yet to see one in my yard. Neighborhood cats visit regularly since there is plenty of birds: blue jays, sparrows, doves, catbirds, cardinals, warblers, gold and other finches, robins, crows, and woodpeckers. Many bugs and "creepy" crawlers live here as well: bees (like Charlie), bumblebees, wasps, flies, mosquitoes, worms, fireflies, butterflies, moths, ants, stink bugs, sow bugs, ladybugs, occasional dragonflies, and many, many, others. The trees and bushes are diverse and produce different foods: crabapple trees, black walnut trees, mulberry trees, cherry trees, winterberry bushes, and blackberry bushes. Squirrels make a feast every winter of the frozen crabapples. I like to call my yard the local forest. The way my lot[1] is divided means I have two neighbors on the north side, two on the west side, and one on the south side. These yards are manicured and mine stands out as exceptionally wild and unruly. Any attempt at some ordering and controlling is done around my back patio, which looks upon the hustle and bustle of the yard. It is a yard in which I and other critters cohabitate with the plants and the land with its buildings—my house and garage—and fences—protecting neat adjacent lots from the lush growth of my yard—although the one fence to the north was taken down by an exceptionally strong and stubborn vine.

What does this cohabitation mean? Every year, one mother raccoon gives birth to a litter under my back deck, which is covered by a corrugated plastic roof. The deck is raised by some 60 centimeters from the ground and full planks enclose the area under it rather than wooden trellis. It is a perfect spot, which I would also choose if I was looking for a quiet and safe space, with two entrances: critters have dug the ground under the planks to gain access to the area under at the north and south end of the deck. The raccoon litters are anywhere between four and seven kits. I know that they are supposed to get between two and five kits, but I remember vividly one very early morning by a mulberry tree when I heard cracks in the branches above me and then counted seven curious kits up in the tree, observing my every move. That litter was exceptionally large as there are usually four or five of them each year. So, they live under my deck. The trick though is that

FIGURE 9.1 Kits up the crabapple tree.

FIGURE 9.2 Kits by the water bowl.

as the weather gets nice, I set up my back deck as my outdoor office and spend my entire day there working. It converts to my living leisure space in the evening as I have dinner there and usually watch a movie on my computer with earphones on so as not to disturb neighbors and cohabitants in my yard. During the day, the raccoons' presence was mostly felt through the light wild smell of their furs sifting through the planks of the deck.

Raccoons come out at dusk, although this past summer they also came out a few times during the day. The north entrance to their den is next to a crabapple tree that grows on the corner of the deck. Every night, while we cohabitate, they come out and climb the trunk (Figures 9.1 and 9.2).

They go up the tree or start wandering in the yard, stopping at the water bowl I have out there for them.[2] I also leave them some snacks: apple cores and vegetable scraps. At the beginning of my outdoors season, they usually come out when I am silently watching a movie. Since everything is so quiet, they venture out and are always surprised to find me there. As they get used to my presence and understand I am happy to share the space with them, they come out even if I am busy preparing dinner on the barbecue, which is very close to the crabapple tree they climb. I talk to them and they sometimes talk back. They are extremely curious and sometimes come way too close to me on the deck. I say "too close" not out of my personal discomfort—I don't have any—but because it is not good for them to get used to getting so close to humans as other humans may not have my gentle demeanor with them, to put it mildly. So, I shoo them away gently, under mama's watch from where she is monitoring her kits a couple of meters away from the deck by the water bowl. After a bit of frolicking around involving running on my railing and fighting in the bushes by the deck, mama gathers them and leads them off into the yard. They sometimes come back later for a quick visit. One night I was quite startled to see a kit right between my feet under the table as I was watching a movie. I laughed and the kit went away. They also like to wander on the corrugated roof. One morning I completely took them by surprise by talking to them from my upstairs office window that looks out just over the roof. Hearing my voice, they rushed to the window and saw me inside through the window screen. "What on earth was the back deck human doing up there?"

In the summer of 2020, one of the kits was pretty rowdy. It was always the first one out, would pick fights with siblings, and wander off from the pack. One night, a very loud dog started barking as they were out drinking, eating, and washing their paws at the water bowl. They all scooted back to the crabapple tree with mama climbing up last. But the rowdy kit was missing. Mama stopped halfway up and looked at me. I had counted only four up the tree too so I knew why she was concerned. She hung out there searching intently with her concerned look, looking to her right and to her left, at me who was now standing about 2 meters from her, also searching the yard. I asked her, "Where did it go?" And then said, "It will come back." The dog finally stopped barking and after some two minutes the little bugger came back running from the willow tree in the middle of the backyard where it had climbed for safety. I laughed in relief as it rejoined its mother and litter up the crabapple tree. I think it was the same bugger that was so rowdy during the day sometimes. It would start fighting with siblings and they would bump and bang around

FIGURE 9.3 Kits playing on the railing.

right under my feet. They would also play with the vine growing along the old chimney that comes out from under the middle of the deck by the house. I sometimes would take a break and play with them, pulling the vine with them pulling back. Rowdy kit showed its snout the one time in the little cutout space by the chimney as if to say, "Hey! That's my vine!" I am always sad when they leave. They always do, eventually, until the following spring. I hope rowdy kit hasn't gotten into too much trouble since the last time we saw each other. That summer they were followed by a pair of skunks that wandered around the deck every evening. Their visits were a little stinkier and not as rowdy (Figures 9.3 and 9.4).

Other occupants of the back deck were a couple of mourning doves. They nested in the vine growing up the old chimney. Again, a perfect spot as they would not be visible to predators through the corrugated plastic roof and they were protected from rain and snow. Their first brood was too early in the spring for me to be a bother to them. The summer office was not open yet. But when it started being nice and I started to sit outside for an hour or two to read, they were up to their second brood. While one of the parents is nesting, the other fetches food. It happened more than once that a startled dove would land on the deck railing less than a meter from me because this was their landing spot to

FIGURE 9.4 Curious kit.

then hop into the nest. What was I doing there? Was I to share this space with them? Of course, this was not in the doves' plans, but there I was. I would talk to them gently when coming out or moving about on the deck so as not to startle them. I entreated them to not be scared. They continued their business as I did mine. It was a little tricky having to set up the deck for the summer since the patio table was by the wall right next to the old chimney. I managed to pull it away from there carefully, avoiding too much noise and reassuring them as I was doing so. By then, two babies had hatched. So I was doing this whole operation under the watch of at least three doves. If I was inside the house, they would use the patio furniture once the babies started trying to fly. Once everyone left, I could see the parents decided to build a new nest for their next brood as I saw them fly around with pieces of twig and weeds toward the front of the

FIGURES 9.5&9.6 Doves nesting in the vine.

house. All my carefulness was not enough to convince them to try that third brood close to me. Or maybe it was the raccoons under the deck pulling on the vine? (Figures 9.5 and 9.6).

There are many ways in which one could experience one's yard. There is big business in helping homeowners to keep theirs well-ordered and manicured. Yard tools, furniture, and decorations are vastly advertised at the tail end of winter because one must exercise control on this space if one is to enjoy it. Gardening advice abounds on how to exercise said control, all for the enjoyment of the human. Products are sold to facilitate such enjoyment and combat the proliferation of weeds and undesirable bugs and pests. I use "combat" purposefully here as this is all portrayed as a battle one must wage and one must win. Traps are sold and "pest" control companies advertise their services for you to have a critter-free yard. This, however, is yet another way for humans to ignore their entanglements, place themselves in a position of exception, and impose their tight—and detrimental—control on their surroundings and the beings they share them with. The most common way of existing in one's *environs* is not by way of cohabitation, it is not a careful approach that lets beings be and fosters sharing the world and one's experiences. Now I still exercise some level of control. Not all critters are welcome. Rats are not as they will come inside the house and chew wires. When they started visiting the yard a couple of years back to feed off the spillovers from the

MEANDERING 9   149

bird feeder I had traps set up by the garage, but I also removed the feeder that was attracting them—sorry birds, but you have plenty to eat in the vegetation and I only set up the feeder in my sight so I could observe you and enjoy your flying around. Now I have to settle for watching you bathe and hearing you ruffle in the bushes, except for when a catbird or two comes and mocks me on the deck railing, which they often do. I only tolerate mice—the other wire chewers—in the yard and not in the house. Traps are set in the basement if they are so unlucky as to make noise in a spot that tells me they are inside. Carpenter ants are also not welcome because they will cause structural damage to the house. But when I get offered to treat the outside of my house with chemicals to keep them away from there as well, my answer is no. Outside is their turf as much as it is mine. I occasionally collect wasps and bees inside the house trying to get out and bumping into a window, wondering why they can't get through. I catch and release them outside. House centipedes are not so lucky. I know it is beneficial to keep them and that they are doing real work of keeping things clean, but they trigger a visceral reaction in me. As a friend of mine says, "Too many legs!" Yet, I have learned to sweep them out of my sight instead of smashing them if I do encounter them in the basement. Spiders are okay. Flies fly in and fly out.

As much as is possible, I embrace an ethics of grace, of letting be. I understand that our beings cohabitate, share the world. We mostly are minding our own business, a business that is never entirely autonomous and crosses paths or is dependent on or shaped by the business of others. Understanding this entails providing care in the form of putting out a water bowl, not blocking the access to the area under the deck, not raking all the leaves, and leaving areas of the yard wild so that we can all come to enjoy it.

7 ETHICAL THRIVING

Reconceptualizing the human, and all other beings, in terms of transjectivity does not evacuate the question of ethics. Quite the contrary! This reconceptualization exacerbates it and requires that we rethink ethicality, or what it means for a human to thrive ethically. If we no longer conceive of the human as an individual but as a dividual—a radically entangled assemblage who does not have agency but instead has agentic capacity intertwined with the multiple agentic capacities permeating it—the question of ethics is muddied. Is it perhaps rendered impossible? Indeed, if an ethics must offer a set of rules and guidelines for practical deliberation and action, then an ethics for transjective beings will be impossible. Any attempt at designing such an ethics would amount to a hubristic move that rests on a misconception of the type of "agent" the human is. An ethics that provides rules and guidelines must hold on to a notion of an autonomous rational agent capable of directing its will according to said rules and guidelines and pursuing a course of action that aligns with them, pursuing the good with some degree of success. However, as we have seen, the human as transjective is anything but this type of agent. And more than this, there is no notion of absolute good or bad, which we could aspire to achieve or combat. Such measuring sticks for moral judgment do not exist. Beauvoir's ethics of ambiguity, the situational existential ethics of Sartre, and Aristotle's virtue ethics and its more recent iterations—in the works of Rosalind Hursthouse or Alasdair MacIntyre—also recognize this.[1] But, they also all more or less depend on a conception of the moral subject that still posits it as capable of practical deliberation and enacting its choice willfully and rationally. Aristotle's *phronemos* is a rational person who possesses the practical wisdom allowing them to recognize the virtuous path to take in any given situation, the mean between a vice by excess and a vice by default. While we can appreciate that this ethics is adaptable to circumstances and does not posit fixed ethical goals and behaviors—courage is a virtue but to be courageous will look very different according to the person involved and their situation—it remains that rationality is the key tool animating this ethics and its pursuit of the good life and *eudaimonia*.

While I am not denying that humans engage in practical deliberation and attempt to carry on their choices in a rational manner or at least with some intent, what I have discussed throughout this book shows that there is a lot more going on than these relatively simple processes of rule assessment and following. What I am proposing is that we need to shift from hubris to humility: we need to recognize that our capacity to act in the way we intend is very limited, no matter how rationally informed our assessment of the situation and our choice of action may be, and that this intention itself is the outcome of entangled collective agentic capacities. We can't ascribe praise or blame to an individual since there is no such thing as an autonomous individual: all we have are transjective beings. This poses an important problem as it seems we need some way to police and regulate behavior if we are to live together and thrive as a collective.[2] Quite simply, we are looking for the means to encourage behavior that is positive for the collective as well as for the means to punish behavior that is detrimental. For this, we need to be able to ascribe responsibility.

A New Ethos: Joyful Orientation

I agree with Barad, Braidotti, and many others that the new onto-epistemology we are adopting requires a new ethics. Or is it the other way around? What if our concern with the care of the self leads us to a new onto-epistemology because we recognize that the existing one is alienating for the self along with its type of ethics that operates with norms and prescriptions that amount to ideals impossible to fulfill? But what we need is not an ethics that is new with regard to its content—that is, new sets of norms and prescriptions—because this kind of approach to ethics is flawed and alienating. Instead, we need a new ethos, an attitude toward ourselves and toward life. This ethos will guide our decision-making differently. Let us consider Spinoza's take on virtue. As Gatens and Lloyd explain, according to Spinoza, passions modulate the intensity of reason. This means that "[w]e are always determined by the necessities of our natures" (1999: 49). Spinoza's virtue lays in the "joyful passage from passivity to activity" (Gatens and Lloyd 1999: 7). This passage is effected once one recognizes the role passions play alongside reason and one orients oneself accordingly. "By understanding the passions we restructure them into rational affects . . . understanding the operation of the causes that determine us is the source of our becoming free" (Gatens and Lloyd 1999: 50). If we apply this to the reconceptualization of the human as transjective, this means that an understanding of the fact that we are radically entangled beings—permeated by multiple agentic capacities and permeating them as well, beings that are done and undone by their intertwined entanglements—will modulate the way in which we engage in practical deliberation and moral judgment. As Karen Barad puts it, "[l]earning to intra-act responsibly as part of the world means understanding that 'we' are not the only active beings—though this is never justification for deflecting our responsibility onto others" (2007: 391). Responsibility remains key even in a transjective ethics.

My reflections on ethical thriving attempt to weave together the various elements of transjectivity that I have explored in the previous chapters and also attempt to make vulner—ability the path to that thriving.[3] Recall that I advocated for a performance of exposure, as put forward by Stacy Alaimo.[4] Performing our exposure, embracing our vulner—ability, is the key to the affirmative ethics of joy I am proposing. Consider the active verbs used: perform and embrace. Not merely accept, which seems much more passive. Not a "Yeah, sure, I guess this is how it is" but rather a "Yes! Of course, this is how things and beings are and I will nurture this as best I can!" One accepts a state of affairs. One enacts a dynamic becoming. An affirmative ethics of joy considers the "self as a question rather than a being" (MacCormack 2016: 106n2). We can only ask the question if we already acknowledge that we are transjective beings. If we hang on to antiquated notions of autonomy, individuation, and agency, then the self is not a question but rather something fixed, some kind of ideal one has to aim for. A transjective affirmative ethics of joy does not have a fixed ideal. It focuses on the process and what attitudes inflect this process.

What does it mean concretely to embrace vulner—ability? To orient oneself with joy? To perform joy and celebrate life? To affirm life in all its instances and give it a "sacred yes" as Nietzsche would have it?[5] Rosi Braidotti calls for an affirmative nomadic ethics which "proclaims the need to construct collectively positions of active, positive interconnections and relations that can sustain a web of mutual dependence, an ecology of multiple belongings" (2006: 250).[6] She also says in her more recent work that "[f]reedom is written into our system as the desire to expand and enhance our existence; this is desire as *potentia*" (Braidotti 2019: 155). As zoe/geo/techno framed subjects, we are "transversal entit[ies], fully immersed in and immanent to a network of human and non-human relations" (Braidotti 2019: 158). The ethical ideal then, according to her, is to "mobilize the active powers of life in the affirmative mode of *potentia*" (Braidotti 2019: 158). It is a *zoe*-driven ethos (Braidotti 2019: 161).

Before discussing what this may mean concretely, let us consider the notion of "joy." Joy is not necessarily glee, although it can be. The Spinozist-Nietzschean affirmative stance and ethos which is portrayed as joyful and delightful does not evacuate tensions or pain. As Massumi explains, "[j]oy can be very disruptive, it can even be very painful. What I think Spinoza and Nietzsche are getting at is joy as affirmation, an assuming by the body of its potentials, its assuming of a posture that intensifies its powers of existence. The moment of joy is the co-presence of those potentials, in the context of a bodily becoming" (2015: 44). Or, as Rosi Braidotti puts it, "[t]o assert the force of affirmative ethics . . . does not mean to dismiss the reality of conflict and pain" (2019: 154). This can entail a lot of pain as one experiences oneself as the radically materially entangled being one is, as the vulner—able being one is. But the opening is an increase of *potentia*, which is at the heart of ethical thriving. The goal is not merely to survive, but to thrive. MacCormack explains: "Enriching ethical encounters are also expressions of power. Affective expressions which elicit joy and novel passions emerge through each entity's capacity to act and be affective not as what they are but that they are.. . . Ethical encounters are jubilant, joyous encounters of both affectivity and liberty" (2016: 16).[7]

So again, and with this in mind, I ask: How does a transjective ethos of life affirmation and orientation toward joy modulate our decision-making and action? First, it forces us to embrace humility. If we understand ourselves as transjective, we know that the practical deliberation process is impacted by the multiple entanglements (of) which we are.[8] As Barad explains, "[e]thics is therefore not about right response to a radically exterior/ized other, but about responsibility and accountability for the lively relationalities of becoming of which we are a part" (2007: 393).[9]

In previous chapters, I have discussed the various negative outcomes of opening oneself, of performing the exposure. Negative traumatic experiences provide a good lens through which we can understand our entangled beings. But, as you will also recall, I have claimed that this insight applies to any and all experiences. Traumatic experiences are a kind of magnifying lens. Still, this attention paid to trauma begs the question of how we can achieve ethical flourishing while experiencing both types of experiences—those that contribute to an affirmation of life and those that disrupt and tear it apart, or in any case try to. As I have also explained, experiences had by other beings also become our experiences, no matter how much we may try to withdraw from them. In fact, as the radically entangled beings we are, we cannot. While we may be much more readily willing to accept communicative joy and happiness instead of the violent assaults on life—that of others as well as ours—it is essential that we also not only accept but actively embrace those assaults. As already established, any kind of assault—big, small, racially motivated or not, gender or sexual orientation driven or not—affects the transjective web of relations that constitutes us and in which we exist. The violent and lethal assault of a Black man affects that Black man's being the most radically when he loses his life, but we are also all affected by it as the affective fabric in which we live is transformed, so that even this white privileged lady typing these words is at the receiving end of the assault. Granted: never to the same magnitude but still potentially very powerfully as one can choose to open oneself to it and commit to action to change things or not. Ethicality is always political. The ethical orientation one chooses for oneself is always also political because we never exist in isolation from our relations. Therefore, the pressing questions are: How will one orient oneself to others and to life following this violent tear in the affective fabric of transjectivity? Will one ignore or will one engage? And how will that inflect the affective fabric of our existence?

Relational Care

We must transform the ontological fact of our vulner—ability into an ethical stance through which we embrace it, in which we actively perform it and open ourselves to the acts of violence and assaults on life so that we may better resist them. This openness may lead to affirmative empathy: saying yes to affects, whatever they may be—and orienting our action accordingly, as much as this is possible. As Sara Ahmed says, "the very project of survival requires we take something other into our bodies. Survival makes us vulnerable in that it requires we let what is 'not us' in; to survive we open ourselves up, and *we keep the orifices of the body open*"

(2015: 83). Replacing "survival" and "survive" with "thriving" and "thrive" captures what I am advocating for as a transjective ethics: only through such an opening and joyful embrace will ethical thriving be possible. As I have argued earlier in the book,[10] vulner—ability is generative, thanks to the multiple entanglements of which we are. Understanding and embracing this is the only pathway to the thriving I am advocating for. This requires an affective orientation toward joy and a performance of our exposure and that of others, a nurturing of ontological vulner—ability in oneself and in all others.[11] With Patricia MacCormack, I see the ethical address as grounded in a view that "sees the dividuation of life in opposition to identity, as it acknowledges the inevitable connection between living bodies . . . the individual is constituted only by its connection to other individuals" (2016: 4).

This represents a new version of the care of the self, encountered famously in the later writings of Foucault. This new care of the self is a relational care, a care that understands the relational nature of transjective being and exercises itself with relationality as the heart of its preoccupation and decision-making. An essential part of the ethical orientation that is needed is the acknowledgment and nurturing of our ontological vulner—ability. Understanding our vulner—ability as grounded in our manifold entanglements opens the way for embracing our being and embracing an ethos that can lead to an existential mode of delight: that of living as entangled, which comes with both generative and not so generative affect. We are like Pando the Trembling Giant, a grove of quaking aspens in Utah—or, more accurately, only one tree since all trees share the same root system and are genetically identical to each other. Pando is the largest living organism on Earth, covering 107 acres, and is one of the oldest organisms, clocking in at some eighty thousand years old. Pando is also a complex ecosystem, host to numerous nonhuman animals and plants. It is a transjective being, vulner—able, multiple, an assemblage of intermingled collective agentic capacities on which its thriving depends but that can also threaten it. It is also itself part of a wider assemblage through its entanglements with the Earth and other ecosystems. We are also like polyps, as discussed in Chapter 2. We are inosculated trees. We are one of many transjective critters inhabiting land, entwined with it. Relationality . . . entanglement . . . interconnectivity . . . whichever way we want to refer to it, that ontological fact which calls for the compound word I have chosen to express how impossible it is to exist without relations, to disentangle, to shut off connections: transjectivity. Care for the self as care for transjectivity is an ethics of care that understands the self's well-being as entirely dependent on the well-being of the whole. As Brian Massumi explains, "[w]e participate jointly in life. We don't have to give up care for the self, however—only the self-centeredness. We have to embed care for the self in relational becomings—for the existential empowerment of the self and the other" (2015: 201). As I have argued earlier in the book, and continuously throughout it as well, conceiving the human in terms of transjectivity does not entail rejecting the notion of selfhood, rather it means understanding it as always done and undone, entangled in its relations, and as being able to exercise a different type of agency. A transjective ethics still cares for the self. While its care is not self-centered, it is no longer anthropocentric and rejects any notion of human exceptionalism. We are transjective just like all other beings we are in relation with. As such, the care of our self is intimately intertwined with, indeed inseparable from, the care of/for others. Puig de la Bellacasa claims, "[c]are is a force distributed across a multiplicity of agencies and materials and supports our worlds as a thick mesh of relational obligation" (2017: 20). Being in charge of our well-being entails also being in charge of that of others. Thus, rather than decrease human responsibility, the reconceptualization of the human as transjective exacerbates it, rendering us responsible for the thriving of all.

Responsibility/Response—ability

In a world of transjectivity, responsibility is increased and our duty to care magnified because no being can thrive on its own.[12] As Puig de la Bellacasa indicates, the carer is implied in a doing that affects them: "Care obliges in ways embedded in everyday doings and agencies, it obliges because it is inherent to relations of interdependency" (2017: 120). Ethical responsibility is in fact very limited in a world of autonomous agents who can look after themselves and whose well-being is not dependent on other beings or their relations to them. The increased responsibility generated by transjectivity, which we should understand in terms of response-ability—I come back to this below—is only so for the human who can understand itself as the kind of being it is, can assess its agentic capacity, and can embrace humility and exercise care. To those who may be tempted to take this as a return of human exceptionalism and anthropocentrism, I would respond with Stephanie Clare who rightfully claims "it is humans whom we address in our writing and it is, arguably, human lives, enmeshed in more-than-human-worlds, that we care most about" (2016: 68).[13] Indeed, our interpellation is to transjective beings like us. I write this book for human readers. I make my plea for a transjective ethos as one that can concern other human transjective beings and lead them to ethical thriving. We are the beings that are preoccupied with ethicality and with regulating our living together.[14] We are or can be made aware of the power of our agentic capacity, of the limitations we face, of our entanglements, of our duty to care because, in a web of well-intentioned humble care, we are also cared for. We ought not to engage in ethical relations or embrace a specific ethos because we might gain something from it but rather because we care. We care because we are concerned. But caring, "to care," entails an active undertaking that concern lacks, as Puig de la Bellacasa reminds us (2017: 42). Because we care we end up caring more.[15] As the kind of being that can know and reflect on one's own being as transjective, there is a duty for us to exercise our agentic capacity in the least negative way. Now, of course, we can never entirely predict the range and amount of impact of our deeds, and what was construed as a careful and respectful course of action might turn out wrong. We need to accept the idea that we cannot fully know and therefore cannot entirely predict outcomes, but we also need to accept the responsibility, even when the outcomes differ from what we planned. This amounts to a relational ethics of care that rests on humility.

Before turning to responsibility, let us dwell a bit more on the notion of care as a practice, an active mode of relating and existing. If, as Rosi Braidotti claims, "[e]thics starts with the composition of transversal subject assemblages ... that actualize the unrealized or virtual potential of what 'we' are capable of becoming" (2019: 54), then we must actively seek to exist as the transjective beings we are and foster any and all relations in which we are entangled.[16] Posthumanist subjectivity being a practical project, according to Braidotti, requires our ethical orientation needs to be articulated in a praxis (2019: 74). This must be accomplished in the mode of care. Any doing, any practice, needs to be infused by care whereby "caring [is] a transformative ethos rather than a normative ethics" (Puig de la Bellacasa 2017: 67).[17] Importantly for Puig de la Bellacasa, care is a doing that always already unfolds in and through the intermingled relations of the world. Care is not only a human doing but rather the doing of all beings. It is "embedded in the practices that maintain webs of relationality and is always happening in between" (Puig de la Bellacasa

2017: 166). While all beings exercise care, not all beings may be aware of their own relationality and attached response—ability. That is why an ethical address to the human, an interpellation, can remind the transjective human of its embeddedness, which comes with a duty to care and a duty to embrace response—ability. To cite Puig de la Bellacasa once more, "[c]are obliges in ways embedded in everyday doings and agencies; it obliges because it is inherent to relations of interdependency" (2017: 120). Care can take many shapes and forms and, surprisingly, can also entail an ethics of grace, of letting be, which requires active affirmation of the radical alterity of those others with whom we are still entangled and respecting their own projects and assemblages, refusing to superimpose our human constructs on them (MacCormack 2016: 69–72). That too is an affirmation of life and its differential thriving.

Let us delve into the notion of responsibility here: What can a transjective ethical responsibility be? How can anyone be responsible for anything as transjective beings? This passage from Barad expresses the challenge rather nicely:

> There are no singular causes. And there are no individual agents of change. Responsibility is not ours alone. And yet our responsibility is greater than it would be if it were ours alone. . . . We are accountable for and to not only specific patterns of marks on bodies—that is, the differential patterns of mattering of the world of which we are a part—but also the exclusions that we participate in enacting. Therefore, accountability and responsibility must be thought in terms of what matters and what is excluded from mattering. . . . There is no discrete "I" that precedes its actions . . . even in our becoming there is no "I" separate from the intra-active becoming of the world. (2007: 394)

Ethical responsibility and reciprocity are intertwined but are not evenly distributed. Transjective beings are all transjective but not in the same way. Their selves, their bodies, their entanglements, their locations, their temporalities, and their ways of existing in a collective—subjectively and materially—will vary to a great degree. Accordingly, we need to understand reciprocity in different terms, as discussed earlier, and we need to focus on the "ability" of response—ability. Donna Haraway says "[c]ompanion species infect each other all the time. . . . We are all responsible to and for shaping conditions for multispecies flourishing in the face of terrible histories, and sometimes joyful histories too, but we are not all response-able in the same ways. The differences matter—in ecologies, economies, species, lives" (2016b: 29).[18]

I already quoted Puig de la Bellacasa who claims that care entails an obligation at the heart of our interdependent relations. But, and very importantly, "[c]are troubles reciprocity . . . because the living web of care is not one where every giving involves taking, nor every taking will involve giving . . . reciprocity in as well as possible care circulates multilaterally, collectively: it is shared" (Puig de la Bellacasa 2017: 121). While there is widespread agentic capacity and multiple webs of interconnectivity, not all agentic capacity is the same in its nature, its scope, or strength. While the relationality of transjectivity is manifold, relations are asymmetrical, as I discussed earlier in the book. And because agentic capacity unfolds in the way it does, reciprocity is asymmetrical as well. As we have seen in considering Myra Hird's work in the previous chapter, there is a whole environmental dimension to the transjective human vulnerability as vulnerable to "living and non-living earth processes. This vulnerability, in turn, calls for a *heightened*, not diminished, assumption of responsibility" (2013: 107). According to Hird, we are reminded that "nature relentlessly flows, but not in ways that are necessarily compatible with human flourishing" (2013: 115). This flow is asymmetrical, forcing us to review our notion of reciprocity, but it does not do away with responsibility. This responsibility is tied with a duty to earnestly seek an understanding of our being and, following that, embrace it. Discussing her notion of transcorporeality, which, as we have seen, is an inspiration to my notion of transjectivity, Stacy Alaimo explains that

> the ethical space of trans-corporeality is never an elsewhere but is always already here, in whatever compromised, ever-catalyzing form. A nearly unrecognizable form of ethics emerges—one that demands that we inquire about all of the substances that surround us, those for which we may be somewhat responsible, those that may harm us, those that may harm others, and those that we suspect we do not know enough about. A trans-corporeal ethics calls us to somehow find ways of navigating through the simultaneously material, economic, and cultural systems that are so harmful to the living world and yet so difficult to contest or transform. (2010: 18)

We need to acquire this knowledge and understanding and put it to work in terms of embracing the ethos we need. What I propose is that the only possible ethics for transjective beings is one that does not focus on rules and guidelines for action but instead puts its whole emphasis on embracing an ethos, an orientation toward life, an attitude toward oneself and others—human and nonhuman—that seeks their thriving, individually and collectively.[19] This ethos entails a few things: knowing oneself and others and embracing oneself and others as transjective and ontologically vulner—able; adopting an affective orientation toward joy; making affirmation of life the core of one's approach to existence.

Performing the exposure does not mean stopping oneself from putting up any resistance to anything that is done to someone. It does not amount to passivity. On the contrary, it means protecting the thriving of life in oneself and in others.[20] Therefore, if one is assaulted—physically or otherwise—one is justified in defending oneself. Embracing our vulner—ability is not a simple opening up of oneself to any and all injuries and abuses. It is also the ability to relate with other beings while recognizing and respecting the vulner—ability of all and orientating relations toward thriving rather than impeding life. I have discussed Judith Butler's views on vulnerability in Chapter 5 as they relate to precariousness and the relational self at the heart of Cavarero's, Brison's, and Freedman's analyses. Since *Precarious Lives*, Butler has continued to investigate the ethical and political problems we face when we live in collectives that render some lives precarious and non-grievable.[21] In her *The Force of Nonviolence*, she explores an ethics of nonviolence that recognizes relations and rejects individualism. Recall that, for her, relations "can be as destructive as they can be sustaining" (Butler 2020: 9). Here again Butler's analysis focuses on the social fabric of our existence all the while discussing life and saying that it requires infrastructure "not simply as an external support but as an immanent feature of life itself. This is a materialist point we deny only at our own peril" (2020: 198).[22] They argue that the social bond is infused with destructive potential and, as we have seen, it is not only the social bond but any relation, any entanglement, that has this destructive potential. As unbearable as it may be, or as it may be felt and experienced, it has to be preserved.[23] This means that in protecting oneself from violence, one needs to engage in protective action that does not enact violence. As they put it:

> the self I am trying to defend is not just me but all those relations that define and sustain me, and those relations can, and should be, extended indefinitely beyond local units like family and community.

If the self I'm trying to defend is also in some sense related to the person I'm tempted to kill, I have to make sure not to do violence to that relation, because that's also me. One could go further: I'm also attacking myself by attacking that person, since I am breaking a social bond that we have between us. (Gessen 2020: np)

Again, Butler's preoccupations are with the social and so are mine. After all, as I said at the start of this chapter, ethicality and living together are central to the transjective human. What Butler says here applies to any relations—social, intersubjective, intrasubjective even, and, of course, material.

This affirmative ethics, with its joyful pursuit and affirmative empathy, is an ethics that affirms life, a *zoe*-driven ethics. What does the "affirmative" mean here? Importantly, and as already said, it does not consist in "denying negativity, but in reworking it outside the dialectical oppositions. That is necessary because negative passions diminish our relational competence and deny our vital interdependence on others" (Braidotti 2019: 167). The affirmation is of what fosters life, what supports and sustains webs of entanglements and potential new experiences of growth. As Braidotti adds, "[a]n ethically empowering mode of relation increases one's *potentia* and creates one's ability to take in and on the world, which is the common nature, or rather the common ground, for all living entities" (2019: 169). It is a dynamic articulation of our capacity to affect and be affected (Braidotti 2019: 171). Thus, the answer to the common objection to this approach to ethics can be articulated. This objection offers that an affirmative ethics seems to require that one affirms the good and the evil and that it makes it impossible to disavow evildoers or even to consider anything as evil or bad given that these would presumably be the outcome of a pursuit to thrive. Quite simply, the mass murderer or psychopathic torturer of humans or nonhumans is pursuing what they deem to be good and their own affirmation of life, the satisfaction of their passions and desires. Why can't that pursuit be affirmed and how can we label it as bad? Quite simply, "ethical behaviour is what can activate and increase relational capacities (*potentia*) and the unethical is what restricts or hampers them" (Braidotti 2018: 221).

In their "Postscript" to *The Force of Nonviolence*, Butler declares: "[A] new imaginary is required—an egalitarian imaginary that apprehends the interdependency of lives" (2020: 203).[24] This egalitarian imaginary can truly be unearthed and embraced once we consider all modes of relationality that constitute us, the subjective and the material. This is what transjectivity offers and what a transjective ethos entails: thinking ourselves, others—human and nonhuman—and the world as the ongoing dynamic web of relations they are, always in flux, always being done and undone, always vulner—able. This is a view that brings delight as we revel in the joy of life affirming itself and thriving, in whatever form it comes. Braidotti claims that transformative energy is at the core of affirmative ethics (2019: 175). There is what she calls an "inexhaustible potential" to engage in "multiple actualizations of yet unexplored interconnections, across and with humans and non-humans" (2019: 175). This is the portrait of transjective beings thriving through their affirmation of their ontological reality as vulner—able beings and through their active and joyful pursuit of the multiple entanglements of which they always already are a part and which always already constitute them.

* * *

What are some concrete, mundane, everyday enactments of a transjective affirmative ethics of joy? Keeping one's yard somewhat wild and resisting the urge to rake all the dead leaves that cover the grass and provide a good shelter for little critters, pollinators, and other bugs when spring makes itself known. Helping a bee in its project, whatever it might be. Opening one's body to a foreign substance to sustain oneself—drinking, eating, and breathing—or to support one's immune system—inoculation. Playing with a rowdy kit and welcoming its racoon family under one's deck each spring—in fact, eagerly waiting for them to settle and manifest themselves instead of calling the pest control company. Thanking the land as multiple and as the ground of our entanglement and therefore of who we are. Experiencing fear but digging into the experience and understanding the multiple affects traversing it so as to no longer fear. Feeling deep affirmative empathy: seeing, acknowledging, embracing, and seeking to unearth the manifold that moves all that is—the good, the bad, and the ugly. Bearing witness and committing to change, all the while embracing humility as one of many agentic capacities with which we dance our dance of living and thriving. The world is in rough shape and the task may seem daunting. But it only seems so if we do not adopt the transjective ethos of joy and affirmation I have discussed. Embracing it, we can take a deep breath and move forward, changing all our relations, ourselves, and the world as we do so.

NOTES

Introduction

1 In his *The Thing: A Phenomenology of Horror* (2014), Dylan Trigg responds to some philosophical attempts to focus on materiality, mostly speculative realism and object-oriented ontology (he targets Meillassoux in particular), by offering to reinstate phenomenology as xenophenomenology: a phenomenology of the human and the nonhuman (5). By focusing on Merleau-Ponty's notion of the flesh, Trigg is able to tackle the human and the unhuman that are at the heart of the subject, with porous boundaries between the two (2014: 52-53). This, as he explains, means that there is an alien materiality to the body that breaks us away from the self (Trigg 2014: 77). After a detailed analysis in which he also invokes Freud's notion of the uncanny, he concludes: "[W]e have encountered the unhuman realm manifest precisely at the edge of experience, as that which evades language, reshapes subjectivity, and, finally, establishes itself as that most familiar thing—*the body*" (Trigg 2014: 146). While Trigg's approach is certainly of interest to me, and the notion that there is an ineffability of the material inscription of experiences resonates with what I will discuss in Chapter 5, I do think that Merleau-Ponty's notion of the flesh still falls short of talking about materiality itself.

2 My approach therefore aligns with diffractive reading as introduced by new materialist and feminist materialist thinkers I will be working with. Geerts and Carstens define it in the following: "Diffraction does not foreground rejection and denial . . . but focuses on stimulating dialogue between divergent and convergent points of view" (Geerts & Carstens 2019: 919). Dolphijn and van der Tuin also speak of the new reading, or new metaphysics, that new materialism offers indicating that it "says 'yes, *and*' to all of these intellectual traditions, traversing them all, creating strings of thought that, in turn, create a remarkably powerful and fresh 'rhythm' in academia today" (2012: 89). Their work offers a great analysis of the key elements making what they call "new materialism" an essential mode of thinking such as transversality and anti-dualist thinking.

3   I return to this philosophical anxiety related to nihilism and relativism in the first section of Chapter 4.

4   A claim made in a November 2020 talk by Gorazd Andrejč.

5   There are many books that aim to define posthumanism and provide an introduction to it for readers. I only mention a few here: Francesca Ferrando's *Philosophical Posthumanism* (Bloomsbury, 2019); Stefan Herbrechter's *Posthumanism: A Critical Analysis* (Bloomsbury, 2013); Cary Wolfe's *What Is Posthumanism?* (University of Minnesota Press, 2010); and David Roden's *Posthuman Life: Philosophy at the Edge of the Human* (Routledge, 2015). I have also attempted to circumscribe a definition in the introduction I co-authored for *From Deleuze and Guattari to Posthumanism: Philosophies of Immanence* (Bloomsbury, 2022) and in a couple of articles (Daigle 2021 and 2020).

6   Donna Haraway may be the most notorious example of that when, in *Staying With the Trouble* (2016), she states that she prefers to think in terms of compost and humusities (32).

7   The notion of curation was suggested by Matthew Hayler in his talk "Posthumanism in Practice" (April 21, 2022, https://www.youtube.com/watch?v=hKlijvOZU9g).

Meandering 2

1   Sharing those worries, Indigenous scholar Hayden King, who contributed to drafting Ryerson University's (now Toronto Metropolitan University) land acknowledgment, expressed regrets in doing so. See https://www.cbc.ca/radio/unreserved/redrawing-the-lines-1.4973363/i-regret-it-hayden-king-on-writing-ryerson-university-s-territorial-acknowledgement-1.4973371.

2   This is a very important endeavor for Canadian Indigenous peoples as I write this. Representatives of First Nations have recently met with Pope Francis to communicate the history of their ancestors, of those who never returned from the residential schools but also of survivors, thereby seeking a papal apology for the wrong doings of the Catholic church on Canadian soil. At the same time, various Indigenous groups and communities are pushing for a systematic search of former residential school locations to identify potential burial sites containing bodies and unmarked graves. At the time of writing this meandering, more than 1,800 confirmed or suspected unmarked graves have been identified with possibly many more to be found.

3   Thanks to Mitch for giving me permission to include it here.

Chapter 1

1 Kim TallBear reminds posthumanist and new materialist scholars that the novelty of their views is far from novel. She points out that Indigenous standpoints "never forgot the interrelatedness of all things" (2017: 180). TallBear further points out that Indigenous ontologies have been rendered invisible or devalued, considered as mere "beliefs" by Western thinkers. She wants the new materialists to reconsider their claim to newness, saying, "The new materialists may take the intellectual intervention that grounds vital-materialist creed as something new in the world. But the fundamental insights are not new for everyone. They are ideas that, not so roughly translated, undergird what we can call an indigenous metaphysic: that matter is lively" (2017: 198–9). In this regard, Simone Bignall proposes that a genuine conversation between Indigenous and non-Indigenous scholars take place for the decolonization of disciplines and academe to unfold (2022: 12). She says: "Indigenous philosophies contribute material for a cosmopolitan (and therefore less Eurocentric), nonhumanist conceptualization of humanity, which we might properly refer to as 'alter-humanism'" (2022: 15). Bignall advocates for the paradigm of excolonialism, a contraction of "exit-from-colonisation," "an ethos of relationality and a political program of intercultural alliance" (2022: 16). This amounts to a collaborative pathway that I aspire to in future work. At the moment, I still find myself in need of much learning about Indigenous ontologies and ways of knowing but wanted to acknowledge TallBear's critique. In this spirit, I refer to material feminism instead of new materialism except in those instances where I discuss a scholar's take on what they choose to refer to as "new materialism."

2 The French original is *Les données de la biologie*, which has been most recently translated as "Biological Data." Beauvoir's aim in her study is to demonstrate how female human beings become women due to how their situation is constructed socially, culturally, religiously, economically, and biologically. What is interesting with this title is that not only does it indicate that she will talk about biological facts about human bodies—and many other types of bodies as the reader soon discovers—but it also indicates that this is how biological science understands the facts it encounters.

3 For a more detailed analysis of Beauvoir's chapter on biology and its importance to posthumanist material feminism, see my "Can Existentialism be a Posthumanism?: Beauvoir as Precursor to Material Feminism."

4 This is noted by Rosi Braidotti in her *La Philosophie . . . là où on ne l'attend pas*. However, in her more recent *Posthuman Feminism*, Braidotti notes that Beauvoir's view according to which one is not born, but becomes a woman, may have the unintended effect of reinforcing a nature-culture dichotomy (Braidotti 2022: 72).

NOTES   167

5 Or an "ambiguous humanism" as Sonia Kruks has labeled it in her *Simone de Beauvoir and the Politics of Ambiguity*. I return to Kruks's position in Chapter 4. Braidotti remarks that Beauvoir's humanist feminism is tied with her socialist leanings (Braidotti 2022: 21).

6 In *The Second Sex*, Beauvoir explained how the glorification of females as goddesses was in fact a way for patriarchy to disempower actual women. Worshipped and placed on a pedestal, women are taken out of human spheres of decision-making and action. Perhaps counterintuitively then, to be a goddess is far from desirable.

7 As mentioned in the introduction, in *Staying with the Trouble* she does away with "posthuman" and instead adopts the notion of "com-post" (*cum panis*, at the table together) (2016: 11) and prefers to think of humusities (2016: 32).

8 I come back to the notion of assemblage in Chapter 3. See also the concise and clear discussion of this notion in Radomska (2016: 61–4). Grounding her analysis in, among others, Barad's and Haraway's theories, Radomska offers the concepts non/living and uncontainable life to refer to materiality that is always in process and dynamic and to emphasize that, just as we cannot separate nature and culture as per Haraway, we cannot separate the living and the nonliving, the organic and inorganic (Radomska 2016: 35). The non/living bears a resemblance to my notion of transmateriality, to which I come toward the end of this chapter.

9 In her fascinating work on bacteria, Myra J. Hird describes humans as symbionts made up of bacteria. Pointing to the fact that bacteria are the last universal common ancestor and are the beings that have generated, and continue to generate, the world and conditions for us to emerge and live, she says "bacterial liveliness suggests a profound indifference to human life" (Hird 2010: 56). She also explains that "[b]acteria weave all organisms into material, cultural and social co-constructions through ongoing symbiotic and symbiogenetic relations" (Hird 2010: 60). I return to Hird's work in Chapter 6.

10 As Victoria Pitts-Taylor remarks about the new materialisms (another label for material feminisms), "The new is best understood to signal not a wholly novel moment for feminism or social theory, but rather a fresh vision of the physical and biological world, engendered through engagement with contemporary scientific fields such as quantum physics, epigenetics, and neuroscience" (2016: 5). As she also says, and as I will argue, this does not entail a disregard for the social: "new materialism aims to rethink the terms of social theory, such that the social is seen as a part of, rather than distinct from, the natural, an undertaking that requires a rethinking of the natural too" (Pitts-Taylor 2016: 4). I have some qualms with the use of "natural" here, especially since Pitts-Taylor invokes Haraway's concept of natureculture. But the general sentiment seems right to me.

11 It is quite fruitful to examine their works in parallel. As Frost mentions, there might be a high degree of unpredictability, indeterminacy, and openness in the quantum field but when energy takes form as matter, "the constraints through which energy relates to itself make it congeal in fairly stable form, not to the extent that it never changes—because it does, and often—but rather in such a manner that we cannot really say that there is a 'radical openness' or 'an infinity of possibilities'" (2016: 51). An analysis grounded in biochemistry thereby complements an analysis grounded in quantum physics. Both serve to dismantle long-standing humanist constructs. It is also interesting to note that the theorizations brought forth by Barad and Haraway stem from a feminist science studies approach that meshes with poststructuralist and Foucauldian concepts. It makes them open to the same suspicions that these philosophies faced with regard to a supposedly inherent moral relativism. I am thankful to the anonymous reviewer of my manuscript who made this point. As we will see, though, while there may be flexibility in how relational care is exercised throughout asymmetrical relations among transjective beings, we are not dealing with a moral relativism whereby anything goes. One worry of those critical of poststructuralism is the potential loss of agency. I discuss, and dismiss, this worry at the beginning of Chapter 4.

12 This, of course, is the story of Genesis, which has permeated much of Western thinking about humans and their world.

13 An anonymous reviewer remarked that there seemed to be some slippage in my discussion of relationality, agency, and entities (beings) whereby I would seem to, at some time, deal with being as emerging from relationality and, at other times, as preexisting relations. Beings indeed only exist as assemblages emerging from relationality, from the affective fabric I will discuss further in Chapter 3. If slippage happens, and it very well may, it is because, as I explain, we approach this problem from our very human perspective and the mundane every day experience we have of existing as individuals that "enter into relations." This may be what we experience, and this makes it a real thing, but it remains that the ontological foundation of that experience tells a different story that posits relationality as primordial. Quantum physics, biochemistry, and also Spinozist philosophy are all clear in this regard. I will return to this in subsequent chapters while discussing affects in Chapter 3, and while revisiting the notion of agency and embeddedness in Chapters 4 and 6, respectively.

14 Humans from the so-called developed world have been harshly confronted with this reality with the 2020–3 pandemic. I return to this in Chapter 6.

15 I will revisit this fundamental point when I revisit the notion of agency in Chapter 4.

16 Agents are tenuous things since "[b]odies are not objects with inherent boundaries and properties; they are material-discursive phenomena" (Barad

2007: 153) whereby matter is "substance in its intra-active becoming—not a thing but a doing, a congealing of agency" (Barad 2007: 151).

17 This points to the ontological vulnerability that is the fabric of our beings, a vulnerability that can be problematic in a humanist context wherein we try to deny it or guard ourselves against it. I come to this in Chapter 5.

18 Barad complained that "[t]here is an important sense in which the only thing that doesn't seem to matter anymore is matter" (2007: 132). The work of material feminists aims to remedy this situation.

19 Alaimo says: "Trans-corporeality entails a radical rethinking of the physical environment and human bodily existence by attending to the transfers across those categories.... As a type of material feminism, trans-corporeality is indebted to Judith Butler's conception of the subject as immersed within a matrix of discursive systems (Butler 1993), but it transforms that model, insisting that the subject cannot be separated from networks of intra-active material agencies (Barad 2007)" (2018: 49).

20 In their study on Spinoza, *Collective Imaginings*, Moira Gatens and Genevieve Lloyd explain: "Our bodies retain traces of the changes brought about in them by the impingement of other bodies" (1999: 18).

21 Kroker is investigating the works of Butler, Hayles, and Haraway and is interested in how the body is construed, claiming "[n]othing is as imaginary as the material body" (2012: 3). While this may be true and we may experience the body via our interpretations and relations to it, the material body still needs to be investigated. The drift Kroker identifies is even more extensive as it drifts in the material.

22 This is reminiscent of Barad's claims about the constructivist approach.

23 For more details, one can consult Brian Epstein's entry on Social Ontology in the *Stanford Encyclopedia of Philosophy* (https://plato.stanford.edu/entries/social-ontology/#FlatOnto).

24 SR and OOO have a few proponents—such as Manuel de Landa, Graham Harman, Timothy Morton, and Levi Bryant—each centering their thinking on objects and adopting a resolutely anti-anthropocentric position. However, there are diverging views among this movement. My aim here is not to examine the details of these but the general points that SR and OOO make with regard to the flatness of ontology. I should also add that Harman distances his own view from Latour, arguing that ANT ends up focusing on the action of the object rather than the object as it *is* in itself.

25 Bryant specifies that while this realist ontology is anti-anthropocentric and a direct response to phenomenology's overemphasis on the human, it is not anti-human. The debate between SR and OOO and phenomenology revolves around whether we can know objects and what the status of various beings are. I have coedited a special issue of *PhaenEx: Journal of Existential and Phenomenological Theory and Culture* (2018) on "Speculative

Realism." With my coeditor Marie-Ève Morin, we discussed the details of the debate in our "Editorial Introduction."

26 See my *Nietzsche as Phenomenologist: Becoming What One Is.*

27 A claim found at the most global level such as here: https://www.un.org/en/un-coronavirus-communications-team/we-are-all-together-human-rights-and-covid-19-response-and.

28 This view is powerfully explored by Zakiyyah Iman Jackson in *Becoming Human* (2020). Because existing fields and theories "position blackness in the space of the unthought, and therefore are not *sufficient* grounds for theorizing blackness" (2020: 17), Jackson proposes to put material feminist theory to work in analyzing matter and race and posing the question: "If being recognized as human offers no reprieve from ontologizing dominance and violence, then what might we gain from the rupture of 'the Human'?" (2020: 20) Importantly, she investigates "the agentic capaciousness of embodied somatic processes and [. . .] how matter's efficacies register social inscription." (2020: 40) Matter matters but how we exist it and how it is inscribed culturally and socially also matters.

29 Braidotti rejects the notion of a flat ontology in the following manner: "The emphasis on immanence, situated perspectives and creativity does not constitute a form of undifferentiated or 'flat' ontology. On the contrary, this neo-materialist vital philosophy foregrounds the unity of matter, or immanence, as a differential principle. It allows for individuation and diversity, while connecting humans to non-human forces" (2019: 50).

30 She makes this argument in her "Constructing the Ballast: An Ontology for Feminism."

31 Nietzscheans will have recognized the argument against the metaphysical-religious tradition that he aims to dismantle: its ascetic ideal based on a worldview that champions the transcendent over the immanent makes impossible demands on humans. In such a view, one is always bound to fail and can never be good morally.

32 In my *Nietzsche as Phenomenologist*, I do make the case for including Nietzsche among phenomenologists, arguing that his was a "wild phenomenology."

33 Karen Barad offers a potent critique of Butler and Foucault on this issue. They say: "Butler's theory of materiality is limited to an account of the materialization of human bodies or, more accurately, to the construction of the contours of the human body. Moreover, as her reading of materiality in terms of Foucauldian regulatory practices makes clear, the processes that matter for her are only human social practices (thereby reinscribing the very nature-culture dichotomy she wishes to contest. Agential realism [Barad's own proposal] provides an understanding of materialization that

goes beyond the anthropocentric limitations of Butler's theory. Significantly, it recognizes matter's dynamism" (Barad 2007: 151).

34 My first formulation of the concept of transjectivity produced a horrendously impossible term: "trans((sub)(obj))ectivity" (see Daigle 2017). I was toying with intersubjectivity and interobjectivity as parallel terms that reflected the mind/body split. The "objectivity" in question here is not some kind of detached, god's eye view on reality, but rather objectivity as it pertains to the being of objects. The "objectivity" of "interobjectivity" refers to the body as material object and not to some kind of truth independent from individual beings. What I have in mind, therefore, is really "transmateriality," which does not work as elegantly to form the compound term I was looking for. The initial term I coined to refer to my concept, the insufferable "trans((subj)(obj))ectivity," contains parentheses whose action was meant to mark the intertwinement of subjectivity and objectivity and the impossibility to sharply distinguish them. I find squishing the term to "transjectivity" does a better job, makes the disentanglement even more impossible, and is definitely easier to both pronounce and type. Sometimes concepts are named following such mundane considerations, but the tale is not always told.

35 As it is now clear from the earlier section in this chapter, Alaimo's notion of transcorporeality is an inspiration to me.

36 In reaction to this, and after having contributed herself to the push toward materiality, Elizabeth Grosz is worried by what she now sees as the excess of materiality. Material feminists were troubled by our lack of attention to the excess of subjectivity. In response, they turned their attention to the material all the while trying to avoid the trap of anti-subjectivism. Likewise, and having grown skeptical of the excess of materiality, Grosz offers an "extramaterialism" that does not do away with materialism but reintroduces idealism. She wants to explore "the incorporeal conditions of corporeality, the excesses beyond and within corporeality that frame, orient, and direct material things and processes, and especially living things and the biological processes they require." (Grosz 2017: 5). She is really seeking to think ideality and materiality together, and not in opposition, showing how they interrelate. To parallel the new materialism, she wants to "call into being a new idealism" (Grosz 2017: 5). I think Grosz's reaction is potentially excessive. If we embrace the human, and all other beings, as transjective, the incorporeal is never evacuated but also never stands by itself.

Chapter 2

1 For an in-depth analysis of this passage of "On the Despisers of the Body" from *Thus Spoke Zarathustra*, see my *Nietzsche as Phenomenologist:*

Becoming What One Is. Likewise, I offer an extensive analysis of the passage grounding this chapter in that book and how it relates to his other views about the human-world relation.

2 I will revisit the question in Chapter 4.

3 It was Rebecca Bamford's and Keith Ansell-Pearson's study on Nietzsche's *Daybreak* that alerted me to this thread and possible origin of Nietzsche's use of "polyp."

4 I will return to this important concept in the next chapter.

5 See Daigle (2022a).

6 See Coral Reef Alliance (n.d.) "Coral polyps: Tiny builders." Available at: http://coral.org.org/coral-reefs-101/coral-reef-ecology/coral-polyps/ and National Geographic (n.d.) "Corals." Available at: http://animals.nationalgeo-graphic.com/animals/invertebrates/coral/.

7 They also feed on the sugar produced by the algae they host and, in return, provide the algae with carbon dioxide and shelter.

8 The multiplicity of the polyp manifests in various ways: as divisible and regenerable; as a member of a colony forming the reef; as a host to algae with which it shares a nourishing relation. The reef is an assemblage of individual polyps which themselves are dividuals and assemblages of themselves and hosts.

9 Hayward's approach is focused on interspecies relations and their haptic encounters in the specific environment of a saltwater lab. Discussing Hayward's approach, María Puig de la Bellacasa says, "What these visions that play with vision as touch and touch as vision invite [us] to think is a world constantly done and undone through encounters that accentuate both the attraction of closeness as well as awareness of alterity" (2017: 115).

10 I did come to *O. wendtii* after thinking Nietzsche's polyp metaphor and researching marine invertebrates. It is while going through my extensive notes on Barad for Chapter 1 that I (re)discovered that Barad discussed that same creature. As I mentioned in the preface, influence works in interesting ways. Having started to think the polyp well before I even read Barad, it is interesting to me that I was not more struck when I read this whole section of *Meeting the Universe Halfway* (369–84). Granted, Barad's discussion is of a different nature and in support of their notion of intra-activity. Barad is also interested in the motivations driving the researchers in their approach to *O. wendtii*. I am more interested in the points made about knowing, the mind, and the brain, which coincide with what I am about to argue.

11 An alternate spelling for man-of-war is man o'war (https://oceanservice.noaa.gov/facts/portuguese-man-o-war.html, https://www.nationalgeographic.com/animals/invertebrates/p/portuguese-man-of-war/).

12   Going back to Nietzsche again here, we could think of this as an illustration of the role of the body as grand reason in creating the little reason (the mind). The human body creates the little reason as a tool for itself. It creates it because it feels a need for it. But it is the grand reason of the body that is primordial. If a creature like a marine invertebrate does not feel a need for this tool, then it just does not create it and exists as a brainless creature. It still has thoughts as a body with a grand reason, "grand" being relative to the body of a being compared to that of others. But it is still a body that thinks, even if we cannot access these thoughts. We will see later in this chapter that other forms of thinking or being conscious might be even more alien to us since they are engaged in by vegetal and, possibly, mineral beings.

13   It was objected to me very early on as I was beginning to think through the polyp analogy that one cannot compare a human being to a polyp because polyps do not have brains and therefore cannot be conscious. The simplicity of marine polyps as digestive tubes that engage in only three functions, ingesting, digesting, and secreting, was the ground of the objection. It seems possible to reduce the life of the polyp to "digestive being." It certainly does not give signs of being conscious or exercising any volition, even if it engages in motion to secure its nutrition. But it is only because we have traditionally conceived of consciousness from a human point of view that we are unable to conceive of nonhuman ways of being conscious and of thinking.

14   Barad adds, "Brittlestars are phenomena intra-actively produced and entangled with other phenomena. They are agentive beings, lively configurations of the world, with more entanglements than arms" (2007: 381). *O. wendtii* is transjective.

15   Indeed, more and more studies demonstrate how our bodies are permeated by multiple elements from our environment at a cellular level. See a brief compilation here: https://sciencing.com/effects-pollution-body-8792.html. We have seen Frost's and Alaimo's analyses of this transcorporeal porosity. I will revisit this fundamental idea when discussing vulnerability and ethical potential.

16   It could be argued that we have already entered the slow process of extinction. In his *Flight Ways: Life and Loss at the Edge of Extinction* (2014), Thom van Dooren explains that extinction is a process that unfolds over time as relations between species and individuals' ways of life are significantly altered. He says: "the edge of extinction is more often a 'dull' one: a slow unraveling of intimately entangled ways of life that begins long before the death of the last individual and continues to ripple forward long afterward, drawing in living beings in a range of different ways" (van Dooren 2014: 12). Visiting Turku in the summer of 2021, I encountered an alley of Linden trees that I named the "Broken Hearts Alley." All the Linden trees appeared to have a dying, rotting core, some of them with a

quite dramatically big hollowed out trunk and yet the trees were still alive and growing with a healthy looking crown. As transjective beings, trees are multispecies assemblages and their "dying," their rotten core (their broken hearts), invites a different type of growth. This also applies to humans: living as humanist humans and cutting ourselves off from our relations to the more-than-human and having caused the disappearance of many nonhuman animal and plant species, our way of life as entangled beings has long been extinct. The humanist human is not human. That humanist human must now become extinct, indeed is becoming extinct. But this opens up new potentialities as we reconceptualize ourselves and rediscover ourselves as transjective. This unfolding extinction/generation is in some ways the perfect moment to conceive a transjective ethos. I return to this in the last chapter.

17 As we will shortly see, stones are also part of various versions of hierarchies of beings and they are at the very bottom as inorganic, the mineral foundation afforded to other beings.

18 *Umwelt* as "lived world" is a connotation added by the French translator of *Streifzüge durch die Umwelten von Tieren und Menschen*. The German sentence reads: "Merkwelt und Wirkwelt bilden gemeinsam eine geschlossene Einheit, die Umwelt" (Uexküll 1965: 21). The French reads: "Monde d'action et de perception forment ensemble une totalité close, le *milieu*, le *monde vécu*" (Uexküll 1965: 15). Translated in 1965, at a time when the influential movement of existentialism is waning, it is understandable that the translator would have added this existentialist spin to the notion of *Umwelt*. This is reminiscent of another existentialist bending of a German concept in Henri Corbin's translation of Heidegger's *Dasein* as "réalité humaine," only in this case, the existentialist bend preceded—and some may want to argue, caused—the movement itself. With regard to Uexküll's concept of *Umwelt*, I think it is justified to add this existentialist dimension as it is really through their existence and by giving meaning to their world that beings create their own environment. This is the meaning Marder takes from Uexküll as well in his discussion of human and nonhuman worlds.

19 See Marder (2013: 20). This resort to etymology allows Marder to engage in a critical analysis of Aristotle's notion of vegetative soul and the views that took roots—no pun intended—in it. The point, for Marder, is to offer a vegetal "anti-metaphysics." He says: "Western metaphysics commences then with the *inversion of the earthly perspective of the plant*, a deracination of human beings, uprooted from their material foundations and transplanted into the heavenly domain, and the correlative devaluation of the literal plant, mired with its roots in the darkness of the earth as much as in non-conscious existence" (Marder 2013: 57).

20 In his *What a Plant Knows*, Daniel Chamowitz explains that "[p]lants are acutely aware of the world around them . . . an 'aware' plant is not aware of us as individuals. . . . A plant is aware of its environment, and people are part of this environment. . . . For all the rich sensory input that plants and people perceive, only humans render this input as an emotional landscape" (2017: 138). In the opening pages of his book, Chamowitz recognizes that his use of "know" in relation to plants is unorthodox and explains that when he uses verbs like "smell" or "see" he is not implying that plants have the same organs as we do. He hopes that using language in this way and referring to what we readily recognize as human and nonhuman animal sensory capacities and experiences in relation to plants will open up our thinking and "challenge us to think in new ways about sight, smell, what a plant is, and ultimately what we are" (Chamowitz 2017: 5).

21 Marder claims that it is "the cornerstone of [the plant's] 'sagacity'" (2013: 12).

22 This process of material inscription is the same for humans whose bodies retain memories of experiences and trauma. I return to this in Chapter 5.

23 In her "Symmetry and Asymmetry in Conceptual and Morphological Formations," Karen Houle speaks of a plant ethics, one that would "cause a mutation in our dominant conceptual habits" (2022: 93). Indeed, by considering the way in which plants exist, by contemplating a becoming-plant, Houle asks, "Could we, tutored by the example of plant bodily being, experience intense positional vulnerability and yet come to know and value ourselves as singular through that very impingement?" (2022: 100). We can develop a different ethicality through thinking plants and their mode of existing as interconnected and resilient, as the expression of vitality but also as exposed and turned outward. The plant's vulnerability is its strength and, as we will see in Chapters 5 and 7, it is necessary for the human transjective to uncover its own vulnerability and develop its potential.

24 Trovants absorb the minerals from the rain, allowing them to grow. Their supposed movement is not explained anywhere that I can find and it looks like this may be a "fact" of folklore more than an empirically observed fact. It is conceivable that as a stone grows it may find itself tipping over if it loses its balance, thereby engaging in motion. But it seems that anything more, such as a stone changing location, would not be possible or at least has not been observed. On the trovants, see: https://whenonearth.net/trovants-growing-stones-romania/.

25 Hird and Yusoff say, "the carbon imaginaries that shape contemporary climate change and petrochemical cultures, are woefully inadequate in their conceptualisation of the range and scope of the kinds (and places) of exchanges taking place" (2018: 277).

26 Barad claims: "Thought experiments are material matters. Thinking has never been a disembodied or uniquely human activity. [. . .] All life forms (including inanimate forms of liveliness) *do* theory. The idea is to do collaborative research, to be in touch, in ways that enable response-ability" (2012: 208).

Meandering 4

1 Feeling out of place would then be yet another disruptive variation on the affective scale of experiences that go from mundane ones to extremely disruptive ones such as trauma.

Chapter 3

1 The oxygen we breathe in and which allows our bodies to survive is all too often mixed in with pollutants that also enter the body and eventually can cause health issues.

2 As Anna Lowenhaupt Tsing puts it: "The question of how the varied species in a species assemblage influence each other—if at all—is never settled: some thwart (or eat) each other; others work together to make life possible; still others just happen to find themselves in the same place. Assemblages are open-ended gatherings" (2015: 22–3). While Tsing is specifically concerned with the interaction among living species here, one can extend what she says to any and all objects.

3 It is interesting to me that Bennett invokes both Spinoza and Merleau-Ponty here, pointing to the fruitful encounter between material feminism and phenomenology I have invoked.

4 Chen is interested in the "specific kind of affective and material construct" that animacy is (2012: 5). Animacy is "conceptually slippery, even to its experts" (Chen 2012: 9). A concept drawn from linguistics, "animacy is the quality of liveness, sentience, or humanness of a noun or noun phrase that has grammatical, often syntactic, consequences" (Chen 2012: 24), it lies within and without the linguistic. Inquiring into this concept, Chen discusses various assemblages, Deleuze and Guattari's body without organs (BwO), and the importance—urgency even—of the new materialisms. The latter allow us to "diagnose the 'facts' by which humans are not animals are not things (or by which humans cannot be animals cannot be things), but simultaneously reveal such 'facts' to be the real uncanny permeating the world we know" (Chen 2012: 236).

5 The unthought is not the unconscious. Rather it is nonconscious. Neither is it like the phenomenological pre-reflective which is a being aware, a being-there, the rawest form of consciousness. As cognitive, the unthought thinks and processes information as well as makes decisions. It need not be human, although there is also a form of cognitive nonconscious that is human, that is grounded in the biological.

6   Hayles defines cognition as "a process that interprets information within contexts that connect it with meaning" (2017: 22).

7   This leads Hayles to say "[w]hen objects join in networks and interact/intraact with human partners, the potential for surprises and unexpected results increases exponentially" (2017: 84). Since this is an ongoing interaction/intra-action, the potential for surprises is constant. This impacts how we conceive of agency. I will return to this.

8   I take this from the early Sartre who proposed such a topology of consciousness (see Daigle 2009).

9   Gerda Roelvink and Magdalena Zolkos posit the following in their editorial introduction to *Angelaki*'s issue on "Posthumanist Perspectives on Affect": "Without trying to exhaust the possible ways in which posthumanism has intersected with, magnified and mobilized the categories of affect, in this opening essay we suggest that one entry into the exploration of their mutual connectedness is the idea of *aliveness*, or *animation*" (2015: 2). As Chen, Hayles, and many others would argue, it is not the affects, events, or bodies themselves that matter so much as the animation their affective relations introduce in the entangled web of relations, in the affective fabric.

One last note on Hayles for now: her view that I just described bears resemblance to Braidotti's notion of the zoe/geo/techno entanglements that she discusses in relation to subject formation—a subject that is framed by these entanglements, that is *of* them (Braidotti 2019). I return to this and Hayles's position in Chapter 6.

10 The title of this section of the *Ethics*, "Concerning the Origin and Nature of the Emotions," should have been more properly translated as "Concerning the Origin and Nature of Affects" since the Latin is "*affectuum*." "*Affectus*" is not common in the philosophical language of the time and Spinoza is using it to emphasize the moral neutrality of the concept. To translate it as "emotion" is not inaccurate but invests the concept with interpretative weight that Spinoza did not intend (see https://spinoza.fr/introduction-au-de-affectibus/).

11 Spinoza concludes from this that one object can cause many conflicting emotions. Brian Massumi says, "[a]ffect as a whole, then, is the virtual co-presence of potentials" (2015: 5).

12 Roelvink and Zolkos point out that "theories of affect challenge the idea of the human as a singular, cohesive and bounded unit, characterized by relative stability over time ... the perspective of affect undermines the idea that a subject position emerges in a process of dichotomous differentiation" (2015: 7). They further say that "[a]n affect-oriented theory of the subject ... aligns with the posthumanist insistence on materiality and ecological situatedness of the body, and with the 'corporeal turn' in the humanities, by offering an imaginary of energetically permeable and animate subjects"

(Roelvink and Zolkos 2015: 8), which opens up to the idea of the processual body. This has important repercussions for the notion of a subject or agent, as we will see.

13 Seigworth and Gregg note that "[i]t is this relationality . . . that persists, in adjacency and duration, alongside the affects and bodies that gather up in motley, always more-than-human collectivity" (2010: 13).

14 In *Politics of Affect*, Massumi explains that "[a]ffective-thinking-feeling is transindividual . . . affect is a differential attunement between two bodies in a joint activity of becoming" (2015: 94).

15 Elena del Río's analyses of Deleuze and Guattari's notion of the BwO along with Spinozist/Deleuzean theory of affect are particularly illuminating. She is mostly interested in the powers of affection and the role cinema can play in letting those unfold and serving a political role. del Río points to Deleuze and Guattari's most radical thought: "the existence of an incorporeal materialism that calls on us to become attentive to a micropolitics of the affections, a virtual plane, no less real than the actual, on which affects, thoughts, and desires continue to brew and transform long before and after they take a shape that we can see, name, or recognize . . . [there is] an ongoing impact of the affections on the ways bodies negotiate, balance, or unbalance power relations with other bodies" (2012: 210).

16 Recall my discussion of Beauvoir's views as anticipating some insights of posthumanist material feminism in Chapter 1.

17 Braidotti discusses difference in the following terms: "To be embodied and embrained entails decentring transcendental consciousness. To view the subject as differential implies to extract difference from the oppositional or binary logic that reduces difference to being different from, as in being worth less than. Difference is an imminent, positive and dynamic category. The emphasis on affectivity and relationality is an alternative to individualist autonomy" (2019: 11–12).

18 For Whitehead, there is no primacy of the body or of the subject. Experience happens and processes of worlding and bodying take place from it. Whitehead's superject is the subject of the event, which is not a subject as we typically conceive of it. Whitehead's views are complicated and worth considering, but this analysis will have to wait for another project. Suffice it to say here that Whitehead is informing Manning's and Massumi's views. In her article, Manning explicates the shift that is initiated in Merleau-Ponty's later writings and attributes it to his increased interest in Whitehead's process philosophy. She thinks that, had Merleau-Ponty had the opportunity to continue working with those ideas, he might have been taken to the point of reneging his earlier phenomenological views from the *Phenomenology of Perception*, views that were entrenched in a notion of human subjectivity. But all we have, due to his premature passing, is the beginning of a shift toward a focus on process and a decentering of

subjectivity in *The Visible and the Invisible*. For a full explanation of this, see Manning (2014). For an examination of the concept of superject in Whitehead, see Stenner (2008).

19 Phenomenologists have often taken an interest in visual arts as one specific form of sensory experience that an embodied consciousness can engage in. The explanatory power that a sensory encounter with a work of art can provide is useful for their analyses. Many have specifically considered cinema and the peculiar nature of perceiving and reacting to moving images. Deleuze also famously devoted a lot of his thinking to the cinema, its different types of images, and their affective power. Sobchack's analyses stem from her interest in the culture of the moving image.

20 This synesthetic system could be referred to as a "cognizer," as per Hayles.

21 Particularly *Eye and Mind*, *The Visible and the Invisible*, and *Signs*.

22 This is a view shared by Mark B. N. Hansen. For him, there is always a strong correlation between the lived body, our embodied experience, and the media we encounter. It is in a body that the image—his focus is on the digital image—is formed and created and that body "gives rise to an affective 'supplement' to the act of perceiving the image, that is, a properly haptic domain of sensation" (Hansen 2004: 12). Against what he sees as Deleuze's attack on the body, Hansen revisits Bergson and puts the emphasis on the vital role of embodiment, even in such experiences as virtual reality and speaks of "new media as a source for the technical contamination of embodied time consciousness" (Hansen 2006: ix).

23 As I will argue in Chapter 5, traumatic experiences provide us with magnifying lenses to understand how we are constituted. Horror and melodrama that deal in heightened emotional and affective relations perform a similar role.

24 While discussing her concept of orientation, Sara Ahmed claims that disorientation, which is a vital experience that can be experienced as ordinary or deeply troubling, involves becoming an object (2006: 159). I discuss Ahmed's view below.

25 In Chapter 1, I also discuss speculative realism's critique of phenomenology and its charge of correlationism. Sobchack's own discussion of the limits of phenomenology with regard to objects come close to those.

26 See Part III of Sartre, *Being and Nothingness*, especially the section titled "The Look." I argue here that the look need not be alienating.

27 See my discussion in Chapter 1.

28 To illustrate this, Ahmed uses the passage from Sartre's *Nausea* where the main protagonist, Antoine Roquentin, has a bout of nausea in the park as he

is suddenly unable to make sense of things around him as they start existing by themselves, resisting any words or interpretation he may want to affix them. Ahmed says: "In such moments of failure when things do not stay in place or cohere as place, disorientation happens" (2006: 170).

29 We sometimes push things too far and elaborate damaging alienating dualistic views such as the ones Western thinking has put forward.

Meandering 5

1 There were two categories of high-risk in Finland: highest risk and lower risk. I belonged to the latter.

2 As book writing goes, it has now been a while since this first inoculation experience. Since then, I have received a second, third, fourth, and fifth shot. I have also received my two doses of the shingles vaccine and have now started an immunotherapy to train my body to not be so hyperreactive to pollen. I was provided two pills for the odd possibility that I might have an anaphylactic reaction (here we go again!) and instructions to take them if it were to unfold and head for the nearest hospital. As I type this, my left upper arm is itchy as I received a shot this morning. I am much less anxious each time even though I have not developed any kind of liking or even tolerance to needles! I continue to open myself up and reassemble myself through this web of interconnections and traffic of substances that do and undo me.

Chapter 4

1 Rimbaud says: "C'est faux de dire: Je pense; On devrait dire: On me pense.— Pardon du jeu de mots—Je est un autre" (2008: 370).

2 In my "Can Existentialism be a Posthumanism?: Beauvoir as Precursor of Posthumanism," I go into more details in my response to Kruks's early critique and proposal for an ambiguous humanism and do not share her view on posthumanism. As I explained in Chapter 1, I do not claim Beauvoir is a posthumanist *avant la lettre*, but I do see her critique of the subject as more closely aligned with poststructuralism and posthumanism in that it serves as a foundation for them.

3 Hekman quotes Latour on this issue who explains that the modern notion of society has been replaced by the notion of the collective, which refers to the association between humans and nonhumans (2008: 93).

4 The asterisk I added in this quote serves as a reminder that the original German is *Mensch* and not *Mann*. This should therefore read as "human."

5 In my *Nietzsche as Phenomenologist*, I further analyze these passages in relation to a Nietzschean view of consciousness as emerging through language. I also provide a detailed analysis of the topology of consciousness we can find in *Thus Spoke Zarathustra*'s "On the Despisers of the Body."

6 Barad offers the following in relation to touching: "All touching entails an infinite alterity, so that touching the Other is touching all Others, including the 'self,' and touching the 'self' entails touching the strangers within. Even the smallest bits of matter are an unfathomable multitude. Each 'individual' always already includes all possible intra-actions with 'itself' through all the virtual Others, including those that are noncontemporaneous with 'itself'" (2012: 214).

7 Patricia MacCormack argues that "when we speak of the I/Other we are speaking of the self as its own othered multiplicity" (2016: 5–6). She embraces the idea of the "dividuation of life in opposition to identity" (MacCormack 2016: 4). Importantly, she points out that we cannot know the ethical agent in advance of what we are capable of and therefore we must reject the notion of human will (MacCormack 2016: 10). I return to MacCormack's important work and her latest *The Ahuman Manifesto* in Chapter 7.

8 Massumi's notion of the incorporeal here is different yet related to what Elizabeth Grosz discusses in her recent book *The Incorporeal: Ontology, Ethics, and the Limits of Materialism* (2017). See my all too brief discussion in Note 36, Chapter 1.

9 Claire Colebrook also explains: "There 'is' no matter as such, no body as such, only a body that matters—a body known only in so far as it is recognized—and only a matter that is given as there for this body in its potentiality.... The performative is an act that relies on and maintains relations among bodies, granting and sustaining each body in its force. I can be a body that matters, a body who matters, only if 'I' act in such a way that something like an 'I' can be recognized" (2011: 14). Here, too, we find an emphasis on relationality and recognition (which can only happen between at least two, even between oneself as subject and object, although these do not exist as separate). Colebrook's formulation should not be read to indicate that there is an entity directing its will to perform itself. Performativity gives a false sense of an agent enacting a certain plan to make itself one way or another. The performativity indicated here is prepersonal and is what will allow for those tenuous moments of coalescence to emerge, for the body to crystallize for long enough to be recognized.

10 Hayles writes: "Still, it is difficult to see how political agency can be mobilized without some references to subjects, organisms, and signs, the

entities that Deleuze [and many contemporary materialist thinkers] writes against" (2017: 77). Braidotti's strategy here and in *The Posthuman* is one that acknowledges subjects, even though they differ widely (see 2013: 135).

11 Radomska notes, "I am wary of the use of the concept of agency, due to its association with intentionality, in both philosophy and legal theory" (2016: 61). She further explains that, thanks to the work of Haraway and Barad, agency has been divested of intentionality. As we have seen, and as Barad explains again in an interview with Rick Dolphijn and Iris van der Tuin, agential realism posits that "agency is an enactment, a matter of possibilities for reconfiguring entanglements" (Dolphijn and van der Tuin 2012: 55). They further explain that this agential realism is "about response-ability, about the possibilities of mutual response, which is not to deny, but to attend to power imbalances" (Dolphijn and van der Tuin 2012: 56). This relates to the asymmetry of relations that I discussed at the close of Chapter 1. I come back to the notion of response-ability as it relates to my concept of vulner—ability in Chapter 7.

12 Hayles discusses the Deleuzian paradigm and the effects of force driving it (2017: 82). She is concerned that the notion of force remains vague and therefore not helpful in determining agency and the degree to which agency can be attributed to various objects. She examines the different kinds of agencies displayed by a rock crashing through a window, an avalanche, and self-organizing systems. She offers that putting the emphasis on cognition allows for a clearer determination of the forces at work in these various instances of agencies because it is explicit about structures, dynamics, and organizations (Hayles 2017: 82). She claims that "the idea of locating agency within material processes is an intriguing possibility, especially given the desirability of locating agency other than in human actors" (Hayles 2017: 83). This is essential in the complex reality in which we exist, one that is becoming increasingly and exponentially complex due to the proliferation of nonconscious cognitive processes that she focuses on in her book. Importantly, she wants to reserve *actors* for cognizers and "*agents* for material forces and objects" (2017: 32). This distinction mirrors that between agency and agentic capacity.

13 Coole explains that she prefers to use "transpersonal" as opposed to "structural" in order to avoid the reification or reductionism she sees as often implicit in discussions of structure (2005: 138). It is true that "structure" does convey a sense of stability and fixity that we now know is always out of reach for the transjective being. With that said, I agree with Coole who thinks that structuralist and post-structuralist approaches provide key insights in the transsubjective constitution of selves (what she refers to as transpersonal). They assist in moving away from a political agency that is grounded in a subject and instead "imply a novel mode of non-subjectivist political efficacy" (Coole 2005: 139).

Chapter 5

1 Erinn Gilson also makes the following important point: "It is important to note that attempts to secure invulnerability at the price of an ignorance of vulnerability in its myriad forms can make us more vulnerable precisely because it leads us to ignore the real conditions that give rise to particular patterns of vulnerability" (2011: 327n8).

2 Freedman also says: "My body is interminably sensitive to the touch, the violence of the rape imprinted all over it—on my breasts, my neck, my lower back, and everything important below that" (2014: viii).

3 In this sense, their philosophical perspective resembles that of Paul Ricœur who most prominently developed the narrative theory of the self in his *Oneself as Another* grounded in the narrative theory elaborated in his three volume *Time and Narrative*.

4 As mentioned, trauma provides us with a magnifying lens of what is always the case through any experiences we have: we are made through them and through the multiple entanglements we are a part of. Traumatic experiences highlight this for us.

5 This process of narrativization of trauma and rebuilding of the social bond is the recovery process embraced by truth and reconciliation commissions that unfolded in recent decades in South Africa, Canada, and Australia and continue their work today. I am not arguing here that such processes cannot be generative. On the contrary, I truly believe that they are and not only provide grounds for acknowledging our collective troubled pasts but also offer solid foundations for action to improve the transsubjective spaces in which we live. For historically oppressed groups, such as Indigenous peoples, it also entails improving the material conditions of their existence (which is unfortunately still in the making for many communities in Canada, for example, who still do not have access to clean water). When individuals participate in commissions and share their trauma, they make themselves vulnerable all over again. Receiving and acknowledging the narrative as inheritor of past oppression or perpetrator of such oppression is to make oneself vulnerable by giving away one's position of privilege. In Canada, some non-Indigenous folks still find accepting the label "settler" difficult, while others find it impossible as they refuse to engage in the reconciliation process by receiving the narrative and accepting their or their ancestors' roles in colonialism. The strides forward, as minimal and insufficient as they may currently be, are still ways in which the social bond is being rebuilt and selves reconstructed.

6 I thank Brett Robinson for drawing my attention to this. For example, while rape is universally considered to be wrong, it is not experienced in the same way across cultures and across societies.

7   I wish to thank Ilaria Santoemma for her help understanding the meaning of the original title and possible alternatives. I was proposing "You who look after me" as a possibility because of the homophony between the Italian "*Tu che mi gardi*" and the French "*Toi qui me garde.*"

8   Cavarero claims: "The truth is that the human being, when totally exposed, is totally fragile—even, perhaps more so, in its adult flesh" (2000: 113).

9   What is of interest to Butler in Cavarero's notion of the narrative self is its implied fragility, its necessary relation to an other to whom one narrativizes oneself. Cavarero's discussions have to do with the intersubjective but there is also the material which is what Butler considers albeit through the lens of social construction. Their approach is therefore not the same. Susan Hekman has claimed that Butler's interest in Cavarero's work initiates a shift in their thinking whereby the connections between "subjectivity, ethics, and ontology are far more simple" (2014: 461). This shift allows them to pay more attention to the materiality in which subjectivities constitute themselves.

10 Pulkkinen's analysis proceeds from a politics of philosophy that examines the context in which certain concepts are used. This allows her to show the important differences between Cavarero's and Butler's views, the first mostly focusing on singular bodily existents and the second on the changing social and political conditions in which individuals are placed and rendered more or less vulnerable (Pulkkinen 2020).

11 In her own critique of Butler's analysis of precariousness, Rosalyn Diprose points out that the role played by nonhuman elements is often disregarded and by Butler in particular. Now, interestingly and despite this critique, Diprose still ends up focusing on a human-centered shaping of the nonhuman through her favouring of the phenomenological notion of dwelling. And even when she claims that "precisely because human beings are not self-contained individuals, we are open to transformation by the world in which we are embedded and vice versa" (2013: 191), she still ends up hanging on to an emphasis on the subjective.

12 It would be wrong to claim that no attention whatsoever has been paid to materiality when examining the particular trauma of rape. What I am arguing is that the attention paid to the bodily and material trauma has been coming from a perspective on how a subjectivity can handle it. In *Rethinking Rape* (2001), Ann J. Cahill is critical of theorists who ignored the embodied and sexual aspect of rape or considered it to be yet another instance of violence. Cahill turns to thinkers of sexual difference and feminist views on the body and materiality in order to identify the particular ethical wrong of rape as opposed to other trauma that persons may suffer. Despite having discussed Braidotti and Gatens, both inspired by Spinoza's views on affects, it is to Irigaray that she turns to identify that particular wrong. Because Irigaray discusses and emphasizes sexual difference, Cahill can make her case for understanding rape as "a violent

destruction and denial of the difference that underlies the possibility of personhood" (2001: 192) and "a violent, sexual, bodily denial and destruction of a person's sexually specific intersubjective being" (2001: 194). Cahill's approach provides a welcome realignment of thinking about rape and its specific trauma but still misses the concept of material inscription of trauma that I want to put forward here.

13 For the full French lyrics of the song and to listen to it, see https://genius.com/Jean-leloup-lucie-lyrics. I am revisiting here the analysis of this song that I offered along with an analysis of the impact of viewing Luka Rocco Magnotta's "1 Lunatic, 1 Icepick" in my "Trans-subjectivity/Trans-objectivity," my first attempt at theorizing the transjective being.

14 One can look at the triptychs on Lalage Snow's website at https://www.lalagesnow.co.uk along with other fascinating series. I first became aware of the "We Are the Not Dead" series through an article published in 2012 about the exhibit (https://mymodernmet.com/lalage-snow-we-are-the-not-dead/).

15 I am not denying how horrendous the experiences of the *gueules cassées* were. Researching this historical phenomenon, I navigated many images and films about these men and the persons caring for them post-injury, medical personnel including plastic surgeons, but also artists who designed, molded, sculpted, and painted the masks and prostheses worn by many of them to hide the deformities. The courage and resilience of these often very young men and the dedication of those caring for them are very poignant. For more on this topic, see Marjorie Gerhardt's *The Men with Broken Faces: Gueules Cassées of the First World War* (2015). A number of short documentaries are also available through a quick online search. One learns that treating such injuries only started with The Great War. In previous conflicts, soldiers with such injuries were either left behind because they could not cry for help due to their injury or were "mercifully" executed when found because it was thought they could not survive their injuries. Prior to the twentieth century, such injuries were less frequent than during the First World War. The novelty of warfare and weapons in the First World War is the reason for the dramatic increase in head and face injuries. Armed conflicts have always yielded injuries and amputations of all kinds, but facial injuries and caring for them were somewhat rare. The sense of self one attaches to one's face, added to the fact that interpersonal relations are often mediated through the face and facial expressions, made dealing with these injuries particularly challenging and necessary for the social reintegration of the *gueules cassées*.

16 From a perspective that considers art and its dealings with wounds, Rick Dolphijn says: "The non-humanist and untimely ideas of the wound have to be occupied with unease and discomfort. . . . It is too easy just to oppose, to reject, to critique any crisis that befalls us. We have to open ourselves up to

it, to recognize in what way this crisis was always already a part of us and to take responsibility for it" (2021: 101).

Chapter 6

1 A quote from Marilyn Strathern's *Reproducing the Future* (1992) quoted by Haraway. Haraway's variations are as follows: "It matters what matters we use to think other matters with; it matters what stories we tell to tell other stories with; it matters what knots knot knots, what thoughts think thoughts, what descriptions describe descriptions, what ties tie ties. It matters what stories make worlds, what worlds make stories" (2016b: 12); "It matters what thoughts think thoughts. It matters what knowledges know knowledges. It matters what relations relate relations. It matters what worlds world worlds. It matters what stories tell stories" (2016b: 35); "It matters what concepts think concepts, and vice versa" (2016b: 94); "It matters which beings recognize beings" (2016b: 96); "Mathematically, visually, and narratively, it matters which figures figure figures, which systems systematize systems" (2016b: 101); "It matters how kin generate kin" (2016b: 103); "It matters which concepts conceptualize concepts. . . . It matters which worlds world worlds. It matters who eats whom and how" (2016b: 165).

2 Haraway closes *Staying with the Trouble* with "The Camille Stories: Children of Compost" (2016b), a work of speculative fiction that "follows five generations of a symbiogenetic join of a human child and monarch butterflies" (2016b: 8).

3 Haraway claims that "[c]ompanion species infect each other all the time. . . . Bodily ethical and political obligations are infectious, or they should be. *Cum panis*, companion species, at table together" (2016b: 29).

4 This leads Haraway to claim that "I am a compostist, not a posthumanist: we are all compost, not posthuman" (2016b: 101–2).

5 The book closes on this statement, but the phrase, in slight variations, is used throughout.

6 Guattari goes on to explain, "The principle common to the three ecologies is this: each of the existential Territories with which they confront us is not given as an in-itself [en-soi], closed in on itself, but instead as a for-itself [pour-soi] that is precarious, finite, finitized, singular, singularized, capable of bifurcating into stratified and deathly repetitions or of opening up processually from a praxis that enables it to be made 'habitable' by a human project" (53). Since "ecology" deals with beings that exist, their interrelations and their relations to their surroundings, the term should be sufficient to encapsulate the ecological registers proposed. However,

bringing them up to light by naming them allows for really understanding the different types of relations unfolding.

7 Although admittedly, Hayles is not building on a Guattarian position, at least not explicitly.

8 As Hayles points out though, "[t]he same faculty that makes us aware of ourselves as selves also partially blinds us to the complexity of the biological, social, and technological systems in which we are embedded" (2017: 45). The task ahead of us is to uncover and recover the entanglements we are.

9 For a detailed analysis of what the zoe/geo/techno framed subject means, see the article I coauthored with Ilaria Santoemma (Daigle and Santoemma 2022).

10 It also fundamentally rests upon *zoe*: "Life is a generative force beneath, below and beyond what we humans have made of it. *Zoe*/geo/techno perspectives at the core of this heterogeneous definition of life are sites of resistance" (Braidotti 2019: 177). The resistance in question allows for our becoming otherwise, other, and together as entangled.

11 MacCormack explains that the monster catalyzes the "turbulence of familiar and stabilizing vibrations, waves and flows" (2016: 97).

12 I will revisit this notion in the next chapter. MacCormack remarks that "[a]n ethical philosophy does not require a return to humanist transcendentalism. It is a valuation of 'life' not as a concept but as it actually incarnates in everyday flesh-in-the-world as an emergent point of philosophy and bio-physiological existence" (2016: 119).

13 Chauvin's expressionless face gave a face to systemic racism: the oppressive and racist sociopolitical system acted through *and* with Chauvin. This is not to say that he does not bear responsibility for the death of Floyd. He absolutely does and, as I have argued, to claim that our agency is limited and permeated by the agentic capacities with which we are entangled does not amount to a dismissal of our agency or ethical responsibility. On the contrary, and as I will argue in the next chapter, to recognize transjectivity entails engaging in practices of care that are antithetical to murderous actions like Chauvin's. In June 2021, he was found guilty of second-degree murder and sentenced to twenty-two years and a half in prison. Chauvin filed an appeal of the verdict in April 2022.

14 It was truly a troubling experience to be reading this excellent book at the time that the BLM movement unfolded in early summer 2020. With a small group of friends, we had decided to read this new book and it felt like reading a live commentary of what was actually unfolding. As a careful and insightful reading of the ways in which institutions of power recuperate violence and exercise their own violence on those who protest, it offered an incredibly helpful lens through which to read current events as BLM organized and spread its action.

15 See my "Fascism and the Entangled Subject." I have also alluded to the events referred to here in Meandering 7, "World in Turmoil."

16 The onset of the Russian war on Ukraine in February 2022 has meant a radical shift in priorities for the Ukrainian people that now have to defend themselves against a human invader. The most pressing issue is no longer the spread of the SARS-Cov-2 virus but instead the shelling of Ukrainian cities and the need to protect the people and territory from Russian advances. Communities and individuals that are entangled in a manifold of relations will face various toxicities and prioritizing which to address will depend on the specific circumstances in which they find themselves. The capacity to address the stress put on them will also inflect the prioritization. For example, the globally uneven distribution of Covid vaccines has meant that some communities have had to face this toxicity in significantly different ways than the more privileged ones who have had access to up to four doses of vaccines thus far. But again, whether one has access to a booster shot or not is trivial if one is sheltering in a bunker under Russian bombing.

17 The recent global spread of monkeypox is an example of that. It should be added that ironically, it was those countries that regularly deal with outbreaks of severe and highly transmissible diseases that dealt better with containing transmission. They knew what precautionary measures to put in place and the populations were not resistant to those in the way that large portions of populations in North America, for example, became irrationally adverse to what they considered to be a serious impingement on their freedom. Masking and vaccination became politicized in ways that would not make sense to populations familiar with these simple precautionary measures (masking in particular).

18 The exact amount of time it took for the virus to spread globally is difficult to determine since the moment when the zoonotic disease transferred to humans is undetermined. Furthermore, analyses of waste waters in European cities have shown that the virus was present much earlier than generally recognized. In North America, the virus is said to have hit in March but people have reported the same symptoms and severe illnesses in late 2019 and early 2020, indicating that it may have been present but undetected.

19 I am deeply thankful to Ilaria Santoemma who helped me shape these ideas as we were working on our co-authored paper (Daigle and Santoemma 2022). I have also discussed the affectivity of pandemicity in Daigle (2022b).

20 Here I have in mind Vanessa Watts's discussion of Indigenous place-thought. She defines it as "the non-distinctive space where place and thought were never separated because they never could or can be separated. Place-thought is based upon the premise that land is alive and thinking and that humans and non-humans derive agency through the extensions of these thoughts" (Watts 2013: 21). This notion of distributed agency is at the core of an Indigenous worldview as it is in material feminism. A word of caution however: it is often tempting to equate posthumanist thinking to Indigenous ways of knowing. It is important to acknowledge that there is nothing radically new in thinking about entanglements—Indigenous scholars or scholars from other non-Western traditions would rightfully criticize and reject any suggestion that there is. It is also important to acknowledge that there are important differences in how notions that appear to be the same come to be construed as they are and therefore are not in fact the exact same. See note 1, Chapter 1.

21 One contributor to the special section is my colleague Adam Dickinson whose fascinating poetic work is based on analyses of his bodily fluids and what toxins, pollutants, and heavy metals are found in them. See his *Anatomic* (2018).

22 It would seem that the asymmetry of relations and agentic capacities I have discussed earlier is in favor of bacteria in this case.

23 This brings to mind Nietzsche's claim that "[t]he earth has a skin; and this skin has diseases. One of these diseases, for example, is called 'Man'" (*Thus Spoke Zarathustra*, "Of Great Events").

24 Giving this question a different twist, Claire Colebrook and Tom Cohen argue that humanity only became "global anthropos" with the emergence of "the Anthropocene, with the declaration that there is a unity to the species, and that this unity lies in its power to mark the planet" (2016: 8). They say that "all that talk about the post-human, the non-human, the inhuman and the problem of lumping all humans into the Anthropocene provides a way of sustaining the human as a problem. What if the human were an effect of its own delusions of self-erasure?" (Cohen and Colebrook 2016: 11). Thus, they argue that there never was the "human" and that anthropos came along retrospectively when the Anthropocene was declared and an "agent" was identified as its cause: humanity, the "we," we "humans."

25 I have discussed these various terms and their meanings as well as the importance of understanding what further oppressive and colonial moves are inherent to naming the new geological epoch "Anthropocene" in Cielemęcka and Daigle (2019) and Daigle (2022b).

26 As Colebrook suggests, "rather than see the humanity that faces an unjust and catastrophically tragic end as the agent of history whose survival is required in order to achieve a more just future, one should see the end of the world as the beginning of other worlds" (2017: np).

Meandering 9

1 I say "my lot" and "my yard" but it is only so because of relatively arbitrary lines drawn once upon a time by municipal officers and because I paid a sum of money to "acquire" it. However, one never really acquires land. The land and its inhabitants do not care much for boundary stakes, fences, or other human concerns.

2 The yard used to have two ponds, which I had to remove because of neighbor complaints. I then thought that I needed to put some water out for the critters. I put a bowl that I refresh every morning and during the day on hot days, as well as a bird bath, which gets really high traffic with birds sometimes having to wait their turn. The only birds I have seen share the bath were the dove couple hanging around and a robin and a sparrow the one day. All others prefer to bathe solo.

Chapter 7

1 Furthermore, and as my good friend Antonio Calcagno remarked to me, the ethical ideal of authenticity championed by existentialist ethics such as that of Sartre is a moot requirement for a transjective being since too much of what it is, of what constitutes it, lays outside of its reach. Indeed! And that is why a different type of ethical ideal is needed (if indeed we need one). As for virtue ethics, Butler explains that it might too narrowly focus on the individual (2020: 57)—I would personally claim it *does*—which is not helpful if we consider "the embodied subject [as] defined . . . by its lack of self-sufficiency" (2020: 51), leading us to define an "extended region of the self" (2020: 52–3)—one which would far exceed the rationality exercised by Aristotle's *phronemos*, for example.

2 Recall the discussion in Chapter 4 of the worry about the loss of agency and related loss of the possibility to ascribe moral or political responsibility.

3 In this sense, my approach seems to match what Huth and Thonhauser identify as the core project of contemporary authors investigating vulnerability and who "elaborate a critique of the liberal ontology of the subject, and for that purpose they employ vulnerability as an ontological, but also normative category" (2020: 546). Although I would tend to flip this around and claim that it is because the liberal ontology of the subject is understood to be problematic that an investigation is prompted whereby we uncover our ontological vulnerability and its ethical potentiality. With that said, the articles gathered in this special topic section present interesting inquiries in the recent debates around vulnerability with somewhat of a heavy emphasis on Butler's view of precariousness and Erinn Gilson's approach.

4   MacCormack puts forward this notion in the following fashion: "We must introduce the flesh in the risks and experiments of thought we take, allow our bodies to hurt, to not be the occupant but make our flesh available to be occupied as part of a greater assemblage" (2016: 132).

5   *Thus Spoke Zarathustra* "Of the Three Metamorphoses."

6   Puig de la Bellacasa emphasizes that "humans exist only in a web of living co-vulnerabilities" (2017: 145).

7   MacCormack insists that the encounter needs to be with an other whose alterity is recognized. As she puts it, meeting the pre-conceived—an other we have already captured in a category or conceptualized in a certain manner—is not a genuine encounter because it does not amount to the openness needed in the ethical encounter. She says: "Alterity and openness, relinquishing reliance on pre-existing signifiers to become lost in the flows of affectivity, are essential to ethical encounters . . . Ethical desire cannot operate in the positioning of two entities aware of themselves as closed subjects" (2016: 17). Similarly, to our misplaced desire to render ourselves invulnerable, we have a tendency to categorize others as a way to feel comfortable in the encounter. What this does, instead, is prevent it. Making oneself open and recognizing the other in its alterity and openness is a riskier enterprise and yet it is also much more rewarding and enriching.

8   Matt Hayler's exploration of this question alongside that of moral responsibility in his essay "Posthumanism and the Bioethics of Moral Responsibility" articulates the issue very clearly. Along with posthumanist insights about entanglement and their challenges to the humanist notion of agency, he examines Bruce Waller's arguments against moral responsibility (2011), which pay attention to the various ways in which subjects may be constituted and rendered predisposed to make the "right" choice in a given circumstance. According to this view, one may be "lucky to be capable of making better choices" (Hayler 2022: 102). While Waller considers social and cultural factors, Hayler adds considerations having to do with microbiomics. Hayler explains: "The human-as-multispecies-complex (Haraway's unthinkable person as individual) manifests in a number of ways that relate to inherited luck, including gut microbes shaping behaviour and impacting on mental health" (2022: 105). At the end of Hayler's essay, the question remains as to what exactly this may mean in terms of assessing concrete actions and passing moral judgment on them, ascribing responsibility or not. My view on this is that at the same time individual responsibility is deflated by these considerations, another type of responsibility emerges, which is even more pressing than individual responsibility. I come to this shortly.

9   In a chapter of his *Sustainability, Wellbeing and the Posthuman Turn* that considers the links between deep ecology and new materialism, among other things, Thomas S. J. Smith claims: "[W]hile both are regularly

accused of anti-humanism (that is, an active attempt to denigrate the human subject), it isn't clear why it is often taken for granted by critics of approaches such as deep ecology and new materialism that greater care and concern for non-humans implies less concern for, or an intentional downgrading of, humans (Glasser 2011). Indeed, the very opposite is more likely to be the case, as we saw above, whereby human flourishing will ultimately only be stymied more by anthropocentric approaches" (2018: 75).

10 See the last part of Chapter 5.

11 As Barad puts it, "[e]thicality entails hospitality to the stranger threaded through oneself and through all being and non/being" (2012: 217).

12 Haraway suggests that "[c]ultivating response-ability requires much more from us. It requires the risk of being for some worlds rather than others and helping to compose those worlds with others" (2016b: 178n32).

13 Joanna Zylinska puts it in the following manner: "[T]here is no way to unthink ourselves out of our human standpoint, no matter how much kinship or entanglement with 'others' we identify" (2018: 59). As Nietzsche would have it in one of his early formulations of perspectivism: "We behold all things through the human head and cannot cut off this head" (1996: I §9).

14 In an article exploring the complementarity of Barad's and Levinas's views, Alex Christie argues "[e]thics is not something humans, or subjects more generally, choose to be a part of, but is intimately imbricated in their material ontology—the 'ethical call' is inaugurated in our very becoming and intra-acting with(in) the world(ing) (non)humans co(in)habit" (2020: 133). I agree that a material ontology is always already ethical. Zylinska explains, in her discussion of Anna Tsing's views on precarity and the call to responsibility to others, "it entails the necessary task of recognizing that entanglement with others is not just a matter of our acceptance or good will, because it precedes the emergence of the human sense of the self" (2018: 57). Whether we accept this ontological fact or not changes nothing: we are always entangled in this way and therefore always response—able. The question is whether we will act on this ability or not. For an analysis of Levinas in relation to Haraway and other feminist new materialists, see Groen and Geerts (2020).

15 Haraway considers "[m]atters of fact, matters of concern, and matters of care [as] knotted" (2016b: 41).

16 Braidotti explains, "[w]e are indeed becoming posthuman ethical subjects. We do so by overcoming hierarchical dichotomies and cultivating instead our multiple capacities for relations and modes of communication in a multi-directional manner" (2019: 63).

17 Puig de la Bellacasa continues: "As a transformative ethos, caring is a living technology with vital material implications—for human and nonhuman worlds" (2017: 67).

18 In the same way that we are responsible for the onset of the Anthropocene and sixth mass extinction event, all the while we act as environmentally conscious individuals and do not do direct harm but instead try to reverse the harm, we are also responsible for the inequitable conditions under which large groups of humans and nonhuman animals live. Again, transjective intersectionality dictates that we are also spatio-temporally entangled. The actions of our ancestors continue to unfold in and through us and our current actions will likewise have an extended affective impact in the future through the beings we are affecting. Response—ability is far-reaching.

19 As Anna L. Tsing claims, "staying alive—for every species—requires livable collaborations. Collaboration means working across difference, which leads to contamination. Without collaborations, we all die" (2015: 28) and "contaminated diversity is complicated, often ugly, and humbling" (2015: 33). Collaboration, the embrace of transjective affective webs of relations is not a smooth and easy process. It is messy and uncertain but essential not only to stay alive but to thrive.

20 Braidotti explains: "Vulnerability as the power of exposure is defined as an ethical and political means to come to terms with—rather than disavow—the untenable, painful, and unacceptable aspects and disasters of posthuman times" (2019: 169).

21 According to Moya Lloyd, Butler's reconceptualization of the body rests on the notion of vulnerability and it is this "corporeal vulnerability that makes possible ecstatic relationality and thence ethics and politics" (2015: 171).

22 As in previous work, Butler acknowledges the material fabric of life and its importance but chooses to focus on the subjective, the intersubjective, and the social. It is not so much that they ignore this dimension but instead that it is not where their interest lies. In an interview for *The New Yorker*, they say again, "We are all, if we stand, supported by any number of things. Even coming to see you today—the pavement allowed me to move, and so did my shoes, my orthotics, and the long hours spent by my physical therapist. His labor is in my walk, as it were. I wouldn't have been able to get here without any of those wonderful technologies and supporting relations. Acknowledging dependency as a condition of who any of us happens to be is difficult enough. But the larger task is to affirm social and ecological interdependence, which is regularly misrecognized as well" (Gessen 2020: np). My claim is that we can reconcile and support Butler's views with an examination of the materialist theory I have worked with throughout this book. It is as important to understand the subjective and intersubjective fabric as it is to understand the material. Brought together, these understandings give us a clear view of transjective being and how it is constituted. That is why I continue to appeal to their potent analyses and put them to work alongside those of material feminists.

23 For the whole articulation of the argument, see Chapter 2 of *The Force of Nonviolence*.

24 This is reminiscent of Félix Guattari's claim that "it will be a question of literally reconstructing the modalities of 'group-being' [*l'être-en-groupe*]" (2000: 34). Braidotti concurs and claims "[i]n the framework of affirmative ethics, the challenge consists in opening up alternative ways of thinking about what kind of humans we are in the process of becoming: 'we' who are not One and the same, but are nonetheless in *this* posthuman convergence together" (2019: 162).

REFERENCES

Ahmed, S. (2006), *Queer Phenomenology: Orientations, Objects, Others*, Durham: Duke University Press.
Ahmed, S. (2015), *The Cultural Politics of Emotion*, 2nd ed., London: Routledge.
Alaimo, S. (2010), *Bodily Natures: Science, Environment, and the Material Self*, Bloomington: Indiana University Press.
Alaimo, S. (2016), *Exposed: Environmental Politics and Pleasures in Posthuman Times*, Minneapolis: University of Minnesota Press.
Alaimo, S. (2018), "Material Feminism in the Anthropocene," in C. Åsberg and R. Braidotti (eds.), *A Feminist Companion to the Posthumanities*, 45–54, New York: Springer.
Armiero, M. (2021), *Wasteocene: Stories from the Global Dump*, Cambridge: Cambridge University Press.
Barad, K. (2007), *Meeting the Universe Halfway: Quantum Physics & the Entanglement of Matter & Meaning*, Durham: Duke University Press.
Barad, K. (2012), "On Touching—The Inhuman That Therefore I Am," *Differences: A Journal of Feminist Cultural Studies* 23(3): 206–23.
Beauvoir, S. ([1949] 2011), *The Second Sex*, trans. C. Borde and S. Malovany-Chevallier, New York: Vintage.
Benhabib, S. (1992), *Situating the Self: Gender, Community and Postmodernism in Contemporary Ethics*, London: Routledge.
Bennett, J. (2010), *Vibrant Matter: A Political Ecology of Things*, Durham: Duke University Press.
Bignall, S. (2022), "Colonial Humanism, Alter-Humanism, and Ex-colonialism," in Stefan Herbrechter, Ivan Callus, Manuela Rossini, Marija Grech, Megen de Bruin-Molé, and Christopher John Müller (eds.), *Palgrave Handbook of Critical Posthumanism*, 1–22. London: Palgrave, 2022.
Bloodsworth-Lugo, M. K. (2007), *In-Between Bodies: Sexual Difference, Race, and Sexuality*, Albany: SUNY Press.
Bogost, I. (2012), *Alien Phenomenology, Or What It's Like to Be a Thing*, Minneapolis: University of Minnesota Press.
Braidotti, R. (2006), "Affirmation versus Vulnerability: On Contemporary Ethical Debates," *Symposium: Canadian Journal of Continental Philosophy* 10(1): 235–54.
Braidotti, R. (2009), *La Philosophie . . . là où on ne l'attend pas*, Paris: Larousse Publishing.
Braidotti, R. (2013), *The Posthuman*, Cambridge: Polity Press.

Braidotti, R. (2018), "Ethics of Joy," in R. Braidotti and M. Hlavajova (eds.), *Posthuman Glossary*, 221–4, London: Bloomsbury.
Braidotti, R. (2019), *Posthuman Knowledge*, Cambridge: Polity Press.
Braidotti, R. (2022), *Posthuman Feminism*, Cambridge: Polity Press.
Brinkema, E. (2014), *The Forms of the Affects*, Durham: Duke University Press.
Brison, S. J. (2002), *Aftermath: Violence and the Remaking of a Self*, Princeton: Princeton University Press.
Bryant, L. (2011), *The Democracy of Objects*, Ann Arbor: University of Michigan Press.
Butler, J. ([1993] 2011), *Bodies That Matter: On the Discursive Limits of Sex*, London: Routledge.
Butler, J. (2004), *Precarious Life: The Power of Mourning and Violence*, London: Verso.
Butler, J. (2009), *Frames of War: When is Life Grievable?*, London: Verso.
Butler, J. (2020), *The Force of Nonviolence: An Ethico-Political Bind*, London: Verso.
Cahill, A. J. (2001), *Rethinking Rape*, Ithaca: Cornell University Press.
Cavarero, A. (2000), *Relating Narratives: Storytelling and Selfhood*, trans. P. A. Kottman, London: Routledge.
Cavarero, A. (2009), *Horrorism: Naming Contemporary Violence*, New York: Columbia University Press.
Chamowitz, D. (2017), *What a Plant Knows: A Field Guide to the Senses*, New York: Scientific American/Farrar, Straus and Giroux.
Chen, M. Y. (2012), *Animacies: Biopolitics, Racial Mattering, and Queer Affect*, Durham: Duke University Press.
Christie, A. (2020), "'Flying at Our Hand': Toward an Ethics of Intra-Active Response-ability," *Configurations* 28(1): 117–43.
Cielemęcka, O. and C. Åsberg (2019), "Introduction: Toxic Embodiment and Feminist Environmental Humanities," *Environmental Humanities* 11(1): 101–7.
Clare, S. (2016), "On the Politics of 'New Feminist Materialisms,'" in V. Pitts-Taylor (ed.), *Mattering: Feminism, Science, and Materialism*, 58–72, New York: New York University Press.
Cohen, J. J. (2015), *Stone: An Ecology of the Inhuman*, Minneapolis: University of Minnesota Press.
Cohen, T. and C. Colebrook (2016), "Preface," in T. Cohen, C. Colebrook, and J. Hillis Miller, *Twilight of the Anthropocene Idols*, London: Open Humanities Press.
Colebrook, C. (2000), "Is Sexual Difference a Problem?," in I. Buchanan and C. Colebrook (eds.), *Deleuze and Feminist Theory*, 110–27, Edinburgh: Edinburgh University Press.
Colebrook, C. (2008), "On Not-becoming Man," in S. Alaimo and S. Hekman (eds.), *Material Feminisms*, 52–84, Indianapolis: Indiana University Press.
Colebrook, C. (2011), "Time and Autopoiesis: The Organism Has No Future," in L. Guillaume and J. Hughes (eds.), *Deleuze and the Body*, 9–28, Edinburgh: Edinburgh University Press.

Colebrook, C. (2014), *Death of the PostHuman: Essays on Extinction Vol. 1*, Ann Arbor: University of Michigan Library.

Colebrook, C. (2017), "Fragility, Globalism and the End of the World," *Ctrl-Z: New Media Philosophy* 7: np.

Coole, D. (2005), "Rethinking Agency: A Phenomenological Approach to Embodiment and Agentic Capacities," *Political Studies* 53: 124–42.

Crutzen, P. J. and E. F. Stoermer (2000), "The 'Anthropocene,'" *IGBP Newsletter* 41: 17–18.

Daigle, C. (2009), *Jean-Paul Sartre*, London: Routledge.

Daigle, C. (2017), "Trans-subjectivity/Trans-objectivity," in H. A. Fielding and D. E. Olkowski (eds.), *Feminist Phenomenology Futures*, 183–200, Indianapolis: Indiana University Press.

Daigle, C. (2020), "Can Existentialism be a Posthumanism?: Beauvoir as Precursor to Material Feminism," *Philosophy Today* 64(3): 63–80.

Daigle, C. (2021a), "Moving Beyond Humanism in a Constructive Manner: The Case for Posthumanist Material Feminism," *Rivista Per la Filosofia. Filosofia e insegnamento* XXXVIII(113): 81–95.

Daigle, C. (2021b), *Nietzsche as Phenomenologist: Becoming What One Is*, Edinburgh: Edinburgh University Press.

Daigle, C. (2022a), "Deleuzean Traces: The Self of the Polyp," in C. Daigle and T. McDonald (eds.), *From Deleuze and Guattari to Posthumanism*, 41–62, London: Bloomsbury.

Daigle, C. (2022b), "The (Post)human and the (Post)pandemic: Rediscovering Our Selves," in T. Topuzovski and S. Newman (eds.), *The Posthuman Pandemic*, 27–42, London: Bloomsbury.

Daigle, C. and M.-E. Morin (2018), "Editorial Introduction," *PhaenEx: Journal of Existential and Phenomenological Theory and Culture* 12(2): i–vi.

Daigle, C. and I. Santoemma (2022), "Pandemicity and Subjectivity: The Posthumanist Vulnerability of the zoe/geo/techno Framed Subject," *Matter: Journal of New Materialist Research* 3(2): 30–59.

Davis, H. (2015), "Toxic Progeny: The Plastisphere and Other Queer Futures," *philoSOPHIA: A Journal of Continental Feminism* 5(2): 231–50.

del Río, E. (2012), *Deleuze and the Cinemas of Performance: Powers of Affection*, Edinburgh: Edinburgh University Press.

Deleuze, G. (1968), *Difference and Repetition*, New York: Columbia University Press.

Deleuze, G. and F. Guattari (1980), *A Thousand Plateaus: Capitalism and Schizophrenia*, Minneapolis: University of Minnesota Press.

Deleuze, G. and F. Guattari ([1972] 1983), *Anti-Oedipus: Capitalism and Schizophrenia*, trans. R. Hurley, M. Seem, and H. R. Lane, Minneapolis: University of Minnesota Press.

Deleuze, G. and F. Guattari ([1991] 1994), *What Is Philosophy?*, trans. H. Tomlinson and G. Burchell, New York: Columbia University Press.

Diderot, D. (1966), *Rameau's Nephew: And D'Alembert's Dream*, Harmondsworth: Penguin.

Diprose, R. (2013), "Corporeal Interdependence: From Vulnerability to Dwelling in Ethical Community," *SubStance* 42(3): 185–204.
Dolphijn, R. (2021), *The Philosophy of Matter: A Meditation*, London: Bloomsbury.
Dolphijn, R. and I. van der Tuin (2012). *New Materialism: Interviews and Cartographies*, Ann Arbor: Open Humanities Press.
Drichel, S. (2013), "Introduction: Reframing Vulnerability: 'so obviously the problem . . .'?," *SubStance* 42(3): 3–27.
Epstein, B. (nd), "Social Ontology," *The Stanford Encyclopedia of Philosophy*. Available online: https://plato.stanford.edu/entries/social-ontology/#FlatOnto.
Fanon, F. (1967), *Black Skin, White Masks*, trans. C. Lam Markmann, New York: Grove Press.
Freedman, K. L. (2014), *One Hour in Paris: A True Story of Rape and Recovery*, Chicago: Chicago University Press.
Frost, S. (2016), *Biocultural Creatures: Toward a New Theory of the Human*, Durham: Duke University Press.
Gatens, M. and G. Lloyd (1999), *Collective Imaginings: Spinoza, Past and Present*, London: Routledge.
Geerts, E. and D. Carstens (2019), "Ethico-onto-epistemology," *Philosophy Today* 63(4): 915–25.
Gehrhardt, M. (2015), *The Men with Broken Faces: Gueules Cassées of the First World War*, New York: Peter Lang Publishing.
Gessen, M. (2020), "Judith Butler Wants Us to Reshape our Rage," The New Yorker. Available online: https://www.newyorker.com/culture/the-new-yorker-interview/judith-butler-wants-us-to-reshape-our-rage/amp.
Gilson, E. (2011), "Vulnerability, Ignorance, and Oppression," *Hypatia* 26(2): 308–32.
Groen, A. and E. Geerts (2020), "Philosophical Post-anthropology for the Chthulucene. Levinasian and Feminist New Materialist Perspectives in More-Than-Human Crisis Times," *Internationales Jahrbuch für philosophische Anthropologie* 10(1): 195–214.
Grosz, E. (2017), *The Incorporeal: Ontology, Ethics, and the Limits of Materialism*, New York: Columbia University Press.
Guattari, F. (2000), *The Three Ecologies*, trans. I. Pindar and P. Sutton, New Brunswick: The Athlone Press.
Hansen, M. (2004), *New Philosophy for New Media*, Cambridge, MA: The MIT Press.
Hansen, M. (2006), *Bodies in Code: Interfaces with Digital Media*, New York: Routledge.
Haraway, D. (1991), *Simians, Cyborgs and Women: The Reinvention of Nature*, New York: Routledge.
Haraway, D. (2016a), *Manifestly Haraway*, Minneapolis: University of Minnesota Press.
Haraway, D. (2016b), *Staying With the Trouble: Making Kin in the Chthulucene*, Durham: Duke University Press.

Harman, G. (2016), *Immaterialism: Objects and Social Theory*, Cambridge: Polity Press.
Hayler, M. (2022), "Posthumanism and the Bioethics of Moral Responsibility," in D. Sands (ed.), *Bioethics and the Posthumanities*, 99–115, London: Routledge.
Hayles, N. K. (1999), *How We Became Posthuman: Virtual Bodies in Cybernetics, Literature, and Informatics*, Chicago: University of Chicago Press.
Hayles, N. K. (2017), *Unthought: The Power of the Cognitive Unconscious*, Chicago: The University of Chicago Press.
Hayward, E. (2010), "Fingeryeyes: Impressions of Cup Corals," *Cultural Anthropology* 25: 577–99.
Hekman, S. (2008), "Constructing the Ballast: An Ontology for Feminism," in S. Alaimo and S. Hekman (eds.), *Material Feminisms*, Indianapolis: Indiana University Press.
Hekman, S. (2014), "Vulnerability and Ontology: Butler's Ethics," *Australian Feminist Studies* 29(82): 454–64.
Hird, M. J. (2010), "Indifferent Globality: Gaia, Symbiosis and 'Other Worldliness,'" *Theory, Culture & Society* 27(2–3): 54–72.
Hird, M. J. (2013), "Waste, Landfills, and an Environmental Ethic of Vulnerability," *Ethics & The Environment* 18(1): 105–24.
Hird, M. J. (2017), "Proliferation, Extinction, and an Anthropocene Aesthetic," in J. Weinstein and C. Colebrook (eds.), *Posthumous Life: Theorizing Beyond the Human*, 251–69, New York: Columbia University Press.
Hird, M. J. and K. Yusoff (2018), "Lines of Shite: Microbial-Mineral Chatter in the Anthropocene," in R. Braidotti and L. Bignall (eds.), *Posthuman Ecologies: Complexity and Process After Deleuze*, 265–81, London: Rowman & Littlefield.
Hoppe, K. (2020), "Responding as Composing: Towards a Post-anthropocentric Feminist Ethics for the Anthropocene," *Distinktion: Journal of Social Theory* 21(2): 125–42.
Houle, K. (2022), "Symmetry and Asymmetry in Conceptual and Morphological Formations: The Difference Plant Body Growth can Make to Human Thought," in C. Daigle and T. H. McDonald (eds.), *From Deleuze and Guattari to Posthumanism*, 85–105, London: Bloomsbury.
Hume, D. (1985), *A Treatise of Human Nature*, Harmondsworth: Penguin.
Huth, M. and G. Thonhauser (2020), "Introduction," *Philosophy Today* 64(3): 537–55.
Ingold, T. (2011), *Being Alive: Essays on Movement, Knowledge and Description*, London: Routledge.
Jackson, Z. I. (2020), *Becoming Human. Matter and Meaning in an Antiblack World*, New York: New York University Press.
Jamieson, D. (2016), "A Review of 'The Anthropocene Project: Virtue in the Age of Climate Change' by Byron Williston," *Notre Dame Philosophical Reviews: An Electronic Journal*. Available online: https://ndpr.nd.edu/news/the-anthropocene-project-virtue-in-the-age-of-climate-change/ (accessed 29 June 2018).

Joker (2019), Directed by Todd Phillips (copyright). United States of America: Warner Bros. Pictures.
Kosofsky Sedgwick, E. (2002), *Touching Feeling: Affect, Pedagogy, Performativity*, Durham: Duke University Press.
Kroker, A. (2012), *Body Drift: Butler, Hayles, Haraway*, Minneapolis: University of Minnesota Press.
Kruks, S. (2012), *Simone de Beauvoir and the Politics of Ambiguity*, Oxford: Oxford University Press.
Kruks, S. (2019), "For a Modest Human Exceptionalism: Simone de Beauvoir and the 'New Materialisms,'" *Simone de Beauvoir Studies* 30: 252–74.
Lloyd, M. (2015), "The Ethics and Politics of Vulnerable Bodies," in M. Lloyd (ed.), *Butler and Ethics*, 167–92, Edinburgh: Edinburgh University Press.
MacCormack, P. (2016), *Posthuman Ethics*, London: Routledge.
MacCormack, P. (2020), *The Ahuman Manifesto: Activism for the End of the Anthropocene*, London: Bloomsbury.
Manning, E. (2014), "Wondering the World Directly—Or, How Movement Outruns the Subject," *Body & Society* 20(3&4): 162–88.
Manning, E. and B. Massumi (2014), *Thought in the Act: Passages in the Ecology of Experience*, Minneapolis: Minnesota University Press.
Marder, M. (2013), *Plant-Thinking: A Philosophy of Vegetal Life*, New York: Columbia University Press.
Massumi, B. (2002), *Parables for the Virtual: Movement, Affect, Sensation*, Durham: Duke University Press.
Massumi, B. (2015), *Politics of Affect*, Cambridge: Polity Press.
Mbembe, A. (2019), *Necropolitics*, trans S. Corcoran, Durham: Duke University Press.
Neimanis, A. (2013), "Feminist Subjectivity, Watered," *Feminist Review* 103: 23–41.
Neimanis, A. (2017), *Bodies of Water: Posthuman Feminist Phenomenology*, London: Bloomsbury.
Neimanis, A., C. Åsberg, and J. Hedrén (2015), "Four Problems, Four Directions for Environmental Humanities: Toward Critical Posthumanities for the Anthropocene," *Ethics & the Environment* 20(1): 67–97.
Nietzsche, F. (2003), *Writings from the Late Notebooks*, ed. Rüdiger Bitnner, Cambridge: Cambridge University Press.
Nietzsche, F. (1974a), *The Gay Science: With a Prelude in Rhymes and an Appendix of Songs*, trans. W. Kaufmann, New York: Vintage.
Nietzsche, F. (1974b), *Thus Spoke Zarathustra: A Book for Everyone and No One*, trans. R. J. Hollingdale, Harmondsworth: Penguin.
Nietzsche, F. ([1886] 1989), *Beyond Good and Evil: Prelude to a Philosophy of the Future*, trans. W. Kaufmann, New York: Vintage.
Nietzsche, F. (1996), *Human, All Too Human*, trans. R. J. Hollingdale, Cambridge: Cambridge University Press.
Nietzsche, F. ([1881] 1997), *Daybreak: Thoughts on the Prejudices of Philosophers*, trans. R. J. Hollingdale, Cambridge: Cambridge University Press.

Noorata, P. (2013), "Interview: More Portraits of Soldiers Before, During, and After War," *My Modern MET*. Available online: https://mymodernmet.com/lalage-snow-we-are-the-not-dead-interview/ (accessed October 28, 2020).

Pitts-Taylor, V. (2016), "Mattering: Feminism, Science, and Corporeal Politics," in V. Pitts-Taylor (ed.), *Mattering: Feminism, Science, and Materialism*, 1–20, New York: New York University Press.

Plumwood, V. (2008), "Shadow Places and the Politics of Dwelling," *Australian Humanities Review* 44: np.

Puig de la Bellacasa, M. (2017), *Matters of Care: Speculative Ethics in More Than Human Worlds*, Minneapolis: University of Minnesota Press.

Pulkkinen, T. (2020), "Vulnerability and the Human in Judith Butler's and Adriana Cavarero's Feminist Thought: A Politics of Philosophy Point of View," *Redescriptions: Political Thought, Conceptual History and Feminist Theory* 23(2): 151–64.

Radomska, M. (2016), *Uncontainable Life: A Biophilosophy of Bioart*, Linköping: Linköping University.

Rimbaud, A. ([1976] 2008), *Complete Works*, trans P. Schmidt, New York: Harper Perennial.

Roelvink, G. and M. Zolkos (2015), *Angelaki: Journal of the Theoretical Humanities* 20(3): 43–57.

Sartre, J. P. ([1943] 1992), *Being and Nothingness*, London: Routledge.

Seigworth, G. J. and M. Gregg (2010), "An Inventory of Shimmers," in G. J. Seigworth and M. Gregg (eds.), *The Affect Theory Reader*, 1–25, Durham: Duke University Press.

Serres, M. (1982), *The Parasite*, trans. L. R. Schehr, London: The Johns Hopkins University Press.

Sharp, H. (2011), *Spinoza and the Politics of Renaturalization*, Chicago: University of Chicago Press.

Smith, T. (2018), *Sustainability, Wellbeing and the Posthuman Turn*, London: Palgrave Macmillan UK.

Sobchack, V. (2004), *Carnal Thoughts: Embodiment and Moving Image Culture*, Berkeley: University of California Press.

Sontag, S. (2003), *Regarding the Pain of Others*, London: Picador.

Spinoza, B. (2002), *Complete Works*, trans. Samuel Shirley. Edited with introduction and notes Michael L. Morgan. Indianapolis/Cambridge: Hackett Publishing.

Stenner, P. (2008), "A. N. Whitehead and Subjectivity," *Subjectivity* 22: 90–109.

TallBear, K. (2017), "Beyond the Life/Not Life Binary: A Feminist-Indigenous Reading of Cryopreservation, Interspecies Thinking and the New Materialisms," in J. Radin and E. Kowal (eds.), *Cryopolitics: Frozen Life in a Melting World*, 179–202, Cambridge, MA: The MIT Press.

Trigg, D. (2014), *The Thing: A Phenomenology of Horror*, Portland: Zero Books.

Tsing, A. L. (2015), *The Mushroom at the End of the World: On the Possibility of Life in Capitalist Ruins*, Princeton: Princeton University Press.

Tuana, N. (2008), "Viscous Porosity: Witnessing Katrina," in S. Alaimo and S. Hekman (eds.), *Material Feminisms*, 188–213, Indianapolis: Indiana University Press.

Uexküll, J. (1965a), *Mondes animaux et mondes humains: Suivi de théorie de la signification*, Paris: Denoël.

Uexküll, J. (1965b), *Streifzüge durch die Umwelten von Tieren und Menschen: Ein Bilderbuch unsichtbarer Welten*, Hamburg: Rowohlt.

Uexküll, J. (2010), *A Foray into the Worlds of Animals and Humans: With a Theory of Meaning*, trans. J. D. O'Neil, Minneapolis: University of Minnesota Press.

Ulrich Obrist, H. and M. Cohen (2013), "Michel Serres," *O32C* 25: np.

van Dooren, T. (2014), *Flight Ways: Life and Loss at the Edge of Extinction*, New York: Columbia University Press.

Vartanian, A. (1950), "Trembley's Polyp, La Mettrie, and Eighteenth-Century French Materialism," *Journal of the History of Ideas* 11(3): 259–86.

Waller, B. (2011), *Against Moral Responsibility*, Cambridge, MA: MIT Press.

Watts, V. (2013), "Indigenous Place-thought & Agency amongst Humans and Non-humans (First Woman and Sky Woman Go on a European World Tour!)," *Decolonization: Indigeneity, Education & Society* 2(1): 20–34.

White, S. K. (2000), *Sustaining Affirmation: The Strengths of Weak Ontology in Political Theory*, Princeton: Princeton University Press.

White, S. K. (2005), "Weak Ontology: Genealogy and Critical Issues," *Hedgehog Review* 7(2): 11–25.

Widder, N. (2011), "Matter as Simulacrum; Thought as Phantasm; Body as Event," in L. Guillaume and J. Hughes (eds.), *Deleuze and the Body*, 96–114, Edinburgh: Edinburgh University Press.

Yusoff, K. (2015), "Queer Coal: Genealogies in/of the Blood," *philoSOPHIA: A Journal of Continental Feminism* 5(2): 203–29.

Zylinska, J. (2018), *The End of Man: A Feminist Counterapocalypse*, Minneapolis: University of Press.

INDEX

9/11 135

ability 136, 159
Aboriginal people 11
abstract bodies 64
actants 23
Actor-Network Theory (ANT) 23, 170 n.24
affective bodies 22, 118
affective fabric 1–2, 63–71, 75, 83, 92, 95, 117, 119, 131, 155, 178 n.9
affective relations 26, 133
affects/affecting 26, 64–7, 73, 88–91, 93–5, 97, 106, 118, 119, 136, 155, 178 n.12
affect theory 63, 64
affirmative empathy 135, 155, 163
affirmative transjective ethos 142, 154
Afghanistan 115, 116
Aftermath: Violence and the Remaking of a Self (Brison) 107
agency 19–21, 33, 84, 88, 93–7, 157, 183 nn.11, 12
agential realism 20, 171 n.33, 183 n.11
agentic capacity 3, 20, 23, 33, 43, 46, 88, 90, 91, 94, 96, 97, 108, 117, 138–41, 151, 153, 156, 158, 160, 188 n.13
Ahmed, Sarah 29, 63, 70, 74, 75, 105, 155, 180 n.24
Ahuman Manifesto, The (MacCormack) 141

Alaimo, Stacy 16, 22, 106, 119, 153, 160, 170 n.19
Alien Phenomenology (Bogost) 23
allergies 77–9, 82
alter-humanism 167 n.1
anaphylaxis 35, 78, 79, 81
Androcene 141
animacy 63, 177 n.4
Anishinaabe people 9, 10, 13
Anthropocene 48, 130, 138, 140, 141, 194 n.18
anthropocentrism 5, 27, 53, 157
anthropodiscentering 53
anthropogenic activity 140
anthropogenic change 141
Anti-Oedipus (Deleuze and Guattari) 68
anxieties 7, 78, 80, 82, 84, 90, 93, 94, 130
 anthropocenic 138–42
 philosophical 84–7
Aristotle 151
Armiero, Marco 138
Åsberg, Cecilia 138
assaults 64, 109, 131–5, 155
assemblages 15, 18, 21, 22, 28, 63, 169 n.13
 congregational 22
 constitution of 32
 dynamic 30–3, 83, 88, 128, 129, 137
 human transjective 63
AstraZeneca 78
asymmetrical relations 33, 138, 160

bacteria 139
balanced reciprocity 33

Barad, Karen   16, 18–22, 26, 44, 152, 153, 154, 159, 171 n.33
Beauvoir, Simone de   3, 7, 16–17, 26, 29, 67, 85, 151
Becoming Human (Jackson)   171 n.28
Being and Nothingness (Sartre)   25
being as it is   25
being-for-itself   72
being for-others   72
being is in-itself   25
beings. *See also* human beings
    definitions of   28
    existence of   26–7, 30–1
    kinds of   26
    relations among   25–7
Benhabib, Seyla   84, 85, 87
Bennett, Jane   16, 21, 22, 51, 63, 117
Beyond Good and Evil (Nietzsche)   88–9
Bignall, Simone   167 n.1
biochemical process   18, 19, 21, 26, 116
biological body   64
biological cognizers   65
biological determinism   21
biological processes   16–18, 20, 21
biology, theory of   49
Black Lives Matter (BLM)   131, 188 n.14
Bloodsworth-Lugo, Mary K.   32
bodily polyps   47–8
body(ies) without organs (BwO)   41, 68, 69, 177 n.4, 179 n.15
bodying   63, 69–75, 179 n.18
Bogost, Ian   23
Braidotti, Rosi   17, 27, 63, 66, 88, 95, 111, 112, 128, 152–4, 158, 162, 163, 171 n.29, 179 n.17, 195 n.24
Brison, Susan J.   92, 107, 108, 113, 161
Brock, Isaac   10
Brock University   10, 12
Bryant, Levi   24

Burroughs, William S.   41
Butler, Judith   7, 22, 29, 84, 110–13, 118, 119, 133, 161, 162, 170 n.19, 171 n.33, 185 nn.9, 11, 194 n.22

Cahill, Ann J.   185 n.12
callicle   42
cancerous cells   47, 48
Capitalocene   141
care   155–60
Cavarero, Adriana   92, 109–10, 113, 161, 185 n.9
cerebrocentric   44
Chauvin, Derek   124, 131, 188 n.13
Chen, M. Y.   63, 64, 68, 177 n.4
Christchurch mosque shootings (2019)   134
Christie, Alex   193 n.14
chronic condition   107
Cielemęcka, Olga   138
cinema   70, 180 n.19
Clare, Stephanie   157
classical phenomenology   74
coalescence   91, 92, 95, 97
co-constitution   18, 30, 71
cognitive nonconscious   177 n.5, 183 n.12
cognitive unconscious   63, 65
cohabitation   143–50
Cohen, Jeffrey Jerome   52, 53
Colebrook, Claire   31, 64, 118, 182 n.9
collective agency   7, 95–6
collective agent   90, 91, 93
collective individuation   90
colonial history   9–11
colonialism   10, 15
colonization, political process of   11
complexity   33
concretion   91, 92
conscious engagement   19
conscious intentionality   50
consciousness   17, 25, 30, 43, 44, 46, 50, 65, 70, 71, 89, 106, 109
consumer culture   137

INDEX   205

consumerism   138
contemporary film theory   71
Coole, Diana   20, 96, 183 n.13
coral polyps   41–3, 45, 46
coral reef   42–3, 46
correlationism   24, 180 n.25
Covid-19
  pandemic   133–6
  vaccination   77–80
Crutzen, Paul J.   140
culture   137
cup corals   42
cyborg   18
Cyborg Manifesto (Haraway)   17–18

Davis, Heather   139
Daybreak (*Nietzsche*)   40, 41, 46
decolonization   9–11
deep ecology   192–3 n.9
Deleuze, Gilles   21, 29, 31, 41, 63, 67, 68, 84, 90, 91, 94, 119, 179 n.15, 180 n.19
Deleuzian traces   41
del Río, Elena   67, 94, 95, 179 n.15
Derrida, Jacques   27, 28
Descartes, René   83
Diderot, Denis   40
Difference and Repetition (*Deleuze*)   90
digital technologies   136
Diprose, Rosalyn   117, 185 n.11
discrimination   11
discursive systems   22
Dish with One Spoon Wampum agreement   10
disorientation   75, 180 n.24
distributed agency   20, 190 n.20
Dolphijn, Rick   92
Drichel, Simone   105, 106
dualistic approach   67
dynamic multiplicity   90

Earth system   15, 47, 48, 140
ecojustice approach   137
ecological degradation   141
ecological diversity   12

ecosystems   140
"effervescence of agency"   22
egalitarian imaginary   162
embodied consciousness   16, 19, 48, 55, 67, 70, 71, 74, 180 n.19
embodiment   4, 29, 30, 45, 67, 69, 70, 96, 106
emotions   66, 73, 90, 118, 120
entanglements   7, 11, 19–22, 24, 29, 32, 33, 36, 49, 56, 61, 65, 69, 92, 105, 127, 128
  of consciousness   67
  intersubjective   111
  between living and nonliving   139
  manifold   9, 62, 75, 90, 118, 127, 136, 138, 141, 154, 156, 163
  material   19–21, 23, 30, 39, 45, 47, 90, 106, 109, 110, 118
  radical multiple   141
  subjective   109
  techno   136
  transobjective   113
environmental ecology   128
Environmental Humanities   138
EpiPen   35, 77, 79
ethical agent   85
ethical duties   12, 105
ethicality   151, 155, 158, 162
ethical responsibility   97, 117, 157, 159
ethical thinking   28
ethics   112, 151, 152
  affirmative   153, 154, 162, 163, 195 n.24
  of ambiguity   151
  orientation   155, 156, 158
  relational   158
  situational existential   151
  trans-corporeal   160
  transjective   156, 157
  virtue   151, 152
Ethics (*Spinoza*)   66
eudaimonia   152
"Everything Must Go" (*Rumble*, 2019)   123

existentialism   3
existential phenomenology   25, 67, 117
extinction   140, 142, 174 n.16
extracerebral thinking   44, 51
extramaterialism   172 n.36
extraocular vision   43, 44

Facebook   134
Fanon, Frantz   26, 67
feeling/being out of place   55–60
feminism/feminists   85–7. *See also* material feminism/feminists
First Nations   10, 166 n.2
First World War   116, 186 n.15
flatness   25, 26, 170 n.24
flat ontology   23–8, 171 n.29
Flight Ways: Life and Loss at the Edge of Extinction (van Dooren)   174 n.16
Floyd, George   124, 131, 133, 188 n.13
fluidity   32
Force of Nonviolence, The (Butler)   110, 161, 162
Foucault, Michel   26–9, 156, 171 n.33
foundationalist ontologies   28
Frames of War (Butler)   110, 118
Frazier, Darnella   124, 131
Freedman, Karyn L.   107, 108, 113, 161
freedom   86, 88
French materialism   40
Frost, Samantha   16, 18, 20–2, 26, 51, 74, 137, 169 n.11

Gatens, Moira   90, 128, 152
Gay Science, The (Nietzsche)   141
gaze   72, 73
geo-bacterial activity   138
Gilson, Erinn   120, 184 n.1
Giving an Account of Oneself (Butler)   110
global economy   137
global trade   138

grand reason (*große Vernunft*)   3, 39, 174 n.12
Gregg, Melissa   73, 93
grievability   133
Grosz, Elizabeth   172 n.36
Guattari, Félix   21, 29, 31, 41, 63, 67, 68, 84, 93, 94, 128, 179 n.15, 187 n.6, 195 n.24

haecceities   68, 94
Hansen, Mark B. N.   180 n.22
Haraway, Donna J.   16–18, 127, 159, 187 n.1
hard materialism   84
hard postmodernism   85
Harman, Graham   24
Haudenosaunee people   9, 10, 13
Hayler, Matt   192 n.8
Hayles, N. Katherine   63, 65, 89, 128, 182–3 n.10
Hayward, Eva   42
Heidegger, Martin   4
Hekman, Susan   28, 86, 111, 185 n.9
hierarchies   23, 24, 26, 27
Hird, Myra J.   52, 138–40, 160, 168 n.9
holobionts   18
Hoppe, Katharine   112
human agency   86
human/animal distinction   17–18
human-animal/machine distinction   18
human beings   27, 45
  as being-in-the-world   4
  vs. bodily polyps   47
  as embodied consciousness   39, 73
  ethical thriving   151–64
  as humus   18
  interconnectivity with other beings   19, 22
  as material being   20, 22, 31, 61, 71, 72, 88
  in materiality   28
  reconceptualizing   151, 153, 157
  as subjective beings   30, 31, 61

as symbionts   168 n.9
as transjective beings   7–8, 28, 30–1, 47, 61, 63, 64, 67, 71, 84, 105, 108, 114, 117, 118, 125, 127, 128, 134, 152, 153, 158, 159, 162
as transsubjective beings   88
human bodies   22, 29, 31–2, 41, 51, 66, 167 n.2
  as fluid   32
  as grand reason (*große Vernunft*)   3, 39, 174 n.12
  with/without organs   67–70
human cognition   65
human cognizers   65
human exceptionalism   5, 16, 20, 30, 45, 48, 51, 97, 157
humanimal continuums   18
humanism   5, 6, 24, 85, 97
humanist feminism   17
humanist human   5, 6, 141–2, 175 n.16
humanist patriarchy   87
humanist subject   15, 17, 22, 85, 88
human polyps   40
human specificity   97
Hume, David   83, 84
humility   8, 13, 48, 51, 130, 140, 152, 154, 157, 158, 163
Hursthouse, Rosalind   151
Husserl, Edmund   29
Huth, Martin   191 n.3

I   83, 84, 88, 89, 91–3
idealism   172 n.36
immanence   64, 68, 94
immanentist philosophy   31
Imperial Japanese Air Service   135
impersonal affect   67
impersonal politics   118
implicit bias   59
Indigenous people   166 n.2
  accepting settlers   11, 12
  oppression   9
  rights   11–12
Indigenous place-thought   189 n.20

individual as collective   95–7
individualism   20, 22, 66, 123, 161
ineffability   113–17
"inexhaustible potential"   163
Ingold, Tim   52
inoculation   77–82, 99
inorganic beings   51, 52
inosculation   99–101
intentional consciousness   25, 55
intentless direction   51
interactionist metaphysics   33
interconnectivity   19, 23, 33, 36, 156, 160
interobjectivity   30, 63, 71, 172 n.34
intersectionality   129
interspecies collaboration   38
intersubjective relations   29, 90, 106, 113
intersubjectivity   19, 30, 61, 71, 106, 172 n.34
intra-acting agencies   19, 20
intra-activity   19–20
Inuit people   10
involuntary memory   50
Izambard, Georges   84

Jack Daniel's   77, 81, 82
Jackson, Zakiyyah Iman   171 n.28
Jamieson, Dale   140
Johnson & Johnson   78
Joker (2019)   121–3
joy   152–5, 156, 163

Kant, Immanuel   39
Kottman, Paul A.   109
Kroker, Arthur   23, 170 n.21
Kruks, Sonia   85, 87, 88, 97
Kurdi, Alan   124

la Mettrie, Julien Offray de   40
land acknowledgment   12, 13
  definition   9
  as reflective process   11
  as tool of decolonization   10
land appropriation   10
Latour, Bruno   23, 26

Lebenswelt 49
Leloup, Jean 114, 115
Leopold, Aldo 51
Levinas, Emmanuel 50
L'homme machine (la *Mettrie*) 40
life 13, 21, 27
linguistic determinism 86
little reason (*kleine Vernunft*) 39, 174 n.12
lived body 51, 66, 70, 71
lived experience 17
lived worlds 49
Lloyd, Genevieve 90, 128, 152
lockdowns 134, 136
Locke, John 84
"Lucie" (song) 114–15
Lyotard, Jean-François 27

MacCormack, Patricia 130, 141, 154, 156, 182 n.7, 192 n.7
MacIntyre, Alasdair 151
Manning, Erin 63, 69, 70, 179 n.18
man-of-war 44–6
Marder, Michael 48–50, 52, 175 n.19
marine polyps 40–6, 47, 174 n.13
Massumi, Brian 63, 66, 69, 70, 90, 92, 119, 154, 157, 179 n.18
material constitution 29
material feminism 3, 4, 15, 16, 18, 119, 167 n.1, 190 n.20
material feminists 3–4, 16–23, 26, 39, 111, 172 n.36
material feminist theory 171 n.28
materialism 24, 31, 65, 172 n.36
materialist thinking 40
materiality 4, 7, 17, 18, 22–4, 28, 30, 32, 39, 40, 45, 46, 51, 52, 58, 59, 61, 64, 73, 89, 110, 138, 168 n.8, 171 n.33, 172 n.36
materiality of bodies 16, 29, 43, 74, 110, 111
material ontology 193 n.14
material processes 65, 111
material world 86, 88
matter, dynamism of 19, 23

Mbembe, Achille 129
memes 131
memory 30, 44, 50, 62, 78, 79, 83, 89, 107, 109, 132
mental ecology 128
Men with Broken Faces: Gueules Cassées of the First World War, The (Gerhardt) 186 n.15
Merleau-Ponty, Maurice 29, 30, 70, 72, 179 n.18
metaphysical-religious tradition 39, 171 n.31
metaphysics of individualism 19, 20
Metis people 10
microbial progeny 139
Milles Excuses Milady (2009) 114
mineral beings 51, 52
mineral-biological system 52
mineral-microbial chatter 139
Minneapolis 131–3
Mississauga people 10
modernity 87, 118
monism 66
monkeypox 189 n.17
monstrosity 129, 130
Moore, Michael 123
moral philosophies 28
moral responsibility 85, 192 n.8
multiple agencies 94, 118, 151, 153

Naked Lunch (*Burroughs*) 41
natureculture 18
Necropolitics (*Mbembe*) 129
Neimanis, Astrida 29, 32, 140
nervous system 44
neurobiology 107
new materialism 86, 165 n.2, 168 n.10, 192–3 n.9
New York City 135
Nietzsche, Friedrich 3, 7, 25, 26, 39–41, 46, 47, 81, 88, 89, 141, 153, 154, 174 n.12
Nietzschean self 89
Nietzsche as Phenomenologist (Daigle) 182 n.5

INDEX 209

nihilism 85, 141
nonconscious intentionality 50
nonhuman beings 7, 12, 43, 64, 139
nonhuman cognizers 65
nonhuman nonconscious cognition 65
non-intentional consciousness 50
nonsubject 87
non-Western thought 49

objectification 30, 71–3
objectifying approach 50
objectivity 172 n.34
object-oriented ontology (OOO) 23, 24, 26, 27, 170 nn.24, 25
oculocentrism 43, 44
One Hour in Paris (*Freedman*) 107
onto-epistemology 152
ontological fact 155, 156, 193 n.14
ontological perspective 8, 87
ontological reality 49, 163
ontological status 48, 109
ontological turn 27
ontological vulnerability 108
ontos logos 25
Ophiocoma wendtii 43, 173 n.10
oppression 17, 72
organic being 51, 52
orientating 70–5
orientation 63, 74, 75, 118, 180 n.24
other-than-human persons 12

pain 35, 36, 62, 106, 107, 112, 125, 135
Pando 156
Parasite, The (*Serres*) 90
Parmenides 25, 26
passivity 112
patriarchy 15, 17
Pearl Harbor attack (1941) 135
Pentagon 135
people of color 131
personal identity 83
Pfizer 77–9

phenomenology 3, 24, 25, 29, 30, 64–6, 70, 89, 119, 180 n.25
Phillips, Todd 121
Phoenix, Joaquin 121
phronemos 151
physical process 18, 19
Pitts-Taylor, Victoria 168 n.10
Plantationocene 141
plant ethics 176 n.23
plant-thinking 48, 50–1
Plant-Thinking (Marder) 48
plastisphere 139
Plato 65
Plumwood, Val 137
political agent 85
political thinking 28
"politics of renaturalization" 118
post-anthropocentrism 15, 16, 24, 53
posthumanism 3, 5–7, 15, 84–6, 158
posthumanist critique 84, 85, 88
posthumanist material feminism/feminists 6, 19, 24, 28, 39, 106
posthumanist material feminist ontology 7, 15–33
  flat ontology 23–8
  material feminist perspectives 16–23
  transjectivity 29–33
posthumanist theory 4, 15
postmodernism 84
poststructuralism 3, 85
post-traumatic stress disorder (PTSD) 116, 120, 134
potentia 112, 154, 162
power relations 26
Precarious Lives (*Butler*) 110, 161
precariousness 110, 161, 185 n.11
pre-reflective consciousness 65
process philosophy 70
Prude, Daniel 131
psychosomatic diseases 116
Puig de la Bellacasa, Maria 136, 157–60

Pulkkinen, Tuija 110, 185 n.10
pure and practical reasons (*reinen* and *praktische Vernunft*) 39

quantum physics 20
Québec City mosque shootings (2017) 134
Queen Mary College, of University of London 56
queer phenomenology 74

racism 59, 109, 188 n.13
Radomska, Marietta 168 n.8, 183 n.11
rape 106–7, 109, 113, 114, 185 n.12
realism 33
realist ontology 24, 170 n.25
reciprocity 159, 160
reconciliation 10, 11
reflective consciousness 65
Regarding the Pain of Others (Sontag) 132
Relating Narratives (*Cavarero*) 109
relational care 155–7
relationality 21, 52, 64, 69, 70, 92, 119, 133, 156, 159, 163, 169 n.13
relativism 86
Reproducing the Future (Strathern) 187 n.1
reproductive service 16
responsibility/response-ability 157–63
Rethinking Rape (Cahill) 185 n.12
Rêve de d'Alembert (*Diderot*) 40
Rimbaud, Arthur 84
Rudd, Gilian 53
Rumble (podcast) 123

Sand County Almanac (Leopold) 51
Sartre, Jean-Paul 3, 4, 7, 25, 29, 72, 151
sea sponges 44
Second Sex, The (Beauvoir) 3, 16–17
Sedgwick, Eve Kosofsky 119

sedimentation 91, 92
Seigworth, Gregory J. 73, 92
self 30, 39, 46, 51, 68, 72, 75, 83, 84, 86–95, 97, 105, 106, 113, 128, 152
  care of 156–7
  relational 106, 108, 109, 161
  as socio-politico-ethical agent 93
  transjective 129
self- 92, 96
self-centeredness 157
self-constitution 29, 46, 55, 74, 92, 93, 108, 109, 111, 113, 114
selfhood 83, 84, 90, 93, 157
self-ing 75
self-preservation 105
self-reconstruction 107, 109, 113
self-reflective consciousness 65
senses and sense-making 70–1
sensory perceptions 71
Serres, Michel 90
sexual differentiation 16
sex *vs.* gender 17
shadow places 137, 138
Sharp, Hasana 67, 118
Sixth Extinction 5, 130, 140, 141, 194 n.18
Snow, Lalage 115
Sobchack, Vivian 30, 63, 70–2, 180 n.19
social bond 108, 161, 162, 184 n.5
social constructionism 86
social constructivism 33
social distancing 134, 136
social ecology 128
social relations 90, 133
sociopolitical changes 85
somatic agency 96
Sontag, Susan 132
soul 39, 40, 66, 88
Spanish Flu epidemic (1918) 135, 136
speculative realism (SR) 23, 24, 170 nn.24, 25, 180 n.25

INDEX 211

Spinoza, Benedict de   21–2, 63, 64,
    66, 67, 90, 92, 118, 128, 152,
    154
Spinozist affect theory   63
standard of living   10
Staying with the Trouble
    (Haraway)   18, 127
Stoermer, Eugene F.   140
Stone: An Ecology of the Inhuman
    (*Cohen*)   52
Strathern, Marilyn   127
structuralism   3
"structures of experience"   63
subjective multiplicity   89, 90
subjectivity   7, 23, 32, 46, 61, 68, 69,
    72, 94, 95, 116, 172 n.36
subjects
    recognized as   87
    as trace   88–95
    as transversal relational
        entities   95
Sustaining Affirmation (White)   27
"Symmetry and Asymmetry in
    Conceptual and Morphological
    Formations" (Houle)   176 n.23
sympoiesis   18

TallBear, Kim   167 n.1
Taylor, Breonna   131
technical cognizers   65
Tecumseh   10
teratological connectivity   130
Thanatocene   141
*Thing: A Phenomenology of Horror,
    The* (Trigg)   165 n.1
"thing-power"   63
Thonhauser, Gerhard   191 n.2
Thought in the Act (Manning and
    Massumi)   70
thrombosis   78
Thus Spoke Zarathustra
    (Nietzsche)   47
"Toxic Embodiment" (Cielemęcka
    and Åsberg)   138
toxicities   127–31
    concept of   139

degrees of   139
social   131–5
traditional dualisms   67
transcorporeality   22, 160, 170 n.19
transjective beings   18, 21, 30, 45,
    46, 53, 55, 56, 58, 59, 64, 84,
    92, 94, 97, 117, 119, 151, 163
transjective intersectionality   129,
    194 n.18
transjective multiplicity   89
transjective vulnerability   135
transjectivity   7, 23, 24, 29–33, 39,
    53, 65, 83, 88, 89, 105, 106,
    117, 141, 151, 153, 155–7, 160,
    163, 172 n.34
transmateriality   32, 168 n.8,
    172 n.34
trans-medium mediation   42
transobjectivity   32
"transpersonal"   96, 183 n.13
transsubjective constitution   29–31
trauma   7, 106–8, 110, 113–16, 120,
    129, 155, 184 nn.1, 5, 185 n.12
traumatic experiences   7, 75, 93,
    106, 107, 113, 154–5, 180 n.23
Trembley, Abraham   40, 48
Trigg, Dylan   51, 165 n.1
Tsing, Anna Lowenhaupt   63,
    177 n.2, 193 n.14
Tuana, Nancy   32, 33
Twitter   131, 134

überbiological   21
Uexküll, Jacob von   42, 49
Ukraine war   125, 134, 189 n.16
Umwelt   42, 49, 175 n.18
United States   131, 135
Upper Canada Treaties   10

Vartanian, Aram   40
"vectors of subjectivation"   93, 128
vegere   49
Vegetabilis   49
vegetal and mineral extracerebral
    thinking   48–53
vegetare   49

vegetus 49
violence 47, 85, 106–9, 113, 115, 122, 132–5, 155
virality 131, 135–8
viscosity 32
viscous porosity 32, 33
vitalism 31
voluntary memories 50
vulnerability 5, 7, 36, 38, 105, 106, 109–12, 133, 135, 136, 160
vulner—ability 7, 8, 117–20, 153–6, 161, 163

Waller, Bruce 192 n.8
Wasteocene 138, 141
Watts, Vanessa 189 n.20
weak ontology 27, 28
"We Are the Not Dead" (2010) 115–16

Western philosophy 39
Western thought 43, 48, 50, 67
What a Plant Knows (Chamowitz) 175–6 n.20
White, Stephen K. 27, 28
Whitechapel/Mile End Road 57
Whitehead, Alfred North 70, 179 n.18
Widder, Nathan 67, 68
women bodies 86
Woolf, Virginia 132
world-constitution 55
worlding 18, 69–75, 179 n.18

xenophobia 59

Yusoff, Kathryn 52, 139

zoe-egalitarianism 27